From Here to Hogwarts

ALSO BY CHRISTOPHER E. BELL

*American Idolatry: Celebrity, Commodity and
Reality Television* (McFarland, 2010)

EDITED BY CHRISTOPHER E. BELL

*Hermione Granger Saves the World: Essays on
the Feminist Heroine of Hogwarts* (McFarland, 2012)

From Here to Hogwarts

Essays on Harry Potter Fandom and Fiction

Edited by
CHRISTOPHER E. BELL

McFarland & Company, Inc., Publishers

Jefferson, North Carolina

LIBRARY OF CONGRESS CATALOGUING-IN-PUBLICATION DATA

From here to Hogwarts : essays on Harry Potter fandom and fiction / edited by Christopher E. Bell.
   p.   cm.
Includes bibliographical references and index.

ISBN 978-0-7864-9931-1 (softcover : acid free paper) ∞
ISBN 978-1-4766-2246-0 (ebook)

1. Rowling, J. K.—Criticism and interpretation. 2. Potter, Harry (Fictitious character) 3. Fans (Persons) 4. Children's stories, English—History and criticism. I. Bell, Christopher E., 1974– editor.

PR6068.O93Z66 2016
823'.914—dc23   2015034934

BRITISH LIBRARY CATALOGUING DATA ARE AVAILABLE

Front cover: steam train on the Glenfinnan viaduct, Scotland © 2016 MartinM303/iStock/Thinkstock

Printed in the United States of America

McFarland & Company, Inc., Publishers
  Box 611, Jefferson, North Carolina 28640
  www.mcfarlandpub.com

For M & O & H & K & S
After all this time?
Always.

Acknowledgments

As often happens in books, I am going to spend time on this page thanking people who, most likely, are not you. Please feel free to go ahead and skip to the Introduction. I won't mind.

Thanks, firstly, as always go to my Megan and my Olivia and my H & K & S. Thanks for helping me remember every day why I wake up in the morning. Three and four and five.

Thank you to my research assistant, Jayne Simpson, for all of her diligent reading and annotating, despite her flatly abysmal taste in both football and basketball teams.

Thank you friends and family, near and far, for your love and support.

Thanks to the Southwest Popular/American Culture Association, for continuing to provide us time and space to get our fingers into these works. I promise you, we are thriving in the space you've given us.

Finally, thanks once again to J.K. Rowling, for creating such a richly layered and textured world that continues to provide us with a platform for discussing the human condition.

Table of Contents

Introduction

CHRISTOPHER E. BELL

As hard as it may be for some to believe, there was once a time when saying one was going to engage in serious, academic study of *Harry Potter* was looked at with, at best, extreme skepticism. In 2002, when John Granger published his first book on the subject—with the unwieldy title *The Hidden Key to Harry Potter: Understanding the Meaning, Genius, and Popularity of Joanne Rowling's Harry Potter Novels*—few could possibly imagine that within a decade, there would be an entire scholarly organization dedicated to the study of *Harry Potter*. Indeed, over the past four years, *Harry Potter* Studies has become quite a varied and complex area of research, collecting a host of serious academics each applying his or her own disciplinary lens and uncovering new and exciting interpretations of the text. The popularity of the work itself has grown exponentially since its debut in 1998; what was once considered a pleasant read for schoolchildren has blossomed into a cultural phenomenon. It is the cultural touchstone for an entire generation; saying one has not ever read a *Harry Potter* book or seen one of the films is akin to saying one has never seen *Star Wars*, or has never heard a Michael Jackson song, or has never seen a Disney movie. The ubiquity of at least a passing *Potter* experience is becoming a cultural commonplace, an entrée into conversation between strangers who may have little else in common.

This is especially true in the world of academia. As the chairman of the *Harry Potter* Studies division of the Southwest Popular/American Culture Association (SWPACA), I have had the distinct pleasure of bringing together a multidisciplinary, international collection of scholars, year after year, to present a diverse and flatly brilliant array of research. While one might intuitively think there would be a limited number of subjects with which to deal in the *Harry Potter* series, I have been astounded at the

1

amount of research in this area produced in the past few years. Since 2010, more than a dozen essay collections about a variety of *Potter*-related subjects have been published, including the philosophical nature of the works (Bassham, 2010), the psychology of the characters (Mulholland, 2013; Sykley, 2010), *Potter* and history (Reagin, 2011), religion (Trevarthen, 2010), and mythology (Deepa, 2011). I have personally edited two such volumes (Bell, 2012; Bell, 2013), acting as curator for the scholarship generated at the annual SWPACA conference. This wide scope of research, while invigorating, brings with it some of the logistical, existential concerns that any young area of scholarship would have, particularly one so diversely interdisciplinary.

For example, at the last convening of the *Harry Potter* Studies division, a rousing debate was raised as to what exactly constitutes *Harry Potter*. What should we consider canon? By definition, a canon is "the body of rules, principles, or standards accepted as axiomatic and universally binding in a field of study or art" (dictionary.com, n.d.). John Guillory (1993) further extends this definition by first removing the term from its traditional place as an inherently religious one: "by raising the question of whether the process by which a selection of texts functions to define a religious practice and doctrine is really similar *historically* to the process by which literary texts come to be preserved, reproduced, and taught" (p. 6). He then goes on to remind us that defining a canon is as much about the exclusion of texts as it is about inclusion (p. 9). When putting walls around a secular canon for purposes of defining the rules and standards of an academic field of study, it is important to consider not only what is included, but what is expressly not included.

For the scholars of *Harry Potter* Studies, this immediately became a debate about the books versus the films. Do we consider *only* the books to be canonical, since the films diverge so wildly from the narrative at critical junctures (excising key characters such as Peeves, removing vital information like nearly all of Voldemort's backstory from *HBP*, and so on)? Are the films to be forgiven for accelerating the narrative past beloved passages in the novels for the sake of expediency, or does doing so inherently render them noncanonical? And what do we make of ancillary texts, like *The Tales of Beedle the Bard*, which are written by Rowling and exist both as their own texts in the real world and as texts within Harry Potter's fictional universe?

Over the course of the three-day discussion, it was suggested that the novels and ancillary volumes were canon, and the films were their own, insular universe "based on" the canonical texts. Scholars across disciplines proposed a wide range of terms: *auxiliary canon, alternative canon, parallel canon*. Each of these have their benefits and drawbacks. First, though, there is the matter of inclusion or exclusion of the films from the canon at all. I, among others, argued that for some *Potter* fans, the films are their *only* exposure to the texts; there are plenty of people who have seen all of the films and read none of the books. For them, the films *are Harry Potter*. This immediately dismisses the term "auxiliary." As the films do, intentionally, adulterate large portions of the narrative (for expediency, not maliciously), "parallel" is not quite accurate. This, then, leaves us with the books as *canon*, and the films as *alternative canon*.

But, then, the discussion continued, what about all of the other *Potter* stuff: The Wizarding World of Harry Potter at Universal Studios, for example, or the *Pottermore* website, or *Potter Puppet Pals*? There are texts in the world that shape the way we approach the *Potter* texts without actually *being Potter* texts. Quickly, it was determined that because of the nature of *Pottermore*, anything written there as supplementary material by Rowling would, in fact, be considered canon. Most of what Rowling publishes on *Pottermore* is an expansion of existing canonical material, and only enhances our understanding of the texts. However, other material (that which is not written by Rowling herself)—video games, theme parks, *A Very Potter Musical*, and so on—are decidedly noncanonical, although they do inform our interpretations of the canonical texts. These, we categorized as *paracanon*.

Finally, there is the not-insignificant reality that Rowling herself reconsiders the canonical texts in interviews, at book readings, and on social media quite a bit. However, her interpretations or revelations are often off-the-cuff remarks made under direct questioning, and quite often are suggestions made that have no basis in the actual text. That is, they are things she has thought, but not things that she expressly wrote. The most famous of these remarks was the 2007 Carnegie Hall reading, during which she announced that "Dumbledore is gay, actually" (ABC News, 2007). But Rowling has made dozens of such comments, ranging from revealing that Harry's son "James sneaked [the Marauders' Map] out of [Harry]'s desk one day" to the fact that Gilderoy Lockhart never recovers his memory, "nor would I want him to. He's happy where he is, and I'm happier without him!" (Beyondhogwarts.com, 2015). These comments, while fun and interesting, really do exist outside of what is written on the pages of the seven novels and three ancillary texts. However, they are also the product of J.K. Rowling's understanding of the universe she created, and therefore cannot be dismissed. In the end, we have chosen to refer to these as *metacanon*—in the original Greek sense of the term "meta" as meaning "after," "beyond" or "adding to."

Therefore, we arrive at the terms *canon, alternate canon, paracanon* and *metacanon*. Why three days worth of discussion (discussion that continues beyond our annual gathering; I received an email on this subject literally as I was writing this introduction)? Why does it matter? It matters because, as *Harry Potter* studies begins to grow, mature, and coalesce into a well-defined area of study, what constitutes the field of play matters. As I explained to the assembled scholars in New Mexico in February 2015, if we are going to continue to live and work together in interdisciplinary peace and harmony, then it is important that we begin to establish the house rules. That begins with a firm understanding of what is considered to "really be" *Harry Potter*, and what is not. Rowling's novels are "real *Potter*," the films are "also real *Potter*," the theme park is "important, but not real *Potter*," and Rowling's interviews are "really interesting, but also not real *Potter*." Of course, like all canons, this is in no way set in stone, and I anticipate years of arguing over this contentious ground in the spirit of comradery, intellectual sparring, and genuine love for the work that we do. This is the very essence of *Harry Potter* Studies: we are a colloquium in which conversation reigns supreme, not for some vague purposes of "peer review" and its attendant exclusionary nature, but for the purposes of intellectual intercourse. We gather, in spaces like this volume, to cognitively commune with one another over some of the best works that modern popular culture has to offer.

This volume, then, is an attempt to engage in a critical discussion about the nature of society, both internally to the texts themselves, and externally, using the texts as a tool for understanding our real world. It is, by no means, comprehensive or all-inclusive. It is simply a dialogue, one of many conversations being had about *Potter*'s continuing relevance to modern academic study and the world at large. I have broken the collection into two parts: the first, "From Here," contains essays that use the *Potter* canon, alternate canon, paracanon, and (in some cases) metacanon to explore issues in the real world. The second, "To Hogwarts," more closely examines the societal relations of the wizarding world. Each section consists of five essays in colloquy.

"From Here" leads off with Kelly E. Collinsworth's in-depth exploration of the nature of school discipline at Hogwarts, and uses it to address real-world approaches to dealing with schoolchildren. Next, Megan Farnel discusses economics in the *Potter* series and relates it to a fascinating discussion of labor in the real world of fandom practice. Both Chin-Ting Lee and Bronwyn E. Beatty, in their two essays, deal with fan community expressions of *Potter*mania; Lee's chapter delves into the world of Facebook fan groups, while Beatty assembles a focus group of *Potter*'s concurrent fans (those who aged within in the same relative time frame as Harry Potter) for a lively conversation about the impact of the series. Between those two pieces, Elizabeth Morrow Clark weaves an interesting history of the development of *Harry Potter* academic courses at the collegiate level.

The collection then enters Platform 9¾ and heads off "To Hogwarts" to examine the society of the wizarding world. Christine Klingbiel uses rhetorical theory to explicate the nature of propaganda in the *Potter* series. Next, librarian Tolonda Henderson and art historian Amy M. Von Lintel entertain a fascinating dialogue about images, particularly paintings, in the wizarding world. Tracy L. Bealer continues along these lines, moving the conversation from art to books and discussing the meaning of reading in the series. Jennifer M. Proffitt and Juliann Cortese further expand the dialogue to *The Prophet*, *The Quibbler*, and *Potterwatch*, examining other forms of media in wizard society. Finally, Kalen M.A. Churcher and Meghan S. Sanders bring the conversation to a close with a consideration of youth activist movements, both in the muggle world and in the wizarding world.

Who, then, is this book for? I believe it is for anyone who wants to engage in a serious conversation about different aspects of the intersection between popular culture and real societal life. Feel free to start anywhere and read the essays in any order you like. I have attempted to group them together loosely based on their foci, but there is no "through line"; the essays were not ordered with any intention that the book be read front to back. Read with a highlighter and a pen—take notes in the margins, attach sticky notes and scribble down questions, scour the reference pages of the essays and use them as a springboard for your own explorations. Agonize, as the *Harry Potter* Studies stalwarts have, over the nature of the canon. Even better, work your questions and ideas together into an email and shoot them to me at dr.christopher.bell@gmail.com. While I can't promise to respond to every email I receive, I will use your questions to further the scholarly inquiries of the *Harry Potter* Studies division when we next convene. In fact, consider joining us yourself—we welcome independent scholars, undergraduate and graduate students, instructors, all levels of professors, and anyone else who wishes to pursue scholarly inquiry into the nature of *Harry Potter*. More details can be found at http://southwestpca.org.

I hope that this collection not only furthers your own intellectual experience with Harry, Hermione, Ron and the rest, but brings you even a fraction of the happiness I was privileged to enjoy as the editor of this volume. Thank you for being one of us, *Potter* scholar.

References

ABC News (2007). "Dumbledore Is Gay and Some Are Miffed." *ABC News*. Retrieved 1 March 2015, from http://abcnews.go.com/Entertainment/story?id=3755544.

Bassham, G. (2010). *The ultimate Harry Potter and philosophy*. Hoboken, N.J.: Wiley.

Bell, C. (2012). *Hermione Granger saves the world! Essays on the feminist heroine of Hogwarts*. Jefferson, N.C.: McFarland.

_____ (2013). *Legilimens! Perspectives in Harry Potter studies*. Cambridge: Cambridge Scholars.

Beyondhogwarts.com (2015). "Harry Potter—J.K. Rowling goes Beyond the Epilogue—Beyond Hogwarts." Retrieved 1 March 2015, from http://www.beyondhogwarts.com/harry-potter/articles/jk-rowling-goes-beyond-the-epilogue.html.

Deepa, S. (2011). *Harry Potter and indian mythology*. Bloomington: AuthorHouse.

Dictionary.com (2015). "canon." Retrieved 1 March 2015, from http://dictionary.reference.com/browse/canon.

Guillory, J. (1993). *Cultural capital*. Chicago: University of Chicago Press.

Mulholland, N. (2013). *The psychology of Harry Potter*. Dallas: BenBella.

Reagin, N. (2011). *Harry Potter and history*. Hoboken, N.J.: Wiley.

Sykley, J. (2010). *Harry Potter ower*. Carindale, Queensland: Interactive.

Trevarthen, G. (2010). *The seeker's guide to Harry Potter*. Winchester: O Books.

Naming Conventions

For the ease of reading and for the sake of consistency, in this volume, the titles of the books/films will be abbreviated as follows:

Harry Potter and the Sorcerer's/Philosopher's Stone	*SS* or *PS*
Harry Potter and the Chamber of Secrets	*CoS*
Harry Potter and the Prisoner of Azkaban	*PoA*
Harry Potter and the Goblet of Fire	*GoF*
Harry Potter and the Order of the Phoenix	*OotP*
Harry Potter and the Half-Blood Prince	*HBP*
Harry Potter and the Deathly Hallows	*DH, or DH1/DH2*

FROM HERE

"I will have order": A Potterish Examination of Authoritarian School Disciplinary Trends and Reactions

Kelly E. Collinsworth

Not only was Harry Potter incredibly popular with Millennials, but research has also shown that the book series impacts the way members of this generation view political and social justice issues. Both at the Hogwarts School of Witchcraft and Wizardry and in our own all-too-real public schools, discipline is often randomly or harshly applied. And in both, fear creates a pathway for increasing intensification and intrusion of official law enforcement into the educational environment. Given this, it is likely that readers who grew up with Harry Potter view the intensification of law enforcement action in public schools through a lens colored by depictions of these issues in the novels and movies, especially in regards to the actions of Dolores Umbridge. School discipline and juvenile justice and the way these issues impact students' lives is a central theme that runs through the heart of the *Harry Potter* novels.

In his book *Harry Potter and the Millennials*, Gierzynski (2013) posits that Dolores Umbridge is the book series' "best manifestation of authoritarianism" and that the "good characters" defy Umbridge's efforts for control. Unlike Umbridge, our heroes are open-minded towards different people and experiences (pp. 19–21). Having concluded that this was an important lesson in the book series, the author conducted a survey of college students to test whether Harry Potter fans had a "predisposition to authoritarianism," which was defined to measure "the tendency to show obedience to authorities, to conform to rules and norms, and to disdain those not deemed part of the in-group" (p. 55). Harry Potter fans displayed a "significantly lower" predisposition to authoritarianism than nonfans (p. 55). An interview response from the study underscores the series' influence on readers' attitudes toward school authorities: "I was often the only one of my peers that was willing to take a stand against the teacher when we thought we were being treated unfairly.... I believe I dealt with authority figures much like the main characters in *Harry Potter...*" (pp. 68–69).

Given the major role that the theme of school discipline takes in the book series, it is not surprising that Harry's anti-authoritarian readers would focus much of their concern and interest on the issue. When we are introduced to discipline at Hogwarts, we see a system not completely unlike that employed in most American public elementary schools today. The budding witches and wizards can earn or lose points, which cumulatively determine their dormitory's standing in the race for the prized House Cup. Similarly, American first-graders' behavior will often be tracked through a system where color-coded cards are flipped or tokens awarded. While the House Points system incorporates teamwork, as opposed to the commonly used individual system seen in our Muggle world, these discipline methods seem apparently normal and acceptable.

However, as Harry's first school year progresses, student discipline at Hogwarts moves beyond the mere loss of house points. Harry, Hermione, Neville, and Draco are given detention, in addition to lost points, for being out of bed after hours (*SS*, p. 243). While Filch, the school's surly caretaker, laments that "hanging you by your wrists" has been forbidden as an acceptable punishment (*SS*, p. 248), the four students' detention proves vastly more dangerous. They are forced to accompany Hagrid, the half-giant groundskeeper, into the Forbidden Forrest to find an injured unicorn. In the dark woods, Harry confronts Voldemort for the first time (*SS*, pp. 250–257). A short time later, Harry and his friends again break school rules, this time going into the third floor corridor, where Dumbledore has warned students not to go unless they "wish to die a very painful death" (*SS*, p. 127). However, instead of being punished for breaking rules, Harry and his friends thwart Voldemort's quest for immortality, and Dumbledore awards them extra points, securing the House Cup for Gryffindor (*SS*, pp. 305–306) (*SS*, pp. 293–295). Then, the following year, Harry and Ron break "a hundred school rules into pieces," only to receive Special Awards for Services to the School (*CoS*, pp. 328, 331).

In fact, throughout the *Harry Potter* series, the inconsistency with which punishments are applied and with which awards are bestowed becomes a prominent theme. Harry and his friends may be rewarded for breaking rules at one point and then punished harshly for breaking them at another time. Whether they are rewarded or punished seems to be driven by the whims of the faculty,[1] the success of their missions, and by the select status that Harry seems to enjoy with his headmaster. There are, seemingly, no established procedures for dealing with such matters at Hogwarts, and the reader, as pointed out by Fishman (2010) in his article on punishment in the novels, is left to puzzle over the applications of school discipline in his or her own Muggle experience (p. 119). The one exception, of course, is the rule prohibiting the use of transfiguration of a student as a punishment, which we encounter after Mad-Eye Moody turns Draco Malfoy into a ferret (*GoF,* pp. 205–206). Most readers were surely disappointed with this rule's enforcement, which returned Draco to his less furry, human form.

Simply put, though, the *Harry Potter* novels offer a valuable lens through which we might examine the rise of strict authoritarianism at Hogwarts as it compares to school discipline in America's Muggle schools. As stated, such comparisons would have been obvious even to young fans of the series, and they now offer an opportunity to take a closer look at criticisms of discipline in contemporary public schools as well as recent court cases that have attempted to curtail possible abuses arising from authoritarian school discipline.

Legal Rights of Muggle Students and Their Application to Underage Wizards

In America, the development of the legal treatment of juveniles, as differentiated from adult offenders, began in the late nineteenth century (*Application of Gault,* 1967, p. 14). The goal of establishing a separate juvenile justice system was to avoid the "rigidities, technicalities, and harshness" present under our criminal law and instead focus not on punishment but on treatment and rehabilitation (pp. 15–16). The state would act as *parens patriae,* or "the power of the state," to act as "provider of protection to those unable to care for themselves" (Black's Law Dictionary, 9th edition, 2009). While the original objective behind the dichotomy of juvenile and adult criminal law may have had good intentions, the result led to a lack of due process for many juveniles.

In the case of *Application of Gault,* the juvenile, Gerald Gault, was picked up by the Sheriff after a verbal complaint by a neighbor that he and his friend had called her on the telephone to make offensive, sexual remarks. Gerald was already on six months' probation for being with someone who had stolen a purse. Neither of Gault's parents were home when he was arrested, and they were not informed of the arrest until they sought out the deputy probation officer. A petition claiming that Gault was delinquent was filed at the courthouse by the probation officer, but it presented no facts to support the conclusion. Additionally, neither of Gault's parents were allowed to review the petition. A hearing was held, but the offended neighbor was not called as a witness. At the hearing, Gault was also questioned by the judge without being informed of his right not to incriminate himself (*Application of Gault*, 1967, pp. 4–6). The Supreme Court observed that "unbridled discretion, however benevolently motivated, is frequently a poor substitute for principle and procedure" (p. 18). As a result, the Supreme Court recognized a juvenile defendant's right to procedural due process.

Procedural due process refers to the "minimal requirements of notice and a hearing guaranteed by the Due Process Clauses of the 5th and 14th Amendments, esp. if the deprivation of a significant life, liberty, or property interest may occur" (Black's Law Dictionary, 9th edition, 2009). The Supreme Court found in *Application of Gault* that "the condition of being a boy does not justify a kangaroo court" (p. 28). As a result, juveniles facing delinquency proceedings or criminal charges must be given notice of court hearings with enough time to prepare for the court case. The notice must state what the juvenile is accused of doing wrong. The juvenile must be advised of his right to an attorney if the charge could result in commitment outside his or her home. Also, juveniles are entitled to assert their right not to talk to the police. Confessions must be voluntarily given, and juveniles may confront through cross-examination their accusers and other witnesses (*Application of Gault*, 1967).

The wizarding world provides us an opportunity to view the importance of procedural due process for juveniles when we look at Harry's encounter with the Ministry of Magic at the beginning of *OotP*. With the knowledge that Voldemort has returned at the end of his fourth year in school, Harry leaves for the summer for the supposed safety of his Aunt and Uncle's home on Privet Drive only to face an attack on his cousin and himself by Dementors. In order to save his cousin from the deadly Dementor's kiss, Harry produces a patronus charm in the form of a stag that drives the Dementors away (*OotP*, pp. 16–19). Upon returning to Privet Drive, Harry receives a letter by owl from the Ministry's Improper Use of Magic Office, accusing him of breaching the "Decree for the Reasonable Restriction of Underage Sorcery." The letter expels him from Hogwarts and states that his wand will be destroyed (*OotP*, pp. 26–27). He is called to a disciplinary hearing at the Ministry because of his previous violation of "section 13 of the International Confederation of Wizards' Statute of Secrecy" (*OotP*, p. 27). Then, a second letter from Arthur Weasley tells Harry to hold on to his wand and remain at Privet Drive, while Dumbledore "sort[s] it all out" (*OotP*, p. 28). A final letter from the Ministry informs him that he is suspended and may retain his wand until the hearing (*OotP*, p. 33).

Thus, Harry is left very unsure of his fate, batted to and fro by the whims of unknowable adult authorities. He does not know if he will attend school, if his wand, which he needs in order to survive in the wizarding world, will be taken, or even if he will be sent to Azkaban (the wizards' prison) (*OotP*, p. 44). Harry has little comfort in knowing how rules will be applied or if he will even have an opportunity to present his side of the story. His experience over the past four years has taught him that rules are not applied consistently and that they often change. Two times previous to this, Harry had been caught performing magic in view of Muggles only to receive minor reprimands. First, he and his friend Ron had flown a car in full sight of Muggles and had only received a warning from Professor Dumbledore (*CoS*, p. 81). Then the following year, Harry accidentally performed magic in front of his Aunt Marge and was told by the Minister of Magic Cornelius Fudge that "we're not going to punish you for a little thing like that! … It was an accident! We don't send people to Azkaban for blowing up their aunts!" (*PoA*, p. 45).

However, by Harry's fifth year, Voldemort is stronger and fear in the wizarding world more intense, leading to harsher charges and potentially harsher penalties. Much like the juvenile in *Application of Gault*, Harry's first notice of the hearing was presumptive. While he was given notice of what statute he had violated, the notice afforded punishment first without an opportunity to present his side of the story. Luckily, Dumbledore was able to step in and correct this due process violation by allowing Harry to keep his wand pending a hearing. Harry's situation became more complicated because the wizard world ties schooling so closely with the actions of the policing authority. On one hand, Harry may be punished with the destruction of his wand and a jail sentence in Azkaban. On the other hand, he may also be punished by the school with expulsion or suspension.

In the United States, Muggle juveniles are subject to the same procedural due process rights as adults in criminal and delinquency proceedings, but the same procedural due process rights do not all apply when it comes to school disciplinary proceedings. Students facing suspension from public schools where the state has provided them a right to a free education must receive "some kind of notice" and be given "some kind of hearing"

(*Goss v. Lopez*, 1975, p. 579). The extent of the notice and hearing required by the due process clause depends on whether the suspension is for less than ten days. If it is for less than ten days, the student must only be given notice by the disciplinarian, in written or oral form, of the accusations against him. If the student denies the charges, then he must be told of the evidence against him and have a chance to tell his or her side of the story. Students in this situation do not have to be given time to prepare for the informal hearing, which can occur immediately following the notice of the charges. If the student is an immediate danger to the school, the student can be removed before the hearing (*Goss v. Lopez,* 1975, pp. 581–582). According to the Supreme Court, "The Clause requires at least these rudimentary precautions against unfair or mistaken findings of misconduct and arbitrary exclusion from school" (p. 581). However, there is no requirement that students be given the right to call their own witnesses, confront or cross examine witnesses, have an attorney present, or even have time to prepare for a hearing (p. 583).

In cases where students are to be suspended for more than ten days or expelled from school, additional due process, such as a more formal hearing, is provided; however, the extent of that process was left undecided by the Supreme Court in *Goss*. Generally, the procedures are governed by state statute. However absent a state statute requiring otherwise, the Supreme Court has not required that students facing expulsion hearings be advised of their right not to incriminate themselves or be appointed an attorney if they cannot afford one.

Viewed in this context, Harry's hearing at the Ministry had several possible procedural deficiencies. First, while Harry is given sufficient notice in advance of his hearing, he arrives for the hearing only to find that the time had been moved up by several hours, making him tardy (*OotP*, p. 137). If Harry had missed the hearing and been found guilty, his rights would have likely been violated. Moreover, considering the deprivation of his wand and possible sentence to Azkaban, Harry should have been informed of his right to an attorney and provided an attorney if he could not afford one. In fact, Harry is prevented from having anyone enter the courtroom with him (*OotP,* p. 136).

At the hearing, Harry faces the entire Wizengamot, about fifty wizards, apparently in an attempt, as argued by Liemer (2010), by Minister Fudge to publicly discredit and humiliate Harry (p. 28). Fortunately for Harry, Dumbledore manages to enter the courtroom and take an attorney-like role. He introduces himself as "Witness for the defense, Albus Percival Wulfric Brian Dumbledore" (*OotP,* p. 139). In Anglo-Saxon criminal trials, witnesses would "vouch for the good character of the accused." This vouching was more important than witness testimony, and the social prominence of the voucher made success at trial more likely (Liemer, 2010, pp. 24–25). When Harry tries to explain what happened, Fudge, demonstrating that he is not an impartial judge, cuts him off and accuses him of making up a "well-rehearsed story" (*OotP*, p. 142). Luckily, the able-advocate Dumbledore invokes the Wizengamot Charter of Rights, which provides for the right to present witnesses on the accused's behalf (*OotP*, pp. 142–143). Dumbledore is able to illicit testimony from Mrs. Figg, Harry's neighbor, that the boys were being attacked by Dementors and that Harry had used his Patronus to save himself and his cousin (*OotP*, pp. 143–145). Dumbledore then argues that an exception to the restriction on use of magic exists "in exceptional circumstances ... [that] include situations that threaten the life of the wizard ... or Muggles present" (*OotP*, p. 148). After some debate, Harry is found not guilty (*OotP*, p. 151).

During the hearing, Fudge also attempts to address Harry's misconduct at school, although Dumbledore reminds him that "[t]he Ministry does not have the power to expel Hogwarts students" (*OotP*, p. 149). Fudge's response foreshadows what will happen later when he says, "Laws can be changed" (*OotP*, p. 149).

Harry's courtroom trial is successful because he has a competent attorney in Dumbledore, which underscores the importance that juveniles need protection in court proceedings and in school proceedings that may end up in court. A young reader would sympathize with Harry's fear and confusion as he faces the charges against him. They would also surely recognize the hopelessness of Harry's fate until Dumbledore comes to the rescue. Students across America watch situations like these play out in their own schools regularly, and this scene must reflect their own trepidation in the face of nameless authority.

Rise of Zero Tolerance Policies or the Ministry's Interfering at Hogwarts

Early on, Cornelius Fudge, the Minister of Magic, is kindly and sympathetic toward Harry ("We're not going to punish you for a little thing like that!"). However, by the beginning of the fifth book, *OotP*, Fudge has turned accusatory. He is driven by fear of Voldemort's growing power, and, as high officials often do, he scrambles and scapegoats as he pursues Harry's prosecution. He is obsessed with appearances and public opinion as he clings to the power afforded him in his role as Minister. Failing to convict Harry, he opts for full Ministerial control of Hogwarts through the person of his dictatorial Undersecretary, Dolores Umbridge, whose character Stephen King described as "the greatest make-believe villain to come along since Hannibal Lecter" (King, 2009).

Likewise, in America's public schools, fear absent reason also drove the rise of zero tolerance school discipline policies. In response to what school officials believed to be an increasing problem with juvenile crime in the late 1980s and early 1990s, especially with guns and drugs (i.e., crimes often associated with minority juveniles), many schools began instituting zero tolerance policies that required specific punishments for particular violations (Curtis, 2014, p. 1253). Additionally, the passage of the Gun-Free Schools Act of 1994 required Title I funding recipients to pass laws to "expel from school for a period of not less than 1 year a student who is determined to have brought a firearm to a school" (Gun Free Schools Act of 1994). The Act also requires schools to "refer students to the juvenile justice system" if they bring weapons to school (Curtis, 2014, p. 1254). As a result of this mandate, according to Curtis, many schools instituted zero tolerance requirements for other school disciplinary violations (p. 1254). As noted by Hirschfield (2008), zero tolerance policies removed discretion from teachers and principals to deal with discipline issues in alternative ways. This lack of discretion led to an escalation of suspensions and expulsions (p. 82). In addition to the increased use of zero tolerance methods, the schools themselves became more policed with the addition of school resource officers, metal detectors, random searches of students and their belongings, surveillance cameras, and strict dress codes. This level of control of the student's environment, as well as the strict application of the disciplinary code, is seen as necessary to negate the fear of school violence, drugs, and other disruptions (Perry & Morris, 2014, p. 1070).

However, data shows that since around 1985, before the rise in zero tolerance policies, school violence had "remained stable, or even decreased somewhat" and that "incidents of critical and deadly violence remain a relatively small proportion of school disruptions" (American Psychological Association, 2008, p. 853). Despite the decrease in school violence, the rate of suspensions, as reported by Losen, had risen sharply since the 1970s (as cited in Perry & Morris, 2014, p. 1068). In a report by Rausch and Skiba, one study of a state's disciplinary incidents found that 95 percent of suspensions were not for weapon or drug possession and fell into the category of "disruptive behavior and other" (as cited in Losen, 2011, p. 8). While the increased use of suspensions for nonviolent offenses was considered a deterrent, the evidence does not support this conclusion (Losen, 2011, pp. 9–10). In addition to the increase of suspensions, student discipline violations, which may have been handled within the school in the past, are now more likely to be referred to criminal authorities (Perry & Morris, 2014, p. 1070). The impact of the increased suspensions, expulsions, and criminalization of behaviors results in increased recidivism, poorer grades and poor performance on tests. One study by Arcia showed that after a suspension, the studied group was "nearly five grade levels behind the non-suspended group" (as cited in Perry & Morris, 2014, p. 1070). Moreover, research from the Office for Civil Rights indicates that suspensions and expulsions disproportionately impact students of color and students with disabilities (U.S. Department of Education, 2014, p. i).

As depicted in *OotP*, an increase in a school's police and penalizing function can have other consequences, such as "erod[ing] a school's moral authority, producing alienation and resistance" (Perry & Morris, 2014, p. 1071). According to Perry and Morris, a school with a punitive educational environment can "breed anxiety, distrust, and uncertainty, even for students who do nothing wrong" (p. 1071). Significantly, a recent long-term study by Perry and Morris indicates that high rates of school suspensions negatively impacts *non-suspended* students' school achievement (p. 1068). The authors of the study also conclude that "even in the most violent and disorganized schools, exclusionary discipline is an ineffective strategy for creating a positive learning environment and may actually exacerbate hostile conditions that lead to lower academic achievement" (p. 1081). Based on these Muggle world criticisms of zero tolerance policies, we cannot be surprised when we see the detrimental effects of Umbridge's reign during Harry's fifth year at school.

Absurd Outcomes of Zero Tolerance

Even at Hogwarts, where discipline was inconsistent and the rules unknowable, outside behaviors traditionally were not punished in school. For instance, early in the series, Harry and Ron "borrow" Mr. Weasley's flying Ford Anglia to get to Hogwarts after Dobby, an elf, closes the passage to Platform 9¾. They are seen by numerous Muggles and openly violate the Reasonable Restriction of Underage Magic (and the statute of secrecy). However, Harry and Ron do not lose House Points for Gryffindor because "term hadn't started." They only receive detention and letters sent home to their parents (*CoC*, pp. 81–82). But, when Dolores Umbridge comes to

Hogwarts in *OotP*, she institutes her own form of zero tolerance policies, framed rules hung higher and higher on every wall. Harry is even punished after he gives an interview about Voldemort to *The Quibbler*, a newspaper, while away from school. Harry is suspended from future Hogsmeade trips, he receives another week of detention, and fifty points are deducted from Gryffindor. Umbridge then makes possession of *The Quibbler* an expulsion offense (*OotP,* p. 581).

Like the students at Hogwarts, many Muggle students have been punished for behaviors that teachers and administrators view as beyond the norm as a result of the zero tolerance rules adopted by states and schools that encompass behaviors beyond those required to be included by the Gun-Free Schools Act of 1994. For instance, news headlines abound with young children, kindergarteners even, who are suspended or expelled from school for bringing items to school shaped like guns or even making finger-guns. Nathan Entingh, a fifth-grader in Ohio, was suspended from school after making a finger-gun, pointing it at a friend, and saying "boom." He was suspended because the finger-gun was a "level 2 look-alike gun" prohibited under the zero tolerance policy (Cuevas, 2014). A seven-year-old was suspended after ate his Pop-Tart into the shape of a gun (Turley, 2013).

Like Harry, students are now increasingly punished for behaviors that take place off of school grounds and usually for comments made on social media. These cases clearly raise questions of criminalization of speech as well. For example, a high school senior in Minnesota jokingly responded to an anonymous tweet alleging that he had kissed a young gym teacher by tweeting, "actually yes." A police investigation was initiated, and no improper relationship was found. However, the school suspended and then threatened to expel the boy from school and required him to enroll in another high school briefly before graduation. This was done because they found that his tweet had violated a school rule against "threatening, intimidating or assault of a teacher, administrator or other staff member" (FoxNews.com, 2014). In another example, a high school student was suspended from school after he wrote on Facebook that his teacher was a "fat ass who should stop eating fast food, and is a douche bag." The remarks were written on his home computer and after school hours (Turley, 2011).

Jonathan Turley, Shapiro Professor of Public Interest Law at George Washington University, worries "about the type of citizens being shaped in these authoritarian environments." He is concerned that students are forced to "accept arbitrary and often illogical actions by public figures." He specifies a case in Virginia where a student was suspended for taking a doctor prescribed contraceptive pill at school. Turley argues that "the government appears to be training a generation of passive citizens ideal for subjugation and control" (Turley, 2009). Surely in the case of Minister Fudge, he hopes that his appointment of Umbridge to police the halls of Hogwarts will enable him to maintain his position and power. However, as Harry and his friends display anti-authoritarian leanings, they resist Fudge's efforts.

The Impact and Effectiveness of Police Presence in Schools

As referenced earlier, no character in Harry Potter so embodies fearfulness, irrational authority, and vindictiveness as does that of Dolores Umbridge. She is sent to Hogwarts by the Minister of Magic to effectively lock down the school. Rules grow rapidly in both number and complexity. Youthful joy is banished. School, itself, becomes a prison, where every student is either a suspect or an informant. While the examples in the novels are extreme, they do ask the reader to consider what role, if any, police should play in contemporary public schools.

Today, there are around 17,000 police officers housed in America's public schools (Thurau, 2009–2010, p. 978). The rise of school resource officers (SROs) resulted from several factors, including an outbreak of fifteen high profile school shootings in the 1990s (Canady, James, & Neace, 2012, p. 9). Other factors included the availability of federal money for police in schools, zero tolerance policies, a tougher stance towards juvenile crimes, and harsher penalties (Thurau, 2009–2010, p. 978).

Studies seem to show why SROs have proven controversial. While SROs may have a potential deterrent effect with regard to serious violent crime, their presence in schools likely causes less significant incidents to be treated as criminal. One study by Theriot reported that schools with SROs had higher arrests for disorderly conduct than schools without SROs. However, the same study found lower rates of arrest for weapons on schools grounds and assault, concluding a possible deterrent effect with SROs (as cited in James & McCallion, 2013, p. 22). Another study by Na and Gottfredson reported that schools with SROs saw a greater number of students reported to police for "non-serious violent crimes," such as no-weapon fights (as cited in James & McCallion, 2013, p. 22). While reports of serious violent crimes have decreased during the rise of SROs in schools, the limited research has not determined whether that is a result of increased police presence in school or other factors (James & McCallion, 2013, p. 26).

As a result of the increase of police in the schools, discipline violations such as fights on the playground, which would have normally been addressed in the principal's office, are now referred for court intervention. SROs are police officers. They have been trained as police officers, and they bring that mentality and disposition to their work in the schools. Further, many common school discipline issues can be viewed as criminal acts: a school yard shoving match (assault); stealing a notebook (theft); or threatening to punch another student (terroristic threatening). Given these considerations, the only rule breaking left solely in the hands of school administrators is very minor issues, things that would never lead to criminal charges, such as tardiness, dress code violations, and inappropriate displays of affection. However, proponents of SROs argue that they prevent "selective enforcement" of disciplinary policies, which can "create the appearance of deliberate indifference to student victims" (Canady, James, & Neace, 2012, p. 34). By having an SRO, proponents would argue, favoritism like that shown to Harry Potter would not exist.

The National Association of School Resource Officers (NASRO) contends that the duties of an SRO are to be an "educator, informal counselor, and law enforcement officer" (Canady, James, & Neace, 2012, p. 3). When selecting SROs with the best chance of success, officers should be able to "effectively work with students, parents, and school administrators, have an understanding of child development and psychology, and ... have public speaking and teaching skills" (James & McCallion, 2013, p. 12).

In Harry Potter, the functional categories of SRO responsibilities align well with what we might imagine to be Umbridge's duties in her new role at Hogwarts. That she fails utterly to successfully fulfill these responsibilities, burdened clearly by her own particular form of madness, opens up the possibility of examining Umbridge in the role of an SRO, and it enlightens us as to how the books might have influenced young readers' views of officers in their own schools. Additionally, it provides us with an opportunity to consider if an SRO can actually fulfill such a multifaceted and multipurpose position as was enumerated above or if their role in school reverts to that of mere enforcer.

Umbridge as Law Enforcement Officer

Best Practice: In a 2014 resource guide published by the U.S. Department of Education, schools are cautioned that when using school resource officers that they should be "focused on protecting the physical safety of the school or preventing criminal conduct of persons other than students, while reducing inappropriate student referrals to law enforcement. Schools are further directed to prevent involvement of SRO's in "routine school disciplinary matters" (p. 9).

Umbridge's focus is clearly and solely driven by an uncontrollable rage for order: order in the class, order in the hall, and order in what is spoken. She requires hands to be raised before questions are asked in class. She disbands school organizations and requires them to ask permission to reform. She also limits communication in and out of Hogwarts and searches students' mail. In order to try to reign in Harry's continuing outbursts, she gives him recurring detentions in her office, writing painful lines in his own blood.

While SROs are warned against becoming involved in "routine school disciplinary matters," Umbridge thrusts herself into the discipline of students for non-criminal issues. Eventually, Umbridge gains additional power as High Inquisitor to "strip pupils of privileges" where she is granted "supreme authority over all punishments ... pertaining to students" (*OotP*, p. 416). She uses her power to ban Harry and George Weasley from Quidditch for fighting with Draco Malfoy, and even bans Fred Weasley because he would have fought Draco "if his teammates had not restrained him" (*OotP*, p. 416).

In using her power as disciplinarian, she employs methods of corporal punishment beyond the norm. Even Filch must get an "approval for whipping" form signed when he wants to discipline Fred and George Weasley (*OotP*, p. 673). While most Muggle schools have eliminated corporal punishment, many states still authorize the practice and provide a defense to teachers who use it. For example, in Kentucky a teacher is justified in using corporal punishment if the force used by the teacher is "necessary to ... maintain reasonable discipline" and the force used is "not designed to cause or known to create a substantial risk of causing death, serious physical injury, disfigurement, extreme pain, or extreme mental distress" (Kentucky Revised Statute § 503.110). Arguably, Umbridge's punishment of Harry is "necessary to maintain reasonable discipline." Certainly, Harry was not following the rules of her class and was frightening the other students with outbursts about Voldemort's return (*OotP*, pp. 244–246). However, for Harry's punishment, in addition to missing Quidditch practice, Umbridge uses a "special quill" for Harry to write "I must not tell lies" until "the message sinks in." Harry feels "searing pain" as the words appear on his hand while the words appear on the parchment in his own blood. When he finally finishes his first night's punishment, "his hand was stinging painfully," and the skin on his hand was "red raw." After the first night,

Umbridge examines his hand, but decides he must do more lines the next night because, she says, "I don't seem to have made much of an impression yet" (*OotP*, pp. 266–268).

Because Umbridge appeared to want to leave a scar on Harry's hand, her defense of her actions under the justification law would likely not stand, as she seemed to have designed the punishment specifically to cause disfigurement.[2] Additionally, the four goals of the criminal justice system, according to Fishman, may include "deterrence, retribution, incapacitation of the dangerous, and rehabilitation" (p. 119). Umbridge's attempt to use punishment as a deterrence by having Harry write "I must not tell lies" fails to work with Harry or other students and fails to change his attitudes towards her or the Ministry (Fishman, 2010, p. 121).

Umbridge takes great personal satisfaction in her investigatory role as SRO, which reaches its peak when she finally locates "Dumbledore's Army," a group of students led by Harry studying defensive practices. Harry's violation of the decree against unapproved school groups results in the Minister, himself, being called to Hogwarts for Harry to explain his actions (*OotP*, pp. 610–611). Harry denies violating any rules, so in a surprising nod towards procedural protections, Harry is allowed to face the witness against him. However, the student witness refuses to speak; she refuses because Hermione has placed a jinx on all students who unknowingly signed a parchment of allegiance to the "army," which, if a student snitches, will cause the word "sneak" to appear on his or her forehead (*OotP*, pp. 612–613). Harry escapes expulsion after Dumbledore takes the blame for formation of Dumbledore's Army and is forced to abandon his post at Hogwarts (*OotP*, pp. 619–622). Educational Decree Number Twenty-eight quickly follows with the appointment of Umbridge as Headmistress of Hogwarts (*OotP*, p. 624). Umbridge's transformation from an investigatory officer to having complete control over both discipline and education at Hogwarts is completed in only a brief period of time.

Umbridge as Educator

Best Practice: According to the National Association of School Resource Officers, "with SROs in the lead, these topics are brought to life through tales from the SRO's personal experience and their nuanced understanding of the threats and consequences confronting students every day" (Canady, James, & Neace, 2012, p. 27).

Umbridge is sent to Hogwarts pursuant to Educational Decree Twenty-

Two, which allowed the Ministry of Magic to appoint her as the Defense against the Dark Arts Professor when Dumbledore failed to fill the position in a timely fashion (*OotP*, p. 307). However, her talents did not lie in teaching. Like most school resource officers, her time was spent with other duties. In a survey of Kentucky School Resource Officers in 2009, respondents reported spending only about 15 percent of their time as educators (May & Chen, 2009, p. 15). Students in Umbridge's class merely read; there is no practice or lecture. Her teaching style is a "drill in submission before authority" allowing for no independent thinking (Wolosky, 2013, p. 290). Professor Umbridge certainly does not "bring topics to life" like Hogwarts' previous Defense against the Dark Arts Teacher, Mad-Eye Moody (*GoF*, p. 208). Unfortunately, Umbridge refuses to use her own practical knowledge in the classroom and sticks to a "Ministry-approved curriculum" (*OotP*, p. 239). Even though the students must take a practical test at the end of the year, Umbridge assures them that if they "study theory hard enough," they will pass, which, of course, is all that matters to her (*OotP*, pp. 243–244).

While order is the one thing that Umbridge desires most, her strict authoritarian policies and sadistic punishments only serve to foment rebellion amongst the students. The students, in fact, take control of their own education, beginning to practice in secret. At Hermione's urging, Harry agrees to teach students defensive practices. In response, Umbridge forbids all student groups through Educational Decree Number Twenty-Four (*OotP*, pp. 331–332) but that just makes the students more urgent to defy her authority (*OotP*, p. 354). In the end, her role as an enforcer of laws and as an arbiter of punishments subsumes her potential role as an educator. In other words, an authoritarian and inquisitor will not be much interested in encouraging student curiosity.

Umbridge as Informal Counselor

Best Practice: "SROs work to establish rapport with students by keeping up with their academic and extracurricular activities, chatting about mutual interests, and providing an attentive ear for whatever is on the student's mind…. Students come to understand that someone cares and will listen, and SROs come to understand where students' concerns lie and what might be threatening their and others' safety" (Canady, James, & Neace, 2012, p. 27).

Upon her arrival at Hogwarts, Umbridge clumsily tries to establish a rapport with the students by addressing everyone at the Sorting Ceremony.

She begins by remarking on their "happy little faces" and announces that she is certain "we'll be very good friends" (*OotP*, p. 212). But then, she quickly turns critical of Dumbledore by announcing a "new era of openness, effectiveness, and accountability ... pruning wherever we find practices that ought to be prohibited" (*OotP*, pp. 213–214). Hermione quickly surmises that the "Ministry's interfering at Hogwarts" (*OotP*, p. 214).

Umbridge encourages students to confide in her, "[I]f someone is alarming you with fibs about reborn Dark wizards, I would like to hear about it" (*OotP*, p. 245). Professor McGonagall recognizes Umbridge's investigatory roll when she warns Harry against misbehaving in Umbridge's class, "You know where she comes from, you must know to whom she is reporting" (*OotP*, p. 248). In an attempt to garner support of some students and to maintain control of others, she selects students to be members of the Inquisitorial Squad. Members are given the authority to take points away from Houses at random (*OotP*, p. 626).

Soon, Umbridge is also appointed, pursuant to Educational Decree Twenty-Three as "Hogwarts High Inquisitor" to, as Percy Weasley reported to the Daily Prophet, "get to grips with ... 'falling standards' at Hogwarts" (*OotP*, p. 307). In this role, Umbridge continues to abuse her power at every turn (*OotP*, p. 450). Here she is able to "get to know" not only students, but also faculty, as she critiques their teaching and interviews students about their teaching skills. She encourages students to talk poorly about their teachers, especially Hagrid, who she treats like "some kind of dim-witted troll" (*OotP*, p. 450). Her failure to establish an effective rapport with her community, an SRO best practice, quickly turns both students and teachers against her.

Using a Patronus to Rebuff the Dementors of School Discipline

Umbridge's unsuccessful tenure in a role not unlike that of a school resource officer, sheds light on the recent wave of Muggle criticisms of zero tolerance and authoritarian action, such as the presence of police in schools. As a necessary response to the expansion of the police in schools, recent court cases have recognized new protections for students in the context of questioning by SROs and other law enforcement officers.

Take, for example, the way in which Umbridge uses forceful and dangerous interrogation techniques. In her obsessive quest to uncover the "truth," Umbridge invests much time attempting to extract information from students, especially about "Dumbledore's Army." Shortly after taking over as Headmistress, Umbridge invites Harry to her office and attempts to serve him a spiked drink. Harry, remembering earlier warnings from Mad-Eye Moody and his refusal to drink from anything but his own flask, only pretends to drink. Umbridge questions Harry, but to her surprise, she is unable to get information from him (*OotP*, pp. 630–631). Later when Harry is caught trying to use her fireplace to magically communicate with someone, Umbridge asks Professor Snape, the potions teacher, to bring her Veritaserum, a truth serum. Snape cannot comply, because she has already used his stores on students, including Harry (*OotP*, pp. 741–744). Upset with Snape's reply, Umbridge yells, "I wish to interrogate him! ... I wish you to provide me with a potion that will force him to tell me the truth!" (*OotP*, p. 745). With no other alternative in her mind, Umbridge resorts to the use of the tortuous Cruciatus curse to force Harry to talk. Hermione reminds Umbridge that the curse is illegal and that "the Ministry wouldn't want you to break the law," but Umbridge is indifferent (*OotP*, pp. 746–747). Fortunately, Hermione stops her before she can torture Harry (*OotP*, p. 747).

The concern that confessions be given freely is at the heart of the Fifth Amendment's right not to incriminate oneself. To protect that right, Muggles are read their Miranda rights when they are taken into custody and before being questioned. Miranda rights refer to the case of *Miranda v. Arizona*, where the U.S. Supreme Court held that criminal suspects who are "in custody" must be read their rights before being interrogated by law enforcement (*Miranda v. Arizona*, 1966). The question of whether someone is "in custody" looks at whether a reasonable person in those particular circumstances would have felt like they could terminate the encounter with the police and leave (*Thomason v. Keohane*, 1995, pp. 112–113).

A child's age affects how a reasonable person would interpret the situation and must be considered in determining whether to give Miranda warnings (*J.D.B. v. North Carolina*, 2011, pp. 2402–2403). For instance, the court in *J.D.B.* considered whether a thirteen-year-old student would feel equally as able to end a police interrogation at school as might an adult who happened to be at the school for some other reason, such as chaperoning an event (p. 2405). The Supreme Court, in making the determination that a child's age should factor in determining whether a child would feel free to leave, looked at several circumstances in the law that treats minors differently than adults. For instance, in contract law, minors can enter into contracts, but the contracts can be voided by the minors if they choose not to enforce them (pp. 2303–2404). Minors also cannot vote, bring lawsuits on their own behalf, lawfully purchase alcohol, serve on juries, or marry without consent of a parent. The law recognizes an assumed emotional and mental maturity level based on age, even though that level is not always reached by the individual.

The U.S. Supreme Court in *J.D.B.* did not go so far as to say that all minors who are questioned at school would believe that they were not free to go if questioned by the police and would therefore be "in custody" and subject to Miranda warnings when questioned by the police on school grounds regarding possible criminal charges. However, a recent Kentucky Supreme Court case, when applying *J.D.B.*, found that, if law enforcement is present during questioning of students, students must receive Miranda warnings if the police want to use the students' statements against them in later criminal proceedings (*N.C. v. Commonwealth*, 2013, p. 865). In making this ruling, the Kentucky court looked at how "use of zero-tolerance policies has caused a dramatic shift away from traditional in-school discipline towards greater reliance on juvenile justice interventions, not just in drug cases, but also in common school misbehavior that ends up in the juvenile justice system" (p. 863). The greater likelihood of criminal charges being pursued, rather than just in-school discipline, influenced the court to require the warnings.

On the other hand, some have argued that the Kentucky case, as well as *J.D.B.*, may have a detrimental impact on school safety by preventing student confessions. As Justice Cunningham said in his dissent in *N.C. v. Commonwealth*, "[W]e should not be impairing school safety by the enlargement of rights of the students" (p. 871). However, as readers recognize that it is wrong for Umbridge to force a confession from Harry through either potions or pain, it is also wrong to use "school safety" as a justification for curtailing the rights of an individual student.

Conclusion

Throughout her Harry Potter series, J.K. Rowling intently mined a deep vein of issues and imagery surrounding the themes of school discipline, juvenile justice, and punishment. We know that young people who have read and enjoyed Harry Potter would seem to share the novels' anti-authoritarian stance on issues of school discipline and juvenile law enforcement. Whether reading the books gave them these attitudes or whether they were attracted to the books through their own psychological and political dispositions, we cannot yet know. We also know that many jurists are also fans of the novels and that they are sometimes referenced even in opinions from the court.[3] Perhaps then it is of no surprise that as more and more of the millennial generation reaches adulthood and as more adults, including judges and school administrators, become familiar with the books, schools are beginning to question the efficacy of zero-tolerance policies and of referring basic discipline issues to law enforcement.

Rowling laid open a world for young readers where adults, driven by fear and ambition, make repressive choices in the name of protecting children even as they worry most about protecting themselves. The books would seem to call for readers, young and old alike, to question such control. It is not a stretch to argue that, as popular as the novels are, they may effect some change in the way that the western world views issues relating to school discipline and juvenile justice. And, if that is the case, rational order may be restored.

Notes

1. I use the randomness of point deduction and awarding as a lesson in classes I teach on Harry Potter and the law to show the importance of clear law drafting. After my students become frustrated with the randomness of my house point allocations, I make each house draft their own House rules for how points will be distributed during the semester. We then practice implementing these "laws" in class to see how clear they are to interpret and apply.

2. My students prosecuted Umbridge for this offense in a mock trial presented to several student juries. She was convicted every time.

3. In a Westlaw search of appellate court cases, more than fifteen cases, about issues having nothing to do with the Harry Potter series or J.K. Rowling, made casual references to Harry Potter and events that take place in the series (e.g., "During the course of this litigation, parties moved in and out of the complaint faster than Harry Potter's broomstick in a Quidditch match." *Bethesda Title & Escrow, LLC v. Gochnour,* 14 A.3d 670, 671 [Md. App. 2011]).

References

American Psychological Association (2008). "Are zero tolerance policies effective in the schools? An evidentiary review and recommendations." *American Psychologist,* 852–862.

Application of Gault, 387 U.S. 1 (U.S. Supreme Court 1967).

Black's Law Dictionary, 9th edition (2009). Available at Westlaw BLACKS.

Canady, M., James, B., & Neace, J. (2012). "To protect and educate: The school resource officer and the prevention of violence in schools." National Association of School Resource Officers.

Cuevas, M. (2014, March 4). "Ten year old suspended for making fingers into shape of gun." Retrieved from www.cnn.com: http://www.cnn.com/2014/03/04/us/ohio-boy-suspended-finger-gun/index.html?hpt=hp_c2.

Curtis, A. (2014). "Tracing the School-to-Prison Pipeline from Zero-Tolerance Policies to Juvenile Justice Dispositions." *The Georgetown Law Journal*, 1251–1277.

Fishman, J. (2010). "Punishment in the Harry Potter Novels." In J.E. Thomas & F.G. Snyder, eds., *The Law & Harry Potter* (pp. 119–127). Durham: Carolina Academic Press.

FoxNews.com. (2014, June 18). "Minnesota teen sues school district, police chief after suspension over tweet." Retrieved from Fox News: http://www.foxnews.com/us/2014/06/18/minnesota-teen-sues-school-district-police-chief-after-suspension-over-tweet/?intcmp=latestnews.

Gierzynski, A. (2013). *Harry Potter and the Millennials: Research Methods and the Politics of the Muggle Generation*. Baltimore: John Hopkins University Press.

Goss v. Lopez, 419 U.S. 565 (U.S. Supreme Court 1975).

Gun Free Schools Act of 1994, Pub. L. No. 103–382, codified as 20 U.S.C. § 7151.

Hirschfield, P.J. (2008). "Preparing for Prison? The Criminalization of School Discipline in the USA." *Theoretical Criminology*, 79–101.

J.D.B. v. North Carolina, 131 S.Ct. 2394 (U.S. Supreme Court 2011).

James, N., & McCallion, G. (2013). "School Resource Officers: Law Enforcement Officers in School." Congressional Research Service.

Kentucky Revised Statute § 503.110. (2014). Use of force by person with responsibility for care, discipline, or safety. Available at Westlaw.

King, S. (2009, August 1). "Review of Harry Potter and the Order of the Phoenix." Retrieved from Entertainment Weekly: http://www.ew.com/article/2009/08/01/harry-potter-and-order-phoenix.

Liemer, S.P. (2010). "Bots and Gemots: Anglo-Saxon Legal References in Harry Potter." In J.E. Thomas & F.G. Snyder, eds., *The Law & Harry Potter* (pp. 19–32). Durham: Carolina Academic Press.

Losen, D.L. (2011). "Discipline Policies, Successful Schools, and Racial Justice." Boulder: National Education Policy Center.

May, D., & Chen, Y. (2009). "School Resource Officers: Who are they and what do they do?" Kentucky Center for School Safety Staff.

Miranda v. Arizona, 384 U.S. 436 (U.S. Supreme Court 1966).

N.C. v. Commonwealth, 396 S.W. 3d 852 (Kentucky Supreme Court 2013).

Perry, B.L., & Morris, E.W. (2014). "Suspending Progress: Collateral Consequences of Exclusionary Punishment in Public Schools." *American Sociological Review*, 1067–1087.

Price, P. (2009). "When is a police officer an officer of the law? The status of police officers in schools." *Journal of Criminal Law and Criminology*, 541–570.

Rowling, J.K. (1999). *Harry Potter and the Sorcerer's Stone*. New York: Scholastic.

Rowling, J.K. (2000). *Harry Potter and the Chamber of Secrets*. New York: Scholastic.

Rowling, J.K. (2001). *Harry Potter and the Prisoner of Azkaban*. New York: Scholastic.

Rowling, J.K. (2002). *Harry Potter and the Goblet of Fire*. New York: Scholastic.

Rowling, J.K. (2003). *Harry Potter and the Order of the Phoenix*. New York: Scholastic.

Thomason v. Keohane, 516 U.S. 99 (U.S. Supreme Court 1995).

Thurau, L.H. (2009–2010). "Controlling Partners: When law enforcement meets discipline in public schools." *New York Law School Law Review*, 977–1020.

Turley, J. (2009, April 21). "Lockdown High: Zero-Tolerance Policies and Authoritarian Learning." Retrieved from Res Ipsa Loquitur (The Thing Speaks for Itself): http://jonathanturley.org/2009/04/21/lockdown-high-zero-tolerance-policies-and-authoritarian-learning/.

Turley, J. (2011, February 15). "High School Student Suspended for Insulting Teacher on Facebook." Retrieved from Res Ipsa Loquitur (The Thing Speaks for Itself). Retrieved from Jonathan Turley: http://jonathanturley.org/2011/02/15/high-school-student-suspended-for-insulting-teacher-on-facebook/.

Turley, J. (2013, March 6). "Step Away from the Danish: Maryland Seven-Year-Old Boy Suspended for Nibbling Lunch Tart Into Gun Shape." Retrieved from Res Ipsa Loquitur (The Thing Speaks for Itself): http://jonathanturley.org/2013/03/06/step-away-from-the-danish-maryland-seven-year-old-boy-suspended-for-nibbling-lunch-tart-into-gun-shape/.

U.S. Department of Education (2014). "Guiding Principles: A Resource Guide for Improving School Climate and Discipline." Washington, D.C.

Wolosky, S. (2013). "Foucault at School: Discipline, Education and Agency in Harry Potter." *Children's Literature in Education*, 285–297.

Magical Econ 101:
Wealth, Labor and Inequality
in *Harry Potter* and Its Fandom

Megan Farnel

While many aspects of the *Harry Potter* universe have been consistently and contentiously debated since the series was published, one aspect of J.K. Rowling's magical world has been depicted and emphasized consistently, particularly by Rowling herself: the series' reliance on an internal logic and set of governing laws and structures. This logic, we are told, shapes every aspect of the texts and their adaptations, at micro and macro levels. Rowling famously rejected a seemingly minor aesthetic suggestion from the director of the third film, Alfonso Cuarón, a decision she explains on the DVD's extras by stating that she could never green-light a sequence, however small, that was not aligned with her understanding of how and why the magical world works (Columbus et al., 2004). In an oft-cited interview with Anne Johnstone, Rowling expanded upon the importance of these structures to her writing, arguing that it was of vital importance to her that she "knew the laws, both physical ... and legal ... because until you know the boundaries, there's no tension" (Johnstone, 2000, par. 22). Certainly Rowling knows these boundaries intimately, and her continued release of information about the magical world via venues like *Pottermore* clearly illustrates how much more knowledge she continues to possess about her imagined universe than she has offered to her readers thus far.

However, it is also the case that some of the boundaries and structuring logics of the *Potter* world are more transparent and consistent than others. Indeed, this article focuses on several intersecting and interrelated areas of the wizarding universe that seem to operate according to opaque, contradictory, and/or unnecessarily abstracted laws: finance and labor, and the uneven levels and forms of marginalization they create and enforce within the magical population. These crucial aspects of the wizarding political economy, I suggest, more closely replicate the logics of the Muggle world than Harry's, and produce telling and important tensions in the texts that impact both seemingly small, everyday moments in the stories as well as the broader political project of the narrative.

The first part of this chapter, then, reads Rowling's books with attention to the intersecting roles of the series' contradictory financial and monetary systems, as well as the racialized and gendered forms of labor that allow the wizarding world to function. In the second part of this article, I turn to the *Potter* fandom. For I argue that the history and ongoing life of many *Harry Potter* fan communities have also been shaped by the complexities and contradictions of the wizarding political economy, and that these structures are both challenged and reinforced by how fans labor with and for the series, and with/for each other. I read the broader *Potter* universe then, comprised of Rowling's novels and the numerous contributions of the series' millions of fans, as a rich and multi-vocal exploration of the complexities and violences of contemporary global capitalism, and an engagement with the inherently political role of fantasy as a force for imagining and creating alternatives.

Money

Galleons, a History

Harry's, and the reader's, first encounter with wizarding finances takes place during the former's initial venture into Diagon Alley. Harry is understandably overwhelmed by this first entrance into the magical universe and would seem to be content to simply take it in, yearning only for more eyes (*PS*, p. 56), but Hagrid immediately directs them to the bank instead. Before the pair even enters Gringotts, then, we are made aware that Diagon Alley is not the space for a *flâneur* type of wandering or window-shopping; rather, it is first and foremost a site of exchange, and Harry's participation in the space is contingent on his purchasing power.

Thankfully for Harry, he soon learns he has much in the way of purchasing power, courtesy of his inheritance. As he comes to terms with the mountains of coins in the Potter vault, Hagrid offers Harry a brief explanation, noting that there are 17 Sickles to a Galleon and 29

Knuts to a Sickle. "It's easy enough," he somewhat ironically concludes, having helped Harry place an unspecified "pile" of coins into his bag (*PS*, p. 58). Far from easy, however, is understanding *how* rich Harry (or anyone else) is, because the relative worth of wizarding currency, both in isolation and by comparison to Muggle money, is often unclear. There is no indication in the canon that the coins are not actually *made* of the elements that correspond to their colors (that is, gold, silver and bronze). Indeed, one of the Muggle employees at the Quidditch World Cup campsite describes receiving coins we can presume are Galleons as "great gold coins the size of hupcaps" (*GoF*, p. 71). However, the worth of the coins seems to bear little relation to the cost of the metals themselves, a tendency that is satirized in a popular work of fanfiction, *Harry Potter and the Methods of Rationality*:

> "In other words," Harry said, "the coins aren't supposed to be worth any more than the metal making them up?"
> Griphook stared at Harry. McGonagall looked bemused.
>   …
> *So not only is the wizarding economy almost completely decoupled from the Muggle economy, no one here has ever heard of arbitrage* [LessWrong, 2000, p. 34].

While the idea of Rowling's Harry being familiar with the term arbitrage, let alone able or willing to take advantage of the vast differences between Muggle and wizarding prices for his own gain is, of course, what makes the scene funny; the point being made here is nonetheless a question we can sincerely ask of the wizarding economy. The closest thing to an explanation readers receive for this tendency comes in book seven, when Ron angrily counters the goblin Griphook's critiques of the secrecy of "wand-carriers" by noting that "goblins know how to work metal in a way wizards have never" (*DH*, p. 305). That is, perhaps there is something about the way in which goblins work with the metal that transforms not just the material, but the market value of the gold as well. Given the number of Muggleborn or half-blood students in the wizarding world, it is nonetheless surprising that the existence of such a process is not made explicit, even if its details remain highly guarded by the goblin population.

Furthermore, the value, or exchange rate, of these metals, however they are produced, is notably inconsistent throughout the series. In *PS*, for example, Hagrid instructs Harry to pay a delivery owl 5 Knuts for the wizarding newspaper, *The Daily Prophet* (p. 50), while Hermione pays only 1 Knut for the paper in book five (*OotP*, p. 257). A fan wiki titled "A Muggle's

Guide to Harry Potter/Magic/Money" extrapolates from these scenes and, based on newspaper prices in 1991, argues that this places the Knut's worth at anywhere from U.S.$0.20–U.S.$1; such a valuation places the Sickle at U.S.$6–U.S.$30, and the Galleon at U.S.$100–U.S.$500 (par. 2). Such a scale would seem accurate given Harry's observation in the second book that the Weasleys' vault at Gringotts contains only "a very small pile of silver Sickles ... and just one gold Galleon" (*CoS*, p. 47); after all, while the series continually emphasizes the Weasleys' limited funds, they never appear to be in absolute poverty.

Perhaps seeking to clarify matters, Rowling gave an interview on Comic Relief after the publication of the third *Potter* book in which she indicated that, though subject to fluctuating exchange rates, the Galleon is equal to approximately "five British pounds" ("Comic Relief Live Chat Transcript," n.d.). Other than the price of the newspaper in the fifth text, the *Potter* money wiki notes that currency in the series has since been consistent with this valuation. Readers could easily therefore assume that the inconsistencies are the product of a first-time writer finding her feet and focusing on larger laws of the magical world more likely to be of interest to child readers than the intricate details of the wizarding economic system.

However, returning for a moment to the Weasleys' vault should give us pause over accepting this explanation too easily. After all, based on Rowling's own scale, the entire family (or, at least the two adults and the five school-aged children still living at home at this point in the narrative) is subsisting on less than ten pounds. This means either that the family's financial situation is far nearer the poverty line than the rest of the series seems to indicate, or there is something about the context of the magical world that allows prices to remain substantially deflated relative to Muggle goods and services. Even if nothing more than an error, the lack of correction in newer editions of the book implies that other mistakes which have been corrected, including the infamous error in the *Priori Incantatem* chapter in book four ("FAQ"), are more urgent and significant than a clear understanding of the wizarding economy and its very material effects on a popular and important set of characters. Given how little information we have to go on, any of these explanations seems plausible, and it is not my intention to make an argument for the validity of one reading over the other. Rather, I want to work instead from precisely the lack of a clear explanation, because we can read the ambiguity of the Weasleys' fate as a microcosm of a larger issue in the text: the lack of real need for a wizarding currency and capitalist economy at all.

What Do Magicians Want with Money, Anyway?

> *"It's impossible to make good food out of nothing!*
> *You can Summon it if you know where it is,*
> *you can transform it, you can increase the quantity if*
> *you've already got some…"*
> —Hermione Granger, *DH*, p. 241

In between much larger-scale lessons about links between wandlore and the very forces of life and death, book seven of the *Potter* series briefly introduces a critical set of limitations on what magic can accomplish. Gamp's Laws of Elemental Transfiguration, Hermione tells a hungry Ron, have five exceptions, including one that precludes a witch or wizard's ability to simply produce food. Another exception, one can safely assume, is gold. Rowling has not yet offered information about the other three, though we can certainly speculate that human reproduction and medical treatment (particularly of wounds inflicted by Dark Magic), may also be included.

What seems remarkable about these exceptions in relation to the larger political economy of the series is not that they exist, but rather, that there are so few of them. Indeed, while money itself is not shaped or controlled by wand-magic, precious few of the necessities of life would seem to be truly controlled or regulated by money. With everything from buildings to numerous textiles to transportation freely available or easily transformed (not to mention easily repaired or maintained at no cost), it is unclear why the wizarding world seems to view itself as so dependent upon the possession of wealth in the form of currency. In other words, how or why does a world in which material itself, and human relationships toward it, are radically different from the Muggle universe so closely follow the economic logics that govern the latter population?

One explanation, of course, is that the wizarding world is *not* in fact capitalist, and in particular that the exchange process is not fully equitable with the Muggle capitalist exchange of money for commodities. And certainly, some aspects of the magical economy would seem to support such a claim. Numerous scholars have commented, for example, on the fact that advertising in the wizarding world is essentially truthful—that is, while at times magic objects are still associated with grand claims and slogans, the products themselves deliver on their promises. As J. Waetjen and T.A. Gibson note, even the Sneakscope Harry receives in the third book, which initially appears to be "the only magical commodity the characters describe as rubbish … actually *works*" (2007, pp. 14–15). In Marxist terms, then, we could argue that what distinguishes wizarding products from comparable

Muggle commodities is that for the former population, an object's use-value (its function) is given greater primacy than its exchange value (its assigned price). If even objects that seem to be cheap and designed for fooling tourists work, after all, then the profit-motive would not seem to hold nearly as much sway in the magical world as it does in the Muggle one. Such a reading would also be supported by the fact we never see any production facilities akin to factories in the magical world, only small-scale artisanal shops.

While such claims are tempting, however, it is my argument that the wizarding political economy is ultimately far closer to the Muggle version than it might appear. And here is where our lingering questions about the form and value of money intersect with the broader issues we have raised about the seemingly strange reliance of the magical world on currency: put simply, the magical financial system seems to function only by rendering itself simultaneously unremarkable and hopelessly abstract to Harry and to readers. This taken-for-granted abstraction of financial systems, L.C. La Berge argues in a recent (2014) article, is a dominant trope shaping both academic and popular media discussions of (Muggle) global capitalism. The abstract, La Berge says, "is employed as a trope that organizes and structures but that itself eludes definition and representation," such that finance itself is accorded "an essentially abstract character" (p. 96). To position money and finance in such a way, La Berge goes on to contend, is to "preclude the category of representation," particularly the lived realities of these abstract systems (p. 100). In other words, to deem questions of finance and economics necessarily or naturally abstract is to similarly render the daily lives and realities of those living under such systems distant or immaterial too.

La Berge's analysis does not map onto the *Potter* universe entirely, of course, mostly because Rowling does in fact represent some of the *effects* of the inequalities that are endemic within capitalism. Readers know that the Weasleys are poor and the Malfoys rich, and that the effect on the former ranges from small humiliations (think of Ron's out-of-fashion dress robes in *Goblet*) to meaningful limitations on power and influence (information we mostly gain by comparison with the Malfoy's comfortable relationship with powerful members of the government for most of the series). However, these effects remain curiously disconnected from the larger economic system, such that it is unclear *why* the Weasleys are poor, and how it is that their limited income can actually pose such a dramatic problem in a magical world where many of the essentials of life would not seem to depend on money. It is not only, then, as Waetjen and Gibson argue, that

Rowling's class relations "more categorical than relational," when she "never suggests that the poverty of one family can be tied to the wealth of another" (2007, p. 13). Rather, the series also obscures (through what I have called "unremarkable abstraction") the larger relation between witches, wizards, and the economic system that so immediately and forcefully shapes their lives. Thus, in a twist on La Berge's analysis, what becomes unrepresentable in Rowling's world is not the effects of this system, but any real sense of their cause, a tendency which renders inequality and suffering both oddly random and largely naturalized in a way that precludes meaningful resistance.

When considered under these terms, then, the rules that Rowling does *not* break become just as significant, perhaps even moreso, as the ones that she does. By presenting readers with a magical world that not only conforms to but is fundamentally shaped by laws that do not seem to be its own, Muggle capitalism becomes a kind of untranscendable horizon, the effects of which can be obliquely remarked upon or described, but never directly approached or challenged.

Labor

A second factor complicating any attempt to understand the wizarding economy as somehow anti- or even pre-capitalist is the issue of labor. The most egregious representations of labor and its abuses are, of course, the house elves, and the majority of this section is devoted to an intersectional analysis of their work and the characteristics of the Muggle world which the position of house elves closely mirrors. However, because there can also be a tendency to reduce the problem of labor in *Potter* entirely to the mistreatment of house elves, I want to begin by considering how labor functions and is enumerated more broadly.

In the oft-cited commodity fetish section of *Capital*, Marx (fittingly, for our purposes) describes commodities as embodying a kind of magic. This "mystical character of commodities," he tells us, "does not originate … in their use-value" (1978, p. 320). Their "enigmatical character" is instead a product of the process by which the "social character of men's [*sic*] labor appears to them as an objective character stamped upon the product of that labor" (p. 320). As a result of measuring all labor by the same form of value (the money-form), a "definite social relation between men [*sic*] … assumes … the fantastic form of a relation between things" (p. 321). The magical economic system thus comes to resemble capitalism not only because the distribution and production of money and resources is described in unnecessarily abstracted ways, but because the wide range of work that goes on within this world is all ultimately expressed in the same form: those troubling units of currency, the Knut, the Sickle and the Galleon.

That the expression of wizarding labor takes this form might appear entirely self-evident and unremarkable is precisely why we might now take pause over it, for it is just as peculiar (perhaps moreso) in the wizarding context as it is in the Muggle one. The skills involved in Ollivander's construction of wands would seem so utterly dissimilar from the production of broomsticks or cauldrons as to make equating them laughable, yet the fact that all three are sold according to the same scale accomplishes just such a characterization of the work. That the production of currency is, itself, a fiercely guarded mystery to all wand-carrying magical workers truly drives this point home: witches and wizards may exercise some control over the type of work they pursue, but all of this labor is nonetheless expressed in a form that is literally outside of their control or comprehension. While the introduction of the house-elves makes questions of labor and exploitation more starkly apparent, then, the human residents of the magical world are hardly distanced from the forms of alienation and fetishistic "sorcery" that characterize capitalism.

While hardly unique through being part of the wizarding world's version of capitalism, then, house-elves are nonetheless singular in other respects. As a quick reminder, readers learn in book four (after being introduced to a single house-elf, Dobby, in book two) that in many well-off wizarding families, as well as large institutions such as Hogwarts, most manual and service labor is performed by unpaid and enslaved beings, most of whom understand such work to be their sole or primary function in life. The Marxist reading here is likely painfully apparent: the exchange of commodities for money in the wizarding economy more broadly may perform a particular type of magic that turns a relationship between people into one between things, but here there is not even a need for such a transformation. For the working body in the figure of the house-elf is always-already a thing, bred to serve, and to be bought and sold according to utility, with little to no regard for the elves themselves as sentient or individuated beings. The interchangeability of house-elf labor is illustrated early in *GoF*, when Mr. Diggory interrogates Winky (a house-elf who is found in possession of Harry's wand) by repeatedly referring to her only as "elf" (p. 120). Owners can also require that disobedient house-elves inflict physical punishments on themselves (a tendency we see both with Dobby in *CS* and with Kreacher in *DH*), which likewise emphasizes the extent to which a

house-elf's mind and body can be trained and controlled to maximize obedience and efficiency, without the need for the employer/owner to even
witness or be informed about an infraction.

The class reading of house-elves is, however, not the only one available
to us, and *Potter* scholarship has indeed extended this discussion to consider
how their position as laborers also intersects, both literally and metaphor-
ically, with other forms of marginality. Most commonly, these approaches
position house-elves either as racialized or gendered workers, who inherit
much of the additional subjugation that is associated with many workers
of such subject-positions in Muggle capitalist societies. In "Specters of
Thatcherism: Contemporary British Culture in J.K. Rowling's *Harry Potter*
series," for example, K.E. Westman contends that, for British readers, the
slavery of the house-elves evokes not only "a history of race relations, as
for the American reader, but class relations in British schools" (2002, p.
325). These two sets of histories and ongoing struggles thus collude in the
figure of the house-elf, such that Westman reads their race as "determining
their class," powerfully indicating "how one material difference (race) can
naturalize another (class)" (p. 326).[1] F. Mendlesohn (2002) similarly notes
that *GoF*'s plot is often driven by "the loyalty of a house-elf," Dobby, whom
Mendlesohn describes as a "mammy whose first loyalty is her charge" in a
way that clearly echoes representations of slavery in films like *Gone With
the Wind* and *Birth of a Nation* (p. 179). At individual and systemic levels,
then, both scholars understand house-elves' class status to be necessarily
intertwined with their status as racialized, non-human subjects.[2]

Gendered readings of the house-elves' fates, meanwhile, argue that we
must attend not only to the fact of house-elf enslavement, but to the types
of labor they most often perform. R.T. Kellner (2010), for instance, argues
that the largely domestic labors house-elves undertake (such as cooking,
cleaning, and providing material comforts like fires and warmed bed-
sheets), along with their lack of education and surnames, position them
primarily as allegories for women's work and social positions. In much the
same essentialist language that has been used to undermine feminist calls
for paid domestic and reproductive work (as well as larger feminist calls
for gender equity), Kellner draws attention to the continual emphasis on
how house elves are "bred and raised" (p. 381) to not only accept unwaged
work and punishing conditions, but to thrive in and desire them. She also
contends that by introducing Winky, the only female house-elf readers
know by name, as a character who is primarily fearful and obedient, a gendered division is introduced even within the house-elf population which
renders feminine house-elf labor even further naturalized and subjugated.

I would add to that observation that this gendered division takes place also at the level of the wage; it seems significant that Dobby, who is gendered male, eventually identifies himself as free and demands payment for his work, while Winky (who has recently been dismissed from her position) declares herself "properly ashamed of being freed" (*GF*, p. 331), and deems Dobby a "bad elf" for accepting paid work (*GF*, p. 332).

Though clearly some house-elf labor is more inescapably linked to "women's work" (and all its attendant problematics) than others, it seems clear that scholars have demonstrated strong textual evidence for reading house elves both as racialized and gendered laborers. Yet, curiously, very little existing research seems to make both of those claims at the same time; that is, existing work seems to stress the house-elves as *either* raced or gendered laborers, rather than as both simultaneously. Given that much of this work (particularly Westman's) demonstrates an attention to the ways in which different forms of marginality can and often do intersect, the seeming absence of attention to house-elves' position at the intersection of raced and gendered work is striking. Such an approach would, for instance, invite a reading of house-elf labor as most closely analogous to the disproportionate representation of racialized, migrant women in positions involving domestic and child-care labor in affluent North American and Eurowestern homes. This approach would also, I argue, emphasize critical sites of both continuity and tension between witches and house-elves in magical society. House-elf labor is a luxury that is typically available only to the wizarding upper classes. In *CoS*, Fred explains that Dobby's owners (whose identity has not yet been revealed) "will be an old wizarding family ... and they'll be rich" (p. 27). Mrs. Weasley, by contrast, is "always wishing [they] had a house-elf to do the ironing" (p. 27), but the family could never afford it. For all but the magical elite then, there is significant overlap between the types of unpaid work typically performed by women and the labors expected of house-elves.

However, rather than any meaningful acts of coalition or solidarity between the groups, or any sustained recognition of the additional trials borne by house-elves given the racist acts of disenfranchisement and violence they face, Mrs. Weasley's statement (and the family's position throughout the series as a kind of wizarding everyman) suggests that instead house-elves typically come to literally embody a desire for upward class mobility. The important exception to this generalization is, of course, Hermione. After witnessing Winky being rudely interrogated by Mr. Diggory and summarily dismissed by Mr. Crouch at the Quidditch World Cup, and then learning that Hogwarts employs a large staff of house-elves,

Hermione embarks upon a campaign to alter house-elf legal status and working conditions. Humorously titled S.P.E.W. (Society for the Promotion of Elvish Welfare), her political program is often played for laughs in the series, and is critiqued even by those who express some level of agreement with her. In addition to the Weasleys (whose complicity with the house-elf system is perhaps unsurprising), Hagrid, whose working-class vernacular and experiences of racism would seem to make him a natural ally to the cause, informs Hermione that she would be doing the house-elves "an unkindness" by setting them free, and reduces Dobby's acts of resistance to his being a "weirdo" (*GF*, p. 233). Critics argue that this produces a deep ambivalence in the text toward house-elves and the broader political tensions they embody. Westman, for instance, contends that we can read Hermione's campaign as "a satirical look at … numerous left-wing fringe movements," but that her position as somewhat of an outsider to the wizarding world also allows her to convincingly problematize beliefs that have becomes naturalized in magical culture (2002, p. 327). Kellner (2010) adds that even Dobby's acts of resistance in asking for pay and leisure time are somewhat undercut by the "little shiver" he gives when describing the much higher pay and weekends off that Dumbledore had initially offered to him before Dobby "beat [Dumbledore] down" (*GF*, p. 331).

The intersectional framework I have proposed above for reading house-elf labor politics adds a further layer of complexity (and perhaps, a partial explanation) to this ambivalence. For it is not only Hermione's possible gender-related empathy (as Kellner argues), or her definite class-advantages over the house elves (which Westman highlights) that are significant—her whiteness, particularly when read against the racialized depictions of house-elf labor, is equally significant. We might then read her actions as most akin to a particular type of white feminism, which has often similarly well-meaning but deeply problematic efforts to "improve" the lives of racialized populations, often without their input or consent. Indeed, given that Muslim women's head coverings have so frequently been a target of such programs, one specific tactic of Hermione's seems particularly striking in its resemblance (though, of course, by no means interchangeable with real-world subjects and experiences). In *OotP*, Hermione learns to knit, and begins leaving hats around the Gryffindor common room, obscured by garbage, to attempt to free unwitting house-elves. Ron rightly protests that such action is deeply troubling, for she risks "setting [house-elves] free when they might not want to be" (p. 230). Despite having seen the impact of dismissal on Winky, Hermione retorts that "of course they want to be free" (p. 230) and continues on with her efforts. Rather than speaking with or in support of the voiced desires of house-elves then, Hermione often speaks for or even over them, and in so doing not only limits the effectiveness of her work, but showcases the extent to which not only class, but also racial privileges, continue to shape both work and struggles around it in the magical world.

In this section, I have suggested that despite some distinctions between the magical and Muggle economies, both are ultimately capitalist formations. Each, I argued, is powerfully influenced by the "magic" of the commodity fetish, the process by which labor and sociality is reduced to its expression in the form of currency. The gendered and racialized nature of house-elf labor, I have also suggested, indicates that the wizarding world inherits from Muggle capitalism a reliance on and reinforcement of systemic discrimination and inequality, which are naturalized and relied upon in order to extract unpaid and exhaustive labor from particular types of subjects in the name of service and comfort for others. The series' tendency toward financial abstraction, which I noted in the opening sections of the chapter, further collude with these tendencies, allowing Rowling to at once indict and critique individual instances of inequality and violence without truly offering either a clear indicator of their broader causes, nor any serious representation of efforts to alter such conditions. The Muggle Prime Minister's misguided assertion that magical beings "can sort out—well—*anything!*" (*HBP*, p. 24) perhaps then takes on a sad new irony. For it is not only the specific figure of Voldemort, but the Muggle world's own entrenched, unjust and deeply discriminatory political economy that, apparently, "can do Magic, too" (*HBP*, p. 24).

Fandom

In this section, we now turn to what is perhaps an entirely different type of magic: the powerful and potentially transformative work of *Harry Potter*'s massive fandom, particularly online. I do not pretend to offer an unbiased account here, for like many, *Potter* was my first exposure to fandom, and remains an important site of comfort, familiarity and support in my own life and work. Neither, however, is what follows a purely celebratory reading of *Potter* fans and their work. I am just as interested in the moments where the fandom clearly carries over some of the issues within the canonical series (and of global capital more broadly) as I am in the moments when it attempts to explicitly resist or transform them. However, my hope is that my own experience within and care for the fandom can result in an account that is both nuanced and compassionate both towards its strengths and towards its ongoing struggles and challenges as part of a broader emancipatory project.

Methodologically, I limit my focus primarily to digital forms of *Potter* fandom for two reasons. First, as I will argue below in more depth, the massive scope and scale of *Potter*'s fanbase has a history which is very much intertwined with the rise of the Internet and its increasing adoption in homes during the early stages of the series. None of this is to deny the importance of offline fandom (or to position a strong and immovable distinction between fans on and offline more broadly), but rather an acknowledgement of the fact that the digital context was and remains a critical component that allowed for the rapid growth and expansion of *Harry Potter* fan groups. Secondly, I have isolated online *Potter* fandoms because I argue that certain forms of sociality and labor are either unique to that context, or at least significantly more influential within it.

Money/Materiality in Fandom

As I briefly alluded to in the introduction to this section, the rise of *Potter* fandom and the growth of personal computing and the Internet are deeply intertwined. Numerous scholars (Grumpta, 2009, p. 217; Jenkins, 2006, 2012; Jenkins, Busse, Klink & Baym, 2011; Tossenberger, 2008) have noted how a wide range of online venues such as a discussion boards, e-mail listservs and blogs created unprecedented opportunities for fans to come together and bond over shared interests. The popularization of the home or personal computer in particular allowed fans to do so with some feeling of privacy, an important consideration for many given the shame often associated with fandom (Zubernis & Larsen, 2012), at the same time as fans' ability to recognize and form alliances based on the global popularity of the series also highlighted both the size and influence of the *Potter* fanbase to itself (Jenkins, 2006). While it would be a stretch to claim a direct or causal relationship between the immense *Potter* fandom and the growth of the Internet, then, it does seem safe to say that the two shared, and continue to share, a particular form of intimacy which was unprecedented at the time, and which makes their histories particularly relevant to one another.

On the surface, however, the political economy of online *Harry Potter* fandoms would admittedly appear to have little in common with that of the wizarding world. Whereas the capitalism of the *Potter* universe is frequently veiled, particularly given the almost universal truthfulness of magical advertising, much of the Internet (like most of the Muggle world) is openly and unapologetically capitalist, and often bombards users with untrustworthy spam and advertising (which only seem magical in the increasing extent to which they are often "personalized" using the browsing histories of individual users). There would seem to be little, if anything, that is abstract about the economic system that shapes Muggle life on and offline, *Potter* fandom included.

Recall, however, that the La Berge piece cited in section one is not a commentary on *Potter* at all, but an analysis of the increasing depiction of neoliberal capitalism as a force of complexity and abstraction. Where do we see these discourses and their effects at work online in *Potter* fandoms? I argue that the intertwined histories of finance and abstraction are most powerfully at work in these spaces through their alignment with a third term: materiality, or, more precisely, immateriality. For during the same period that the *Potter* series and its fandom were growing and developing, the Internet was itself becoming a more predominant force, and with it arose some curious ideas about the changing role of matter.

In both academic and popular media spaces at the time, there was an intense focus on the idea of the digital as a space that challenges or reworks traditional concepts of space, identity, and embodiment. J. Daniels (2009), for example, notes how pervasive such ideas were within early cyberfeminist thought, which often linked the supposed utopianism of the digital to the "subversive potential of human/machine cyborgs, identity tourism, and disembodiment" (p. 101). Put simply, Daniels contends that much of this work was characterized by a tendency to believe that the supposed anonymity of the Internet allowed users to escape their embodied, material realities (and the accompanying forms of oppression and discrimination that can often come with those conditions). Such ideas, and the attendant fears of the potential consequences of anonymity have hardly been entirely dismissed since that point; one need only think of the 2010 film *Catfish*, in which the central tension is rooted in the anxiety of never being able to truly confirm who one is interacting with while online. Without decades of online sexism, racism, homophobia, and other discriminatory violences, however, such analysis was both more persuasive and more optimistic about the link between the digital and emancipatory political projects.

What does this have to do with finance and economics, though? Quite a lot, I would suggest, particularly when taken in combination with the way the *Potter* series itself was marketed. S. Brown's "*Harry Potter* and the Fandom Menace" (2007), while often dismissive and judgmental of fans in a way that displays both the article's age and a kind of touristing or surface-level approach to fan culture, does offer some useful insight into these P.R. strategies. Brown notes that Rowling's much focused-upon background, and her repeated expressions of discomfort with the growth of *Harry Potter* as a brand, while sincere, also positioned her as a kind of anti-capitalist "rebel" (p. 178). This approach allowed the marketing team behind *Potter* to locate itself in what Brown (building on research from Heath and Potter) notes is a long tradition of "anti-marketing," which has been "employed by copious conveniently counter-cultural CEOs ... rock stars, movie makers and arts industry denizens" (p. 178). Such a move not only effected public perception of Rowling and her texts, I would suggest, but also shaped how fans understood themselves and their role in generating profits for the books, and later the films.

To be clear, I am not suggesting that *Potter* fans, then or now, were somehow duped into purchasing the books and other associated merchandise without really realizing it. In fact, several episodes in fandom history (two of which I will go on to detail shortly) clearly illustrate the strong awareness many fans had about their power and influence as the primary consumers of all things *Potter*. What I would contend, though, is that the marketing of the series presented consumption and fan production as resistant, counter-cultural acts. This tactic, particularly when combined with methods of generating profit online which still felt new and abstract to many (such as page-views and online ad revenues) obscured not only the profit motive of the author, as well as her publishers and the film studios involved with adapting the series for the screen, but also the full extent to which the financial success of all those enterprises was dependent on fans and their actions online, even (perhaps especially) in the moments when they were not actually purchasing something. Much as within the *Potter* series itself, then, there existed within and around its fandom an abstracted conception of finance which neatly aligned itself with popular conceptions of the digital as a space removed or divorced from the material world. The result was a fannish political economy which, though unmistakably capitalist, was nonetheless unclear about fans' position at the intersection of finance and resistance.

We can turn to a specific episode in *Potter* fan history which has since passed almost into the status of legend for confirmation. While the vast majority of *Potter* fan sites had originally been tolerated, even encouraged, by Rowling and her publishers, Warner Brother's purchase of the film rights to the series initially seemed to herald a dramatic shift in that "hands-off" policy. "The studio," Henry Jenkins explains, "had a long-standing practice of seeking out Web sites whose domain names used copyrighted or trade-marked phrases" (2006, p. 186). After locating such pages, they tended to undergo what Warner calls a "sorting out" process, whereby "each site was suspended until the studio could assess what the site was doing with the ... franchise" (2006, p. 187). *Potter* was not the first franchise on which Warner employed this tactic. However, the studio had underestimated not just the P.R. nightmare that would result in sending threatening legal notices to so many sites created and managed by teens and tweens, but the vast size and impressive organization of the *Potter* fandom as a whole. The Defence Against the Dark Arts organization, based in the U.S., soon arose as a collective response, allowing prominent figures in the struggle to "coor-dinate media outreach and activism against the studio"; these efforts included a petition to the studio, as well as several interviews on national news outlets (Jenkins, 2006, p. 186). Warner Brothers eventually admitted to mishandling their relationship with the fandom, and developed what Jenkins calls a "more collaborative policy for engaging with *Harry Potter* fans" (187). This policy often involved the studio partnering with, and even sponsoring, some of the more popular fan sites and programs. Jenkins thus reads participants in the *Potter* fandom as groups who are "mapping out new strategies for negotiating around and through globalization, intellec-tual property struggles, and media conglomeration," and "asserting their own rights even in the face of powerful entities" (p. 205).

Certainly this is true to a degree, and the account Jenkins offers of these events is perhaps more nuanced and balanced than other writing on the mat-ter—such as the understandably celebratory *Harry, a History*, a book on *Harry Potter* fandom written by one of its most prominent members (Anelli, 2008). However, we might also be wary of the extent to which this period in *Potter* fan history has been circulated and re-circulated, as well as the often-heroic way in which it is described. After all, this narrative can, and I argue, has been largely aligned with the set of strategies I identified above in which fandom's financial contributions to the *Potter* franchise are mini-mized, de-materialized, and recast primarily as a tale of grassroots organizing and resistance. And much as I suggested in the opening section of this chapter that the odd inconsistencies and lack of information surrounding the nature of money in *Potter* itself allows for too much to be covered up (particularly the links between that money and various forms of inequality and suffering), we might ask what links this heroizing of the *Potter* fandom similarly dis-courages one from making. For it is not only various circuits of profit which are obscured but (again, much like in the *Potter* books themselves), accom-panying circuits of labor and differential marginalization.

Labor

Perhaps the easiest way into considering labor and its discontents within the *Potter* fandom is through a second of its most famous and contentious debates: that surrounding the *Harry Potter Lexicon*. Initially, the story was a happy one; the *Lexicon*, an encyclopedia of all things related to the *Potter* universe, began as a fan-site which was so comprehensive and well-regarded that Rowling herself admitted to using it for continuity-checking while writing some of the later books in the series (Schwabach, 2009, p. 420). However, the relationship between the two soured when the webmaster of the site, Steven Vander Ark, announced his intention to publish the material from the site in a for-profit text. Eventually, Rowling and her publishers launched a lawsuit aimed at preventing the text's publication, and the ensuing court case provoked numerous debates about how to define concepts like fair-use and derivation in the contemporary context.

The case and the broader debates that went on around it also, blogger Raizel notes, produced a wide-scale split within *Potter* fandom. While there are takes that are more and less complex, Raizel argues that ultimately, the vast majority of positions on the matter are divided into two camps. In the first, Rowling is deemed a "super-rich author trying to suppress a labor of love by a fan," and Vander Ark as "a fan wanting to show is appreciation for the work he loves" (2008, April 24, pars. 3–4); in the second, Vander Ark is cast as "someone trying to make money based on another author's creation," and Rowling as an "author wanting to protect her precious creations from an unauthorized use by another" (2008, April 24, pars. 3–4). Raizel takes issue with the reduction of the issue to these two positions not because each does not hold some validity, but because this binaristic take tends to leave out another very significant population directly involved in the *Lexicon*'s original iteration as a site: the numerous other fans who contributed their own time and labor. This issue came up briefly during the first day of the trial, Raizel notes, as Vander Ark was directly asked if he would be offering any compensation to other fans who had been involved with the *Lexicon* were it to be published. However, on the second day of the trial, the judge quickly dismissed the relevance of this discussion, arguing that "whether or not the fans contributed in part is a side issue" to what was deemed the larger and more pertinent matter of fair use (as cited in Raizel, 2008, April 24, par 12).

The majority of fan (and, I would add, academic) coverage of the topic has largely taken this statement to heart, continually focusing on Rowling and Vander Ark as two opposing forces engaged in a struggle over the shifting context of fair-use (Huggins, 2010; Schwabach, 2009; Siskind, 2009). Indeed, this historicization of the struggles over the *Lexicon* has arguably become even more firmly entrenched in both fanlore and scholarship since Raizel's 2008 post. This makes the blog's reminder that the *Lexicon* "was created … with a large number of fans helping to make the entries accurate," and converted into a monetized book format with "no consideration of the … fans that contributed and made the website a success" (par. 5) all the more significant an intervention. For even fans positioning themselves on Vander Ark's "side" participate, by isolating the *Lexicon* to the work of a single figure, in the erasure of their own work, and the work of their fellow fans, as meaningful labor deserving of recognition and/or compensation.

That this characterization of fan labor, as dismissed and devalued even by fans themselves, echoes much of what I argued about house-elves in the first section is, of course, no accident. Indeed, though there are some meaningful and important distinctions between the two groups (most of which are discussed in depth shortly), they also share several important qualities. First, particular affects are deployed as an explanation or excuse for fair compensation and treatment. The *Potter* canon constantly emphasizes the fact that house-elves' primary source of joy and fulfillment is found through the service they provide humans. Hagrid deems Hermione's efforts with S.P.E.W. an "unkindness," for instance, because serving humans is "what they [house-elves] like" (*GF*, p. 233). George, a frequent visitor to the Hogwarts kitchens, similarly informs Hermione that the house elves are "happy," and that they believe "they've got the best job in the world" (*GF*, p. 211). In fandom, work is often similarly positioned as a labor of love, both in the *Lexicon* case and in other instances of monetized fan production, including, most recently, *Fifty Shades of Grey*, which was originally a work of *Twilight* AU (alternate universe) fanfiction (Jones, 2014).

It is not that we have to read either of these feelings (the happiness of the house-elves or the loving devotion of the fan) as somehow inauthentic or untrue. However, affect theorists such as Ahmed (2010) have demonstrated that affects like happiness are frequently used as a mechanism for disciplining marginalized populations; one famous example she returns throughout her work, for instance, is what she calls the "feminist killjoy," who is deemed the problem for not finding humor in, say, a sexist joke or enjoying the experience of being harassed on the street. And we do see such discipline within both *Potter* and its fandom. Winky, the openly unhappy and alcoholic house-elf, is literally covered over with a table-cloth during one of Hermione, Harry and Ron's visits to the kitchens (*GoF*, p.

467). Numerous high-profile fan groups, including *The Leaky Cauldron*, meanwhile, publicly cut ties with Vander Ark during the trial, citing not the concerns raised by Raizel, but a "fundamental" disconnection with how Vander Ark understands and presents the role of fandom (Anelli, 2008 March 24, par. 9). Both of these limit cases, and the types of responses they evoked from their peers, thus suggest that neither the happy house-elf or the loving fan are quite as natural or uncomplicated as they seem. Instead, both illustrate how specific affects enforce systems of unwaged and marginalized labor.

Furthermore, the gendered dynamics at work in fandom and house-elf labor are often similar as well. Many fan spaces, particularly those that center around the production of fanfiction, are consistently populated primarily by women. The *Potter* fandom certainly conforms to this tendency; while children and adults identifying all along the gender spectrum participate, many of the most influential individuals and *Potter*-related sites in fandom (including *The Leaky Cauldron* and *The Daily Prophet*) were started and run entirely or primarily by women. Moreover, though certain genres of fan work, as well as specific fandoms, maintain a more masculinist culture and population, M. Stanfill (2011) argues that fan labor more broadly tends to be socially gendered feminine.[3] Drawing on a range of popular culture representations of fans, Stanfill notes that men who do elect to participate in fan culture are typically deemed only "questionably masculine," and certainly not "virile or athletic" (par. 3.2). Coverage of the *Lexicon* trials would seem to implicitly support such characterizations of male fans, particularly the innumerable articles that detailed Vander Ark's tearful breakdown during the second day of the trial (Boswell, 2008; Hartocollis, 2008; Pilkington, 2008). Both house-elf and fan work, then, share a tendency to be articulated or represented as forms of "women's work." Given that women's domestic and reproductive work are, much like fan work, frequently deemed labors of love, fandom's labors appear inseparable from, and materially affected by, the gendering of fan participation and representation. Interestingly, however, counterposing Vander Ark with Dobby also seems to suggest one critical distinction: while I suggested that Dobby's gender allows his resistance to be heroized (particularly in comparison to Winky), the blanket femininity that is often used to represent fandom as a whole appears to have worked the opposite way in Vander Ark's case. That is, Vander Ark's gender does not appear to have accorded him the privilege of having his rejection of the typical fandom labor model (particularly its lack of compensation) read in a more complimentary or resistant light. While this in no way indicates that fandom is some kind of gender-neutral or post-gender space, it does suggest that the status of fan labor itself is gendered in such a way that does not necessarily require that the gender identity of fans themselves uncomplicatedly correspond.

Matters only become more complex when, as we did with house-elf labor, we also consider the role of race within discussion of the *Harry Potter* fandom and its labors. In many respects, this is the factor that most clearly differentiates house-elves from Muggle fans. For while house-elf labor is largely essentialized as a natural tendency and desire of their race, the access, time, and ability to be involved in (and represented by) fandom remains a luxury, and one which has often been demonstrated to be unevenly available to differing populations based on numerous factors including race (see Jenkins, 2002, April 1, as well as meta discussions of race within fandom including RaceFail). And despite the global scope of the *Potter* fandom, there have been recurring indications of its pervasive whiteness and the types of conscious and unconscious modes of discrimination that can arise from such demographics. M. Velazquez and blogger LadyGeekGirl (the latter of whom has written extensively on issues surrounding race, gender, and sexuality in fandom) have both noted, for example, tensions within the *Potter* fandom surrounding two characters: the unambiguously racialized Cho Chang, and Lavender Brown. The latter was played by Jennifer Smith, an actress of color, in the early *Potter* films. However, the role was infamously recast when Brown becomes a love interest to Ron Weasley in the sixth film, a move which has sparked intense debate within the fandom about whether the decision constitutes whitewashing, or a stricter adherence to the few canonical indicators Rowling provides about Brown's ethnicity (Velazquez, 2013, p. 100). While Velazquez highlights some of the creative reworkings and critiques of race within the *Potter* fandom (p. 105), LadyGeekGirl argues that the "out and out hatred" (2013, September 2, par. 3) of both Brown and Chang indicates the persistence of whiteness and white supremacist attitudes within *Potter* fan spaces. Moreso than the absence of any magical methods of ensuring oppression and obedience, the factor that most seems to differentiate house-elf labor from that of fan labor is the way in which race often acts as a barrier that keeps certain fans *out* (or inside but marginalized) rather than, as in the case of house elves, ensuring that racialized bodies remain internal to a system of work that much of the rest of the wizarding world depends upon.

How, then, do we read the types of activism that have arisen from within the *Potter* fandom? Many of these projects, after all, have taken on explicitly anti-racist language and causes, and are too nuanced and thoughtful to be simply or carelessly equated with Hermione's well-meaning but often offensive political efforts in the *Potter* canon. Take, for example, the Harry Potter Alliance (HPA). Formed by community organizer Andrew Slack, the group now "has more than 100, 000 members in more than 70 active chapters around the world" (Jenkins, 2012, par. 3.2), and has mobilized around issues ranging from gay marriage to fundraising for Haitians affected by the 2010 earthquake. In perhaps its best known campaign, Not in Harry's Name, the group recently won a major victory when they successfully pressured Warner Brothers to commit to having all *Potter*-branded chocolate produced only by companies that observe fair trade policies (Maggiacomo, 2015). Jenkins contends that the HPA's ability to "organize and mobilize quickly, to frame issues and educate supporters, [and] get the word out through every new media platform and channel" is what distinguishes the organization, and those like it, from "more casual deployment of pop culture references" (2012, p. 23). And certainly, there is no arguing with the very real results the group has achieved, often in support of racialized and otherwise marginalized populations.

If they truly wish to overcome the problems of their own source texts, however, the HPA and other fan activist efforts and organizations also have to reckon with their own exclusivity, and the fact that not everyone is willing or permitted to identify with the heroes of the *Potter*-verse, or to take action based upon their lessons. This does not mean anything as patronizing as "outgrowing" the *Potter* framework as a means of achieving social change. In the context of global capitalism, the time for positioning meaningful socio-political change at the opposite pole from fan culture and consumption has long since ceased to be a useful approach (if indeed it ever was, fraught as such analysis tended to be with class, race and gender-based discrimination). Such shifts might, however, take the form of an emphasis and explicit naming of systemic oppressions, and a move away from the somewhat liberalist tendencies of Rowling and her works, which I have argued tend to divorce or at least mask the relationship between individuals and the larger structures that govern their lives. They might also involve mobilizing around issues with less normative privilege, such as gay marriage,[4] and contributing instead to more controversial causes such as prison abolition movements or efforts to resist the labor practices that go into producing the very digital technologies many fans use to connect with one another. Certainly, any efforts to democratize or extend the reach and relevance of fandom would also involve continuing to develop partnerships and coalitions with other community organizations, a move that has already enriched and enhanced HPA efforts, but which must continue and expand if the group is truly to speak *with* marginalized populations rather than simply *for* them.

Ultimately, I am not arguing for any one particular cause or tactic to supplant or replace the other campaigns undertaken by the HPA and other groups within *Potter* fandom; there is room and need for a range of approaches that account both for small-scale, everyday injustices as well as the larger systems at their root. In order for the latter to take place with more frequency within *Potter* fandom, though, fans must grapple not only with forces like the studios adapting the original narratives, but with the *Potter* canon, which reinforces just as many of the problems of the Muggle world as they challenge, and with fandom's own complicity in those inequities.

Conclusion

While *Potter*'s fandom and canon are often discussed in isolation from one another, I have brought them together in this paper to attend to an ongoing conversation between the two related to labor, economics, gender, and race. Rowling's book, I have argued, repeatedly illustrates individual experiences of oppression and discrimination, but by representing money and the broader financial system in an abstracted and mystified way, also refuses to offer any decisive indication that those very structures are the cause of many of such experiences. Furthermore, by reading the house-elves as a population that is both gendered and racialized, I have suggested that the magical world within the texts inherits from its Muggle counterparts many modes of naturalized, systemic inequality, as well as the complex troubles of creating political movements to counter those systems.

The *Potter* fandom, particularly online, exhibits many of the same tendencies and struggles. I argued that the marketing of the *Potter* series, when combined with larger discourses about the Internet as a space of "immateriality," resulted in a tendency to obscure fans' position as not only consumers, but producers who were critical to the financial success of the franchise even when they were not buying books, movie tickets, or memorabilia. Like the house-elf laborers in the books, too, I noted that fan labor is often gendered in a way that is held up as a justification for its lack of compensation. The racial exclusivity of fandom, however, also sets this population distinctly apart from the house-elves, and, I argued, makes fan activist efforts focused on these inequalities essential if fans do not wish to replicate the limitations of the source texts.

The latter is important, of course, for while the *Potter* canon may be largely concluded, its fan base remains massive, committed, and in possession of significant political, economic, and social influence. Perhaps what remains as perhaps the fandom's largest obstacle, then, particularly if it wishes to continue the aim expressed *on The Daily Prophet* website to make "progress toward revolution" (as cited in Grumpta, 2009, p. 223), is not a turn toward realism, but a further extension of the tremendous imagination of the *Potter* universe, toward a world beyond capitalism and all its violent magics.

Notes

1. One might also reverse the dynamic Westman describes, reading the wizarding world's need for inexpensive labor as a primary reason for the naturalization of this understanding of the house-elves as a race. This approach would align with similar readings (Harvey, 2006, p. 383) of capitalism as a model that (inconsistently) enforces divisions amongst gendered, racial, sexual, and ability-based lines in order to capture the most labor for the lowest cost.

2. House elves' non-human status means that they are an imperfect allegory for any human population in the Muggle world, a point Gumpta (2009) also makes. While house-elves could also fruitfully be read through the lens of a field like critical animal studies, I foreground their close parallels with racialized and gendered human subjects here, partially because I argue that what Grumpta calls house-elves "recognizability" (p. 123) as pseudo-human laborers invites such an approach.

3. Jenkins interestingly argues that this social gendering of fandom was particularly strong for *Potter* fans, whom he identifies broadly as embodying "Fan Girls as a cultural and political force" (2007 May 21, par. 18).

4. This is not to say that marriage equality is an unimportant goal. However, it is also a project that many (Duggan, 2003; Puar, 2007; Spade & Wilse, 2013; Whitehead, 2012) link to what is called homonormativity, or the broader depoliticization and alignment of queer culture with heteronormative ideals.

References

Ahmed, S. (2010). *The promise of happiness.* Durham: Duke University Press.

Anelli, M. (2008). *Harry, a history: The true story of a boy wizard, his fans, and life inside the Harry Potter phenomenon.* New York: Pocket Books.

Anelli, M. (2008, March 24). "Lexicon trial updates and important announcement about the floo network." Retrieved January 13, 2014, from http://www.the-leaky-cauldron.org/2008/3/24/lexicon-trial-updates-and-important-announcement-about-floo-network/.

Boswell, W. (2008). "Steven Vander Ark breaks down in Harry Potter lexicon trial." *Crushable.* Retrieved from http://www.crushable.com/2008/04/16/entertainment/steven-vander-ark-breaks-down-in-harry-potter-lexicon-trial/.

Brown, S. (2007). "Harry Potter and the fandom menace." In B. Cova, R. Kozinets & A. Shankar, eds., *Consumer tribes* (pp. 177–191). London: Butterworth-Heinemann.

Columbus, C., D. Heyman and M. Radcliffe (producers), & Cuarón, A. (director). (23 May 2004). *Harry Potter and the Prisoner of Azkaban* (motion picture). Warner Bros.

"Comic Relief Live Chat Transcript." (n.d.). Retrieved December 18, 2014, from http://www.accio-quote.org/articles/2001/0301-comicrelief-staff.htm.

Daniels, J. "Rethinking cyberfeminism(s): Race, gender, and embodiment." *WSQ: Women's Studies Quarterly* 37 (1/2), 101–124. Retrieved from http://login.ezproxy.library.ualberta.ca/login?url=http://search.ebscohost.com/login.aspx?direct=true&db=edsgao&AN=edsgcl.200538263&site=eds-live&scope=site.

Duggan, L. (2003). *The twilight of equality? Neoliberalism, cultural politics, and the attack on democracy.* Boston: Beacon Press.

"FAQ." (n.d.) Retrieved March 12, 2010, from http://www.jkrowling.com/textonly/en/faq_view.cfm?id=19.

Gumpta, S. (2009). *Re-reading Harry Potter*, 2d ed. New York: Palgrave MacMillan.

Hartocollis, A. (2008, April 16). "Sued by Harry Potter's creator, lexicographer breaks down on the stand." *New York Times.* Retrieved from http://www.nytimes.com/2008/04/16/nyregion/16potter.html?_r=0.

Harvey, D. (2006). "The production of spatial configurations: The geographical mobilities of capital and labour." In *The limits to capital* (pp. 373–412). London: Verso.

Huggins, C.M. (2010). "The judge's order and the rising phoenix: The role public interests should play in limiting author copyrights in derivative-work markets." *Iowa Law Review* 95(2), 695–722. Retrieved from http://login.ezproxy.library.ualberta.ca/login?url=http://search.ebscohost.com/login.aspx?direct=true&db=lgs&AN=502148073&site=eds-live&scope=site.

Jenkins, H. (2002, April 1). "The color blind web: A techno-utopia, or a fantasy to assuage liberal guilt?" *MIT Technology Review*, n.p. Retrieved from http://www.technologyreview.com/article/401404/cyberspace-and-race/.

Jenkins, H. (2006). "Why Heather can write: Media literacy and the Harry Potter wars." In *Convergence culture: Where old and new media collide* (pp. 169–205). New York: New York University Press.

Jenkins, H. (2007, May 21). "Everybody loves Harry?" (weblog). Retrieved from http://henryjenkins.org/2007/05/everybody_loves_harry.html.

Jenkins, H. (Interviewer) & Busse K., Klink F. & Baym N (Interviewees). (2011). *Acafandom and beyond: Week three, part two* (interview transcript). Retrieved from Jenkins' personal weblog: http://henryjenkins.org/2011/06/acafandom_and_beyond_week_thre_1.html.

Jenkins, H. (2012). "'Cultural acupuncture': Fan activism and the Harry Potter Alliance." *Transformative Works and Cultures* 1(10), n.p. Retrieved from http://journal.transformativeworks.org/index.php/twc/article/view/305/259.

Johnstone, A. (2000, July 8). "The hype surrounding the fourth Harry Potter book belies the fact that Joanne Rowling had some of her blackest moments writing it—and that the pressure was self imposed; a kind of magic." *The Herald.* Retrieved from http://www.accio-quote.org/articles/2000/0708-herald-johnstone.html.

Jones, B. (2014). "Fifty shades of exploitation: Fan labour and fifty shades of grey." *Transformative works and cultures* 15(1): n.p. Retrieved from http://journal.transformativeworks.org/index.php/twc/article/view/501/422.

Kellner, R.T. (2010). "J.K. Rowling's ambivalence toward feminism: House elves—women in disguise—in the 'Harry Potter' books." *The Midwest Summer Quarterly 51*(4), 367–385. Retrieved from http://login.ezproxy.library.ualberta.ca/login?url=http://search.ebscohost.com/login.aspx?direct=true&db=edsglr&AN=edsgcl.232311203&site=eds-live&scope=site.

La Berge, L.C. (2014). "The rules of abstraction: Methods and discourses of finance." *Radical History Review 1*(118), 93–112. DOI 10.1215/01636545-2349133.

LadyGeekGirl (2013, September 2). "Fanfiction: Not necessarily a voice for minorities" (web log post). Retrieved from https://ladygeekgirl.wordpress.com/2013/09/02/fanfiction-not-necessarily-a-voice-for-minorities/.

LessWrong. (2000). *Harry Potter and the methods of rationality* (Google Books mirror version). Retrieved from https://books.google.ca/books?id=vrPQAwAAQBAJ&printsec=frontcover&source=gbs_ge_summary_r&cad=0#v=onepage&q&f=false.

Maggiacomo, M. (2015, January 14). "We won! Harry Potter chocolate will be fair trade" (web log post). Retrieved from http://thehpalliance.org/2015/01/we-won-harry-potter-chocolate-will-be-fair-trade/.

Marx, K. (1978). "Capital, Volume One." In R.C. Tucker, ed., *The Marx-Engels reader*, 2d ed. (pp. 294–438). New York: W.W. Norton.

Mendlesohn, F. (2002). "Crowning the king: Harry Potter and the construction of authority." In L.A. Whited, ed., *The ivory tower and Harry Potter: Perspectives on a literary phenomenon* (pp. 159–181). Columbia: University of Missouri Press.

Muggles' Guide to Harry Potter/Magic/Money. (n.d.). Retrieved January 2, 2015, from http://en.wikibooks.org/wiki/Muggles'_Guide_to_Harry_Potter/Magic/Money.

Pilkington, E. (2008, April 16). "Emotions run high at Harry Potter's a to z trial." *The Guardian*. Retrieved from http://www.theguardian.com/books/2008/apr/16/harry potter.law.

Puar, J. (2007). *Terrorist assemblages: Homonationalism in queer times*. Durham: Duke University Press.

Raizel. (2008, April 24). "Lexicon of love? Why the Harry Potter Lexicon lawsuit isn't only about derivative works and fair use" (web log). Retrieved from http://thelearned fangirl.com/2008/04/24/lexicon-of-love-why-the-harry-potter-lexicon-lawsuit-isnt-only-about-derivative-works-and-fair-use/.

Rowling, J.K. (1997). *Harry Potter and the philosopher's stone*. Vancouver: Raincoast Books.

Rowling, J.K. (1998). *Harry Potter and the chamber of secrets*. Vancouver: Raincoast Books.

Rowling, J.K. (1999). *Harry Potter and the prisoner of Azkaban*. Vancouver: Raincoast Books.

Rowling, J.K. (2000). *Harry Potter and the goblet of fire*. Vancouver: Raincoast Books.

Rowling, J.K. (2003). *Harry Potter and the order of the phoenix*. Vancouver: Raincoast Books.

Rowling, J.K. (2005). *Harry Potter and the half-blood prince*. Vancouver: Raincoast Books.

Rowling, J.K. (2007). *Harry Potter and the deathly hallows*. Vancouver: Raincoast Books.

Schwabach, A. (2009). "The Harry Potter Lexicon and the world of fandom: Fan fiction, outside works, and copyright." *University of Pittsburgh Law Review 70*(3), 387–434. Retrieved from http://login.ezproxy.library.ualberta.ca/login?url=http://search.ebsco host.com/login.aspx?direct=true&db=edswss&AN=000267299800002&site=eds-live&scope=site.

Siskind, S. (2009). "Crossing the fair use line: The demise and revival of the Harry Potter Lexicon and its implications for the fair use doctrine in the real world and on the Internet." *Cardozo Arts & Entertainment 27*(1), 291–312. Retrieved from http://login.ezproxy.library.ualberta.ca/login?url=http://search.ebscohost.com/login.aspx?direct=true&db=edshol&AN=hein.journals.caelj27.12&site=eds-live&scope=site.

Spade, D. & Wilse, C. (2013). "Marriage will never set us free." Retrieved November 23, 2014, from http://www.organizingupgrade.com/index.php/modules-menu/beyond-capitalism/item/1002-marriage-will-never-set-us-free.

Stanfill, M. (2011). "Doing fandom, (mis)doing whiteness: Heteronormativity, racialization and the discursive construction of fandom." *Transformative Works and Cultures 8*(1), n.p. Retrieved September 8, 2014, from http://journal.transformativeworks.org/index.php/twc/article/view/256/243.

Tosenberger, C. (2008). "Homosexuality at the online Hogwarts: Harry Potter slash fanfiction." *Children's Literature 36*(1), 185–207. Retrieved from http://login.ezproxy.library.ualberta.ca/login?url=http://search.ebscohost.com/login.aspx?direct=true&db=edspmu&AN=edspmu.S1543337408100096&site=eds-live&scope=site.

Velazquez, M. (2013). "The occasional ethnicities of Lavender Brown: Race as a boundary object in Harry Potter." In M.K. Booker, ed., *Critical insights: Contemporary speculative fiction* (pp. 100–114). Ipswich, MA: Salem Press.

Waetjen, J., & Gibson, T.A. (2007). "Harry Potter and the commodity fetish: Activating corporate readings into the journey from text to commercial intertext." *Communication and Critical/Cultural Studies 4*(1), 3–26. DOI: 10.1080/14791420601151289.

Westman, K.E. (2002). "Spectres of Thatcherism: Contemporary British culture in J.K. Rowling's Harry Potter series." In L.A. Whited, ed., *The ivory tower and Harry Potter: Perspectives on a literary phenomenon* (pp. 305–328). Columbia: University of Missouri Press.

Whitehead, J.C. (2012). *The nuptial deal: Same-sex marriage and neo-liberal governance.* Chicago: University of Chicago Press.

Zubernis, L., & Larsen, K. (2012). *Fandom at the crossroads: Celebration, shame, and fan/producer relationships.* Newcastle upon Tyne, UK: Cambridge Scholars.

Keeping the Magic Alive: The Fandom and *"Harry Potter* Experience" After the Franchise

CHIN-TING LEE[1]

Four years have passed since *DH2* was released, signifying an end to a decade long, worldwide media phenomenon that has caught the hearts of many, regardless of age, race, or gender. This essay examines how and why the *Harry Potter* fans continue to reminisce on what the franchise has brought for them. I will first synthesize work from the distinct fields of fandom and memory studies, in order to highlight the changing practices of fans and the need for new perspectives and insights. I next discuss the methods I used to collect and analyze my data on the fans' perceptions and experiences in their use of social media to remember the *Harry Potter* texts. This is then followed by the results from the textual analysis of posts from the Facebook page, "We Owe JKR Our Childhood," and interviews with Potterheads that follow the page. I argue that the imminent value of the series among the fans and the social nature of Facebook; allow Potterheads to remediate and recreate the "*Harry Potter* experience."

Moving Forward in Fandom: Emerging and Changing Fan Practices

Harry Potter was certainly not the last we saw of young adult movie franchises taking their last bow. The 2010s has been a significant period in which major movie franchises have been finishing: *The Hunger Games*, *The Hobbit* (*The Lord of the Rings* from a broader perspective), and *Twilight* come to mind. With various fandoms supposedly coming to an end, I am therefore interested in how and if fan practices and experiences are different once the text that brought them in as a fan ceases to be ongoing. I chose the *Harry Potter* fandom, and Facebook as the medium to examine and analyze given my own involvement in the fandom itself. Other than my personal engagement, there does not seem to be a study that looks at the Potter fandom in its current context. Studies on the *Harry Potter* fandom were conducted during its prime—often focused on the fan versus intellectual, copyright laws perspective, or reinforced the negative pathology of fans with addiction (Rudski, Segal, & Kallen, 2009). Research on Facebook also leans towards the personal (Almansa, Fonseca and Castillo, 2013) or business sides of Facebook (Lin and Lu, 2010) rather than the social. The first of two research questions that this essay addresses is:

RQ1: How is Facebook used by *Harry Potter* fans to remediate and recreate the "*Harry Potter* experience"?

By the term "*Harry Potter* experience," I mean a *Harry Potter* fan's overall emotions, and memories associated with the *Harry Potter* texts (books and films). My research aim is to understand the current context of the *Harry Potter* fandom. "We Owe JKR Our Childhood" (hereafter referred to as WOJKROC) was created on 2 April 2011, in between the releases of *DH1* and *DH2*—a bufferer for fans to look back on the series before it finally ended. Aside from the unique name, it also highlights the significant value of the franchise for fans. Rebecca Williams (2011) argues that research that looks into fandom once a media text is cancelled or finished is under-examined in the field (p. 266). In her research, she coins the concept of "post-object fandom," to account for, and accurately describe, the transitional period in which the fan object ceases to be ongoing, becoming dormant (Williams, 2011, p. 269). When examining fandoms, the works of Henry Jenkins (1992), Camille Bacon-Smith (1992), and Janice Radway (1991) have laid fundamental frameworks for understanding fan practices, interactions, and relationships with a fan object. They all countered the argument that *Star Trek* fans and female readers of romance novels respectively, were passive consumers—that their acts of creativity (Jenkins, 1992, p. 22; Bacon-Smith, 1992, pp. 92–93), sense of community (Bacon-Smith, 1992, p. 8), and rereading (Radway, 1991, p. 12) mean something deeper and beyond a mindless fad.

Williams's (2011) notion of "post-object fandom" however, illustrates how much fan practices have changed over the past two decades (p. 269). The notion of being a fan has become much more accepted since the 1990s, especially with the rise of Internet use (Hermes, 2009, p. 115; Pullen, 2004, p. 83). With Internet use also came new challenges and issues fans faced, such as fan-websites and fan videos pitted against the original authors and copyright laws (Jenkins, 2003, pp. 290–292; 2006, pp. 198–200; Schwabach, 2009, pp. 387–388; 2011, pp. 117–119; Tan, 2013, pp. 97–100), that new theories and perspectives need to be conceptualized to understand fandoms in the age of the web. Not only that, but new, emerging fan practices and behavior that differ from simply loving the fan object have emerged. For instance, the notion of the anti-fan (Pinkowitz, 2013), trolling (Phillips, 2013), and use of memes (Coscia, 2013; Goriunova, 2013; Harlow, 2013) have been highlighted and discussed in recent years. In this sense, I want to further contribute to the discussion and new direction of fan studies due to all these changes and emerging theories and perspectives in the field.

My question is also an attempt to understand how social media is used in the context of fandom. Williams's (2011) work examined fans of the TV series *The West Wing* on forum boards (p. 268). Through my own observation and involvement in the *Harry Potter* fandom, Potterheads actively remember, discuss, and recreate the experience of the series through not only websites and forums, but also social media: on Facebook, Pinterest, Twitter, Tumblr, and so forth. The interactions and discussions on social media change rapidly and are less in-depth due to limited character lengths for posts in comparison to forums because of this, but are nevertheless worth examining given the popular use of memes, GIFs, and images to convey humor and often larger, deeper messages through the implicit, common understanding of the *Harry Potter* text among fans. WOJKROC is one of the many examples of fan-created pages on Facebook that aims to keep the series alive. Studies have shown that Facebook *profiles* allow individuals to construct and manage their identity and personality (Almansa, Fonseca and Castillo, 2013, pp. 129–130), and *pages* provide businesses a space for social interaction and maintenance of relationships, and product longevity with their consumers (Lin and Lu, 2010, pp. 567–568). Thus, while Jenkins (1992), Radway (1991), and Bacon-Smith's (1992) work remain important— as fans still continue to create their own content, and actively and critically understand their respective fan objects. In this era of the Internet and social media however, questions and issues surrounding identity and social media built based on identity-building have become a significant area of study, and how the functions and nature of different social media networks influence or affect fan interactions.

Identity is an important theme and focus on fandom studies because fans, especially celebrity and media fans, have a strong attachment to an object; they identify, perceive, and understand themselves and other people through a media text or celebrity they like (Click, Lee, & Holladay, 2013; Geraghty, 2007). This attachment and relationship has only intensified with social media, which can either strengthen the feeling of intimacy and the fan-celebrity relationship (Click, Lee, & Holladay, 2013, p. 366), or manifest negatively through hate groups, anti-fandoms, or trolling (Sanderson, 2013; Phillips, 2013; Pinkowitz, 2011). Sherry Turkle (1996) has also argued that our identities are fluid; we transition between multiple online identities, and differentiate between our real and online selves (pp. 178–180). I therefore want to emphasize on how fans interact with *each other* through an online medium, rather than towards an object. Identity theorists (Jenkins, 1996, p. 6; Taifle & Turner, 1986, pp. 15–16) have argued that our perception and sense of identity also comes from the ability to differentiate ourselves from other people. Geraghty's (2007) research also highlights that often an attachment with a text can create an emotional, supportive network among the fans themselves (pp. 89–90). Not only do I want to examine how fan practices have changed due to the status of a media text, but I also want to further explore how fans perceive of their identity, interaction, and experience with other fans through Facebook based on this common investment in a text.

Moving Forward in Memory Studies: Relating Fan Practices with Memory Studies

Fans are known to repeatedly reread and re-watch a text such that they come to have proficient knowledge of it. Although this repeated consumption often forms and establishes the hierarchical distinction between the audience and the fan community (Abercrombie & Longhurst, 1998, p. 148; MacDonald, 1998, p. 138), the nature of the hierarchy and fan knowledge, as in the difference between the knowledge of the text from a fan versus what an audience obtains, and its relationship to *memory* has yet to be explored in depth. I therefore pose a second question:

RQ2: What are the functions of WOJKROC in facilitating a collective identity and memory for the *Harry Potter* fandom?

Through this question, I want to establish a relationship between memory and fandom studies. In the realm of memory studies, the notion of memory equals an embodied experience; we form our perception and knowledge through the ability to collect and recollect information (Richards,

2007, pp. 20–21). It manifests in much broader ways beyond the individual, for instance, the way of culture and traditions, such as rituals, ceremonies (Connerton, 1989, pp. 4–5), the passing down of words that form a collective narrative for a community—a history (Assman, 2011, pp. 36–38). For a group, such as a family or ethnic community, other than these broader forms of memory manifested in objects are also family stories, photos, and videos that are told and remembered, and therefore only unique to the group (Halbwachs, 1992, pp. 22–24; van Djick, 2007, p. 12). Radley (1990) argues that "remembering is something which occurs in a world of things; as well as words, and that artefacts play a central role in the memories of cultures and individuals" (p. 57). I thus want to explore how such forms of collective memory holds true in the context of fandom. In the same way I aim to move studies forward in fandom with the first question, so is my intention with the second question for memory studies. Much of the studies on memory has a socio-cultural focus, I therefore want to bring aspects of fan practices that are major themes in memory studies—the impact of the Internet on the discourse of memory (Pentzold, 2009; Sommer, 2012, p. 139), the social nature in forming collective memory (Sommer, 2012, p. 147), and memories as specific to the group (Gibson and Jones, 2012, pp. 127–128; Halbwachs, 1992)—with fan studies.

Method

I took a multi-method, two-step approach in order to answer my research questions by conducting both a textual analysis of the WOJKROC page, and semi-structured interviews (online messaging) with followers of WOJKROC. The textual analysis aims to get an understanding of how the group works as a whole—the dynamics between users, and users with administrators (and other social media)—with the interviews digging deeper into the results and understanding what WOJKROC and interacting on it means for the individual. This was designed with Halbwachs's (1992) theory of collective memory in mind, where he argued that the group provides and shapes the way we remember, but it is the individual who does the remembering through contributing, in the context of my case, this means by liking, sharing, or posting comments on WOJKROC (p. 40). A combination of textual analysis and interviews also draws on the textual, pictorial nature of Facebook with the personal and social characteristics of the network, and draws strengths from both of the methods to better answer my questions. Posts from WOJKROC were collected between the months of August 2013 to January 2014. I saved three random posts everyday, resulting in a total of 103 saved posts.

As the data collection for the textual analysis finished, I began to seek interviewees. Participants were sought mid–January, 2014 with semi-structured interviews between all eight participants beginning late January until March 2014. I set two criteria when selecting my participants: they had to have liked the page before my initial contact with them, and between the ages of 18 and 25. My basis for the second criteria was that the participants would have grown up with the *Harry Potter* books, as the *PS/SS* book was published in 1997; I am interested in how this particular factor shapes their "*Harry Potter* experience." The participants were selected from those who liked or commented on the Facebook post made by Riddle, the administrator at the time, promoting my project.[2] A total of 72 messages were sent to those who liked and commented the post, with 16 people who replied expressing an interest in participating. Given the limited time frame to conduct the interviews, I chose to have only eight participants for my final sample (six females and two males). The participants were therefore chosen based on a first come, first serve basis. After seeking approval from all of them, they have all given me permission to re-use their quotes for this publication.

My main mode of communicating with the interviewees was through Facebook Messenger. Although with two interviewees the questions and answers were first exchanged through email before moving on to Facebook for follow-up questions, the exchanges with the other six participants were all done over Facebook. Some directly wrote their answers or sent a file attachment through the messenger. *Harry Potter* fans are spread across the globe, it was efficient and convenient to conduct interviews through this method. Given the different time zones, the participants could also respond in their own time. All the names of the participants have been changed to pseudonyms that are constructed by me or ones they have made for themselves.

Results and Discussion

Some themes that stood out from the textual analysis and interviews were: the role of social media in allowing fans to gather and remember the *Harry Potter* series, the subsequent hierarchies and fan interactions established based on the frequency and effort dedicated to remembering it, and the identification and connection with the series and its characters on a personal level such that they would rather keep and preserve the *Harry Potter* text as it is, followed by a reflection of themes that illustrate Radway's (1991) emotional reading, and the multiple ways, aside from WOJKROC, in which *Harry Potter* can be remembered.

Memes: A Collective Memory and Reappropriation of the *"Harry Potter* Experience"

A popular type of post on WOJKROC is the meme. For example, one popular meme combines the words "To those Muggles who said *Harry Potter* was over" with an image taken from a scene in *PS/SS*, where Harry was told by Professor Quirrell that he, not Professor Snape, whom Harry suspected, was the person behind all his near-death experiences in his first year at Hogwarts. The image shows Harry with an angry expression and the words "you liar" as an indicator of what he said. However, "you liar" in this context has changed, and functions as a continuation of the sentence above, complete with an appropriate image that expresses the sentiments of fans. This post shows the fan practices that have continued as Jenkins (1992) has discussed—fans appropriate from the text to construct their own meaning, whether that is through fan fiction, fan art, or fan videos (p. 36). The post is also an exemplar of memes as pictures combined with words to relate to a concept implicitly, and to fit a multitude of situations and contexts (Coscia, 2013, p. 3; Harlow, 2013, p. 63). In short, this post reflects fan practices that have remained and continued, such as fans reappropriating from texts, but also ways in which it has changed from it being in the forms of fan fiction, fan art, or fan videos to now memes.

When examined from the perspective of collective memory and fan hierarchies however, there are new insights and nuances into the workings of WOJKROC. When Olick, Vinitzky-Seroussi, and Levy (2011) spoke of collective memory, they summarized it as not only providing a way for a group to recall memories, but also shaping and providing the materials to do so (p. 19). This is notable in how WOJKROC's posts are provided by individual fans on other social media sites that are then subsequently picked up by the administrators. In this sense, the page operates closely to Halbwachs's (1992, p. 40) notion of collective memory. As the discussions will later show, this shapes how fans remember and perceive of their *"Harry Potter* experience." Fan hierarchies are also established in how the meme uses the word "muggles" to differentiate fans and non-fans. "Muggle" as used by Rowling in the books is a neutral term to describe people who do not possess any magical qualities. It can, however, become a condescending term depending on the context, and the characters who use them. Through this meme the word has been appropriated by fans to describe non-fans, in order to establish a group identity, in this case the Potterheads and the *Harry Potter* fandom, and to differentiate fans and non-fans of the *Harry Potter* franchise. From this meme, it can be gathered that WOJKROC draws on individuals to form a collective identity and memory of the "*Harry Potter* experience," because of how the administrator acts as the sole contributor to the page, with the comment threads acting as other individuals adding their own interpretations, and memes are one type of post that is commonly used to remediate the experience due to the ease in which to create one, and the subtle nuances and implicity that can be shown with only an image and few words.

Rereading and Social Media: WOJKROC Prompting Interaction and Memory of the Text

Of the eight interviewees, seven stated that WOJKROC prompts a rereading of the books, or provides content and materials in which to recall certain parts. Nyx's (female, age 23, from the U.S.), perception of how she views her relationship between the other WOJKROC followers and herself is worth drawing upon here.

> I'd probably say that my relationship with the other fans is something that's not extremely close but in a weird way it is. I may not speak to these people every day or know their personal lives but we all have one passion in common, and that's enough for me.

By describing her relationship with fans as "not extremely close but in a weird way it is," it illustrates the increased distance and effort needed to get to know another fan on a much more intimate level, but the sense of belonging and togetherness based on a common interest remains (Bacon-Smith, 1992, p. 8). Her response validates Sommer's (2012) view that Facebook draws people holding similar interpretations together (p. 147). It also illustrates Bacon-Smith's (1992, p. 9) point that "fans shape their own gatherings over time"; over the course of two decades, fans and their relationships and practices have shifted from the physical to an online space. Padma (female, age 24, Hungary) and Mia (female, age 20, Philippines) express similar sentiments as well.

> *Padma:* Before I've started reading the series again [WOJKROC] revealed a lot of differences between the books and movies, basically it inspired me to re-

reading and thus be able to comment or express my views … having the same thought or think that I understand something better than others is the drive to comment.

Mia: [WOJKROC] does keep the experience alive. It resurfaces all the emotions that came with reading the books, and watching the films. The like page also bridges the gap between HP fans all over the world. It's interesting to see how fans from other countries would react to certain information. It also reminds me just how many Potterheads there are.

While Nyx's answer demonstrates that WOJKROC is a space in which to engage with other fans, Padma and Mia's response illustrates Halbwachs's (1992) theory that memories become stronger when in the context of a group—it is *collective* because materials (posts or comments) are given by various individuals, as indicated in Padma's drive to comment.

Nyx, Padma, and Mia's responses also shows contrasting views and use of social media to interact and retain the "*Harry Potter* experience," and thus their fan identity and sense of being a *Harry Potter* fan. In the case of Nyx, she is content knowing that she and other fans share a common love and interest for *Harry Potter*, and does not feel the need to contribute in the way Padma does. Padma became much more involved and critical of the books and films because of WOJKROC, such that she wants to share her opinions, and showcase her knowledge of the series with other WOJKROC followers. On the other hand, Mia's answer highlights that WOJKROC acts as a virtual meeting point, and a portal of sorts, for *Harry Potter* fans to come together; to share, discuss, and react to what WOJKROC shares on its page. In this sense, Nyx, Padma, and Mia's responses highlight new ways of rereading that are not prompted by relaxation or prior expectations and knowledge of the story as Radway (1991, p. 92) found, but rather by engaging on social media and being exposed to opinions of other fans.

Rereading and Social Media, Part 2: Quizzes

Quizzes are another prominent type of content on WOJKROC that prompts this style of rereading through social media. Quizzes on WOJKROC do not occur very often, but go for a particular length of time. They are however dependent on the time zone which the administrator is in, and the number of users participating. The quizzes on WOJKROC highlight how rereading becomes a form of honing knowledge of the series, as shown in Terry's (male, age, 24, from India) response.

Quizzes generally because of different time zones I'm not able to participate but I enjoy checking my knowledge later on my reading the question and checking how many I got right :p

CL: By doing these quizzes, do they help to refresh your memory of the series? And a new way to remember HP? (Other than interesting posts or photos that is)

Terry: Yeah, they really do. These guys (admins and others) are really good! They remember such minute details I'm forced to reopen the books and find out the answers. They help you revisit things you've forgotten.

Terry's response is similar to Padma's in that rereading is, again, prompted by WOJKROC and its content, indicating that the Facebook page is not only recreating the "*Harry Potter* experience," but also creating new ways of reading it and understanding it through the form of quizzes, illustrating that a group provides the materials and ways in which to remember, in the context of fandom and social media (Olick, Vinitzky-Seroussi, & Levy, 2011, p. 19). Furthermore, it is initiated by fans, thus prompting engagement and discussion. In this sense, WOJKROC is a means in which fans interact and engage with the series. Given the conclusion to the *Harry Potter* franchise, the fan practices and interactions become a competitive performance of memory, or knowledge, over the text with other members.

Fan Hierarchies in WOJKROC and the *Harry Potter* Fandom

The memes highlight how WOJKROC functions as a space for Potterheads to remediate and remember the "*Harry Potter* experience," but the quizzes show a sense of competition and proficient knowledge of the *Harry Potter* text that allow fans to band together. This is reflected in this post on September 9, 2013 (Figure 1).

It shows five users' responses to a scene cut from *GoF*. From a broader perspective, this Tumblr post demonstrates that physical meeting places for fans such as conventions have moved on to a virtual space. Although conventions do still happen, social media sites such as Facebook crosses geographical and financial boundaries, allowing fans from various places to meet and interact much more easily. This post also demonstrates the interconnectedness between different social media platforms given that posts can easily be shared through a screen capture or hyperlinks.

On a minor scale, this post illustrates the workings of a group as argued

sepulchre-by-the-sounding-sea:

　　twatsooooooooon:

　　　　phoenixfire-thewizardgoddess:

　　　　　　lokistimetravelingsassbutt:

　　　　　　　　cumberfields:

　　　　　　　　　　Yes Ron cover your boobs because
　　　　　　　　　　you're a girl

　　　　　　　　He's also wearing a shirt.

　　　　　　Guys... he lived with the goddamn Twins for
　　　　　　YEARS, that's probably an instinctive 'Please
　　　　　　don't throw an experimental potion or giant
　　　　　　spider on me' reaction...

　　　　　...at least he'll never have that problem again...

　　　　Look me in the eye and tell me that was really necessary

　　im not even in this fandom and i know that was a no no

Figure 1: "cumberfields" (2013, September 9). *We Owe JKR Our Childhood.*

by Jenkins (1996, p. 4) and Sommer (2012, p. 147). Although the users' responses reflects Jenkin's (1996) point that our social identity is a product of us processing differing opinions; his argument was based on face-to-face, interpersonal interactions (p. 4), thus does not capture the non-verbal cues and internal nuances of which people arrive to their conclusions. Hence this post also validates Sommer's (2012) view that intertextuality and visibility of interpretations on Facebook influences our personal and collective memories; thus forming groups with people of similar interpretations to our own (p. 147). This is shown in the first two users' replies where the general sentiment is how Ron did not need to cover himself given that he is wearing a shirt. In Sommer's (2012) argument, she mentions that conflicts can also arise from forming a group (p. 147)—this is reflected in the last two users' responses to the post as well as the reactions *to* the Tumblr post on WOJKROC (see page 32 for comment thread)—in which they all agree that the third user's comment was unnecessary. The third comment created such a reaction because while it justifies Ron's reaction it mentions that one of his twin brothers (Fred) passed away by ending the post with "he'll never have that problem again." The death of many favorite characters (such as Fred) towards the end of the series caused numerous upsets among the fans.[3] In this sense, Facebook—as used by WOJKROC—is used to develop and sustain the *Harry Potter* fandom and in doing so, construct a social identity based on not only a collective memory of, but also grief over the deaths of some of the characters in, the *Harry Potter* text.

Another post that also highlights the group dynamics of WOJKROC is one posted on December 26, 2013. This was also taken from Tumblr, exhibiting a six-panel cut of a scene in the *PS/SS*, where Harry receives his first ever Christmas present from the Weasleys, whom have only known him through Ron. Ron is already wearing the Christmas sweater, emblazoned with the letter R, that Molly Weasley made for him. Harry is wearing pajamas. The captions read:

Harry: Happy Christmas, Ron! What are you wearing?

Ron: Oh, Mum made it. Looks like you've got one, too!

Harry: I've got presents?!

Ron: Yeah!

Beneath the six photos is a post from "simplypotterheads" that reads:

For the first time in his eleven years, Harry James Potter got to open proper presents at Christmas, all because Ron Weasley wrote home and told his own parents that Harry wasn't expecting anything. What the Weasleys lacked in galleons, they more than made up for in heart ["simplypotterheads"].

"simplypotterheads"'s text below the image acts as a caption but also a way to read this particular scene. In using "all because" when "simplypotterheads" explains how and why Harry received his presents, and "what the Weasleys lacked in galleons,[4] they more than made up for in heart" as the closing phrase, it becomes a command, an instruction; it gives the post authority over how the scene should be understood and an indicator of how Ron should be perceived from this scene. The comments from WOJKROC users affirm and further add to the interpretation, with comments that indicate a correct way of reading the text in order to better appreciate Ron as a character (see page 35 for comment thread). The crux of "simplypotterheads"'s caption and comments from WOJKROC is that the scene alone, without a deeper understanding of Ron from the books, or looking at it critically, would be less appreciated by a casual or non-fan. It exhibits the hierarchy of knowledge and fandom know-how MacDonald (1998) says fan communities possess (p. 138), where fans remark that those who do not appreciate Ron "clearly haven't read the books," or have only watched the movies. In choosing to illustrate the caption with this scene from the *first* movie, rather than any other Harry-Ron, or Harry-Weasley-family interactions from latter movies demonstrates an extensive knowledge of the books, as well as critical analysis of the differences between the book and film adaptation of the characters—prior knowledge, time, and practices that a casual or non-fan would not question or do—in order to resonate with the post and its intention.

Fan Hierarchies in WOJKROC and the *Harry Potter* Fandom, Part 2: Dedication and Time

Moving out of WOJKROC and looking deeper into how fans come to these conclusions of the differences between fellow fans who have extensive knowledge and those who do not, Riddle's (male, age 22, from India) response from my interviews with WOJKROC followers is a good starting point.

> CL: So in a way, by actively participating in the fandom, it helps you re-experience HP?
>
> *Riddle:* Regularly, yes. So much so that you end up sorting new people you meet in your normal day to day life. Sorting into Hogwarts houses, of course.

In answering "regularly," Riddle alludes to the "*Harry Potter* experience" as only meaningful and fulfilling as the effort fans put into the experience. "Regularly" can also mean frequency, which could be related to repeated practices such as rereading the books, or re-watching the films. In his context, fans are differentiated based on the amount of time and engagement dedicated to it. Padma also replied to this question in a similar way.

> I think Potterheads are more deeply involved, they (or should I say we) are not just [sic] like the series, but really give thought to the happenings and the background. A casual fan will not question anything written in the books or depicted in the movies and will not give it a second thought.

Her response expands on Riddle's views on time and dedication. Out of all the interviewees I asked, Padma's the only one who categorized the fans in this manner. In using "Potterheads" and "casual fans," Padma differentiates the various levels of knowledge apparent in the fandom, the former as more critical and involved compared to the latter, who are less engaged. Moreover, by the "should I say we" in the parenthesis, it implies that there are others out there who have similar opinions to her own. Padma's answer reflects Jenkins's (1996) point that our identities are socially constructed; based on processing and negotiating the distinction and difference between ourselves and other people (p. 86). In the context of *Harry Potter* fans and WOJKROC, this is based on the level of not only the level of interest and engagement with the series, but also an added amount and level of critical analysis compared to casual fans (who do not question the books or films) and non-fans.

Jenkins's (1996) theory however, was social identity in the context of face-to-face, interpersonal communication. Turkle's (1996) notion of identity in an online, mediated context also helps to understand how and why fans engage with WOJKROC. She argued that in the MUD (multiple user domain) experience, online and real life identities of the users merge (Turkle, 1996, pp. 178–180). This is illustrated in Riddle's quote earlier, in which he says he sorts the people he meets in real life into Hogwarts houses. You-Know-Who (female, age 24, from Pakistan) also had a similar answer.

> A little different??? Lol, we Potterheads are wayy, wayyy different from non–Potterheads. Because we've got that special feeling and mental training on friendship, love and bravery. We Potterheads can connect any time and anywhere in the world without feeling [sic] about our cultural and other differences. We just have that special magic that brings us together!!! :D Moreover, I personally feel that whenever I meet a new person and I come to know that he/she is a Potterhead, I don't ask more from them because this connection makes me feel that I'm with the right person. Although this sounds crazy but this connection and bond has

never put me in doubt :) I have always found awesome, passionate and amazing people because of HP. So,we [*sic*] Potterheads are clearly and completely different from non–Potterheads ;)

You-Know-Who's response is significant in that she considers reading the books a "training," meaning values such as "friendship, love and bravery" can be learned and honed from reading the *Harry Potter* series; that such a training results in an unspoken understanding and connection with other Potterheads. Similarly, for Riddle and You-Know-Who, the *Harry Potter* universe has integrated with their real lives in such a manner that it becomes their way of forming friendships. Thus, WOJKROC is not only an online platform to engage with other fans online or in real life, but also a way for fans to position and differentiate themselves based on the differing levels of engagement, and knowledge of the series compared to non-fans and those less engaged with *Harry Potter*.

From the previous posts and comments threads there is the recurring theme that the books are valued more than the films, and the need for deeper appreciation of certain scenes and characters by reading the books. On September 7, 2013 (Figure 2) WOJKROC shared this post from "The Happy Page." "The Happy Page" allows users to comment or send messages to finish off the sentence "Happiness is ____." While most comments on WOJKROC were affirmations to the statement (see page 38 for comment thread), one user in particular said,

> The BEST thing would be getting temporary amnesia and forgetting hp, only to spend an entire day reading the books again and getting to discover how awesome they were again, all without knowing it [Granger, 2013].

The word "best" already indicates the better option, above all others; by writing the word in capslock however, it emphasizes what would make the act of rereading the series the most enjoyable. "Temporary amnesia" means losing the memories and feelings attached to the "*Harry Potter* experience" for a period of time and rediscovering the same depth and meaning ("how awesome they are *again* [own emphasis]." Radway (1991) has pointed out that we reread with the knowledge of how the story ends, including the deeper layers of the text, the nuances, and subtlety (p. 62). Theorists (Cicero, 2007; Connerton, 1989) on memory also highlight that memory is the deeper meaning and knowledge we have collected and gathered through repetition. What this user highlights and suggests with her form of rereading differs from both Radway's (1991) notion of rereading and memory— it essentially means losing the memories and emotions attached to the "*Harry Potter* experience" altogether; reading and watching the *Harry Potter*

Figure 2: The Happy Page (2013, September 7). *We Owe JKR Our Childhood.*

text with fresh eyes and no expectations, only to become a fan all over again. It means the loss of the extensive knowledge and deeper layers to the *Harry Potter* text that can only be gained through repeated rereading and re-watching, along with the memories and recollections associated with it in order to feel that sense of surprise that only a new fan would have. Granger's comment suggests the depth and meaning *Harry Potter* has for her and fan identity in a broader sense, that fans relate and identify with a media text to the extent that rereading would be even more meaningful if it was like reading it for the first time.

Another post that highlights this is desire to keep the *Harry Potter* universe intact is a post by "arrogantmistletoerag" on Tumblr, which was then screen captured and shared by the WOJKROC administrator (see Appendix, page 42 for image).

Can we talk about how Lily and James had survived they would totally be the hot parents of Harry's year? Like, they'd go to pick him up from the platform and all of Harry's mates would be like, That's your mum? And Is that what you're going to look like in a few years? And when people would come over they'd just look at all the pictures like shit, this gene pool. They'd lose their mind when Harry introduced Sirius as his godfather ["arrogantmistletoerag," 2014].

"arrogantmistletoerag" presented an idea of how Harry's life would have been had his parents not been killed. The responses on WOJKROC indicate that this idea undermines the narrative of the whole series. The first two, fourth and fifth commenters argue that had Harry not lost his parents, "there would not have been a *Harry Potter* series" or "that wasn't meant to be" (see page 37 for comment thread). Bacon-Smith (1992) and Jenkins (1992) have discussed on fan creativity and production stemming from wanting to fill plot holes and gaps in that universe, but the responses from the WOJKROC users indicate a deviation from that to one where the fan *does not* wish to change a key and driving plot of the text, which is the death of Harry's parents. Their deaths sparked the conflict between Voldemort and Harry throughout the books as well as for Harry's escape from death in the hands of Voldemort each time. Their deaths were also significant and a major character and plot development as it marked Harry as the only person (the "Chosen One") who can defeat Voldemort. It is however also worth pointing out that the third comment, while also a fan, considers the former two users as taking the post too seriously, that the post is only presenting a "what-if" situation (see page 37 for comment thread). The contrast between the third commenter with the others exhibits an example of the differing levels and extent of fan identity and relationship with the text.

"Keep it the way it is": Preserving the *Harry Potter* Universe, *Harry Potter*'s Generational Impact

The desire to keep the experiences and memories of the "*Harry Potter* experience" intact, rather than creating continuations or alternate universes, points to fan behavior that differs from what has been found in studies on fan fiction. This was discovered in the text post but further explored when I was asking participants what they thought of Warner Bros. announcing the spin-off film, *Fantastic Beasts and Where to Find Them*. While the film will still be related to the *Harry Potter* universe as established in the books and films, the story will be based on a textbook used by the characters in *Hogwarts*, therefore there is no canon material for fans to fall back on to check for authenticity and loyalty to the books. Nor will it include the same characters, as the timeline is set years before the characters studied in Hogwarts, thus most of the participants were worried or hesitant. Riddle, for example, said,

> I think the movies will drag the charm of H.P. to an extent where we won't be as excited anymore. Having spanned years, the movies have established an irreplaceable imprint on us. If they bomb and aren't received as widely as the original 7 movies, then the credibility of Harry potter [*sic*] as a popular fandom might lessen. If I had it my way, I'd rather let the memories stay as they were left when dh2 ended.

In describing the "*Harry Potter* experience" as an "irreplaceable imprint" and describing the fans in plural ("we," "us") instead of simply for himself in singular, Riddle highlights the important value of the franchise, and speaking on behalf of other fans who feel the same way. Nyx similarly said, "I'm kind of worried about them branching out too far away from the book or trying too hard with special effects but I'm staying optimistic." Jenkins (1992, 2003, 2006) has argued and discussed extensively on the contested relationship between producers and fans when it comes to control over the text, fans are in a subordinate position and do not have a say in the plot and direction a text would take. Although Riddle and Nyx's response demonstrates this position, I wanted to dig deeper into the reason behind this hesitance towards the new film further by letting them talk about the significance of *Harry Potter* in their lives.

All my participants agreed that the *Harry Potter* series had an incremental impact during their childhood. Terry, You-Know-Who, and Riddle all stated this explicitly.

> *Terry:* In a lot of ways, I've grown up with *Harry Potter* and associate my childhood a lot with the series. For me it's a series with which I have a lot of fond memories.
>
> *You-Know-Who:* For me HP is life because I grew up with him. Harry Potter is the kind of friend on whom I can trust throughout my life, till my end *Always*[5] ;)
>
> *Riddle:* It's like your home. You can wander [*sic*] about the town but when the sun gets down, you'll return home. The worth of this series got multiplied when I started interacting with fans and like-minded people and the best thing about this was there were no boundaries of region, religion, language or culture.... The mania was, and I hope still is, phenomenal. I practically grew up with Harry. The books have raised a generation, and I am glad I am a part of the same.

I want to highlight Riddle's response here again because he describes the series as a place ("home") you can return to, relating the characters' growth in the series with himself in his own development. What all three quotes illustrate, and have in common, is fan identity as defined by generational experience—*Harry Potter* is not only a franchise that is targeted towards young adults, but a generational one—in which there are fans who started off as young adults from the year Harry started to when it ended.

The *Harry Potter* texts were therefore an integral part of development and growth for the fans, making the identification and relationship with the series a very personal one. Our childhoods are often associated with innocence, purity, and infinite creativity and imagination. The *Harry Potter* universe draws on all of these, but also a realistic progression from this innocence into adulthood and maturity—with each book gradually becoming darker and showing Harry's struggles to come to terms with every bigger conflict and death he faces. I think Padma sums up the "*Harry Potter* experience" and the series significance for her perfectly.

> Recently re-reading the series it means much more.[6] It means a never lost but relived childhood but [*sic*] with the discovery of the depth of characters and meaning. It is now a return to old friends since I grew up with Harry, Ron and Hermione and I know it sounds really sentimental but magic and all the adventures they go through is a strap in a world absurdly serious and adult.

Emotional Reading and Other Ways of Recreating the "*Harry Potter* Experience"

Some other findings worth mentioning include the relevance of Radway's (1991) notion of emotional reading (p. 62). Five out of the six female participants I talked to brought up reading the *Harry Potter* books as a form of escape and relaxation.

> *Nyx:* I think of all the life lessons it taught me. How it helped me escape from reality if I was feeling down and out.
>
> *Padma:* Generally I love reading and I consider it as a bit of a refuge from my worldly problems.
>
> *Hazel Tifiaeh* (female, age 24, from USA): It was the series that made me passionate about reading. It also helped bring me and my older sister together when we were pulling apart. It also helped me escape from some real world issues I was going through. It probably saved my life.
>
> *You-Know-Who:* Whenever I'm bored and I really want to relax, I watch HP or

grab any part, any chapter and go back to Hogwarts because our Queen Rowling herself said that Hogwarts will always be there to welcome us home.

Mia: I can leave the books on my shelves for years; whenever, I feel the urge to read them again, it would be the same experience.

These responses not only demonstrate the continued relevance of Radway's (1991) argument, but also indicate that the same forms of relaxation and escape can be provided by novels outside of the romance genre, as *Harry Potter* is categorized as fantasy. Hazel Tifiaeh's response is worth highlighting here because it validates Geraghty's (2007) view that the point of entry in becoming a fan includes the emotional and mental support a media text can provide (p. 127). In addition, her response also suggests that the same could be said for genres of media text other than sci-fi. Whilst the male and female participants differed in how they reread or engage with the text and on WOJKROC, their responses show that, regardless of gender, *Harry Potter* has left an enormous impact, and the fans remain emotionally attached to it.

WOJKROC is, of course, only one of the many ways in which fans keep the *"Harry Potter* experience" alive. Padma says that she watches reruns of the movies if it is on TV, and has a Pinterest account that also allows her to keep in touch with the series alongside her Facebook one. Hazel Tifiaeh writes fanfiction and is a member of various *Harry Potter* Facebook groups and follows other Facebook pages. Their multimedia activity illustrates that there are different ways in which the *"Harry Potter* experience" can be recreated and remediated. Twenty years ago, Bacon-Smith (1992) highlighted how the cost of postage was an issue when it came to maintaining and sustaining a fan community (p. 9). With a proliferation of social media platforms today, the issue now is that there are too many of them. As Aristo (female, age 20, from Vietnam) says, "it would take a while for me to notice, should the page suddenly disappear," illustrating that Facebook has a personal function aside from its social one that makes WOJKROC only one of the many ways the *"Harry Potter* experience" is sustained and recreated on social media.

Conclusion

I began this essay wanting to find out how Facebook is used to recreate and remediate the *"Harry Potter* experience," and the role of social media in fostering a collective memory and identity for Potterheads, using WOJKROC as the case study. Through the textual analysis and interviews,

I found that given the depth in which fans identify and relate to the series, this leads to creating fan-accounts dedicated remembering and recreating the memories associated with the *"Harry Potter experience."* On WOJKROC and with other fans, this is through liking and sharing memes, a discussion on various scenes and characters, or partaking in quizzes hosted by the WOJKROC administrators; establishing fan hierarchies and group identity at the same time. On a personal level, fans reminisce through the act of rereading, or re-watching the *Harry Potter* text, some expressing this act as prompted by the discussions on WOJKROC, others for knowing that it will be the same experience. Through these revelations, it also revealed how Facebook is used in the context of fandom that illustrates the workings of collective memory. It not only shows new practices of fan behavior in the context of Williams's (2011) "post-object fandom," but also that WOJKROC *provides* the materials in which fans could remember *Harry Potter*, sometimes prompting fans to re-engage with the series. Given the significant value of the series in raising a generation, and the personal value it has for fans individually, this value also suggests the desire to preserve and keep the *Harry Potter* universe untouched and intact. To conclude, WOJKROC functions as a collective memory space, and a means in which Potterheads can re-experience the text in a new context, prompted by the social nature and functionalities of Facebook. As the series has concluded, interactions and the functions of WOJKROC therefore relies not only on administrators providing materials, but also the fans' own proficiency, or memory, of the *Harry Potter* text in order to maintain and keep the fandom alive.

As the project was conducted in a short time frame, my insights into the *Harry Potter* fandom through WOJKROC are by no means aiming to be representative. Given the mass, worldwide following of *Harry Potter*, I only sought eight out of the millions of fans, young and old, out there. Future research into the *Harry Potter* fandom could explore the phenomenon from a socio-cultural, or literary point of view, considering that the franchise began as a literary text. To examine the impact of the books, as much as the films, would also capture the broader and numerous ways in which Rowling's books have influenced and raised a generation. Secondly, Facebook is only one of the many social media channels fans have used to recreate the *"Harry Potter* experience," it would be worthwhile to consider how fan interactions on one social media differs from another given the different functions and features of Facebook from Twitter (an emphasis on short, concise posts), Tumblr (images and GIF-focused), and Pinterest, and if a compare and contrast of this is possible. As my sample and focus was on young adults, and had more females than males, a study that looks into the perspective of male fans, or even the older, adult audience of *Harry Potter* would provide some insights into how the male and older audiences and fans relate and associate with the *Harry Potter* series, and how that differs from the female and younger fans. Moreover, the significance of the series for younger fans in their childhood could also be examined from a psychological perspective. In short, the research could be taken further whether in the field of *Harry Potter* studies, media and audience studies, socio-cultural studies, and so forth—there are numerous ways in which the findings and points in this research that could be expanded upon. I hope my small contribution here has provided a starting point for *Harry Potter* studies, fan studies, memory studies to explore this area in their respective fields.

Notes

1. The author would like to acknowledge her thanks to Dr. Alison Horbury and Dr. Esther Chin for taking the time to provide their feedback on the draft of this essay. This essay was rewritten from the author's Master (by coursework) thesis conducted as a student at the University of Melbourne, Australia.

2. Riddle initially offered for me to be a temporary administrator so that I could introduce myself and the project to the members of the page. This was not granted as contact with Riddle dropped before this could happen. As an alternative, participants were sought from the post Riddle made. "Riddle." (2014, January 19). Facebook status. *We Owe JKR Our Childhood*. Retrieved from http://www.facebook.com/WeLoveJKR/posts/653837807991882?stream_ref=10.

3. In Brown's interview, she asks Rowling of the many character deaths in DH. It was mentioned that fans, and those Rowling met at book signings, expressed their sadness over the death of many of their favorite characters. Brown, J. (2007, July 29). "Rowling: I wanted to kill parents." *Today*. Retrieved from www.today.com/id/20026225#.UzddmPmSzE0.

4. Wizard money.

5. You-Know-Who is using a *Harry Potter* reference that is popularly used among fans. "Always" was Professor Snape's response to Professor Dumbledore's surprise that he still loves Lily (Harry Potter's deceased mother).

6. Padma first read the books in Hungarian and was rereading the series in English during the time I was interviewing her.

References

Abercrombie, N., & Longhurst, B. (1998). *Audiences: A Sociological Theory of Performance and Imagination*. London: Sage.

Almansa, A., Fonseca, O., & Castillo, A. (2013). "Social networks and young people: Comparative study of Facebook between Colombia and Spain." *Communicar* 20 (40), 127–134.

Assman, J. (2011). *Cultural Memory and Early Civilization: Writing, Remembrance, and Political Imagination*. New York: Cambridge University Press.

Bacon-Smith, C. (1992). *Enterprising Women: Television Fandom and the Creation of Popular Myth*. Philadelphia: University of Pennsylvania Press.

Cicero, M.T. (2007). "From the ideal orator (oratore)." In Rossington, M., & Whiteheads, A., eds., *Theories of Memory: A Reader*. Baltimore: John Hopkins University Press.

Click, M.A., Lee, H., & Holladay, H.W. (2013). "Making monsters: Lady Gaga, fan identification, and social media." *Popular Music and Society* 36 (3), 360–379.

Connerton, P. (1989). *How Societies Remember*. Cambridge: Cambridge University Press.

Coscia, M. (2013). "Competition and success in the meme pool: A case study on Quickmeme.com." *International AAI Conference on Weblogs and Social Media*. Boston: MIT.

Ditter, F.J., Jr., & Ditter, V.Y. (trans.). (1980). *The Collective Memory: Maurice Halbwachs*. New York: Harper and Row.

Geraghty, L. (2007). *Living with Star Trek: American Culture and the Star Trek Universe*. London: I.B. Tauris.

Gibson, P.L. & Jones, S. (2012). Remediation and remembrance: "Dancing Auschwitz" collective memory and new media. *ESSACHESS Journal for Communication Studies*, 5 (2), 107–131.

Halbwachs, M. (1992). *On Collective Memory*. (Coser, L.A. Trans.). Chicago: University of Chicago Press.

Harlow, S. (2013). It was a "Facebook revolution": Exploring the meme-like spread of narratives during the Egyptian protests. *Revista de Communication*, 12, 59–82.

Jenkins, H. (1992). *Textual Poachers: Television Fans and Participatory Culture*. Kindle Edition: Taylor and Francis.

Jenkins, H. (2003). Quentin Tarantino's Star Wars? Digital cinema, media convergence, and participatory culture. In Thorburn, D. & Jenkins, H. eds., *Rethinking Media Change: The Aesthetics of Transition*. Cambridge, MA: The MIT Press.

Jenkins, H. (2006). *Convergence: Where Old and New Media Collide*. New York: New York University Press.

Jenkins, R. (1996). *Social Identity*. London: Routledge.

Lin, K-Y., & Lu, H-P. (2011). "Intention to continue using Facebook fan pages from the perspective of social capital theory." *Cyberpsychology, Behavior, and Social Networking* 14 (10), 565–570.

MacDonald, A. (1998). "Uncertain utopia: Science fiction media fandom and computer-mediated communication." In Harris, C., & Alexander, A., eds., *Theorizing Fandom: Fans, Subculture and Identity*. Cresskill, NJ: Hampton Press.

Olick, J.K., Vinitzky-Seroussi, V., & Levy, D., eds. (2011). *The Collective Memory Reader*. New York: Oxford University Press.

Pentzold, C. (2009). "Fixing the floating gap: The online encyclopaedia Wikipedia as a global memory space." *Memory Studies* 2 (2), 255–272.

Phillips, W. (2011). "LOLing at tragedy: Facebook trolls, memorial pages and resistance to grief online." *First Monday* 16 (12), http://firstmonday.org/ojs/index.php/fm/article/view/3168.

Pinkowitz, J.M. (2011). "'The rabid fans that take [Twilight] much too seriously': The construction and rejection of excess in *Twilight* antifandom." *Transformative Works and Cultures* 7, http://journal.transformativeworks.org/index.php/twc/article/view/247/253.

Pullen, K. (2004). "'Everybody's gotta love somebody, sometime': Online fan community." In Guantlett, D., & Horsley, R., eds., *Web Studies*, 2d ed. London: Arnold.

Radley, A. (1990). "Artefacts, memory and a sense of the past." In Middleton, D., & Edwards, D., eds., *Collective Remembering*. London: Sage.

Radway, J. (1991). *Reading the Romance: Women, Patriarchy and Popular Literature*. Chapel Hill: University of North Carolina Press.

Richards, J. (2007). "Section I: Classical and early modern ideas of memory—Introduction." In Rossington, M., & Whitehead, A., eds., *Theories of Memory: A Reader*. Baltimore: John Hopkins University Press.

Rudski, J.M., Segal, C., & Kallen, E. (2009). "Harry Potter and the end of the road: Parallels with addiction." *Addiction Research and Theory* 17, 260–277.

Schwabach, A. (2009). "The *Harry Potter Lexicon* and the world of fandom: Fan fiction, outsider works and copyright." *University of Pittsburgh Law Review* 70 (3), 387–434.

Schwabach, A. (2011). *Fan Fiction and Copyright: Outsider Works and Intellectual Property Protection*. Surrey: Ashgate.

Slade, C. (2006). "The mediated space: Technology and personhood." In Volkmer, I., ed., *News in Public Memory: An International Study of Media Memories Across Generations*. New York: Peter Lang.

Sommer, V. (2012). "The online discourse on the Demjanjuk trial: New memory practices on the world wide web?" *ESSACHESS Journal of Communication Studies* 5 (2), 133–151.

Taifel, H., & Turner, J. (1986). "The social identity of intergroup behavior." In Worchel, S., & Austin, W.G., eds., *Psychology of Intergroup Relations*. Chicago: Nelson-Hall.

Tan, D. (2013). "*Harry Potter* and the transformative wand: Fair use, canonicity and fan activity." In Hunter, D., Lobato, R., Richardson, M., & Thomas, J., eds., *Amateur Media: Social, Cultural and Legal Perspectives*. London: Routledge.

Turkle, S. (1996). *Life on Screen: Identity in the Age of the Internet*. London: Widefield and Nicolson.

van Djick, J. (2007). *Mediated Memories in the Digital Age*. Stanford: Stanford University Press.

Teaching *Harry Potter*:
How the Wizarding World
Has Transformed Higher Education

Elizabeth Morrow Clark

University course offerings in subjects from Marketing to Literature to Speech draw upon the content and context of the Wizarding World, both as a means of keeping student attention and as a subject worthy of study in and of itself. The successes and failures of teachers and learners at Hogwarts parallel the successes and failures of university faculty and students. This essay will address issues in education as depicted in J.K. Rowling's works, as well as how educators approach teaching the "*Harry Potter* Generation." At many levels, faculty find that Harry brings an automatic audience, whether among intermediate readers or college seniors. As a faculty member known for esoteric content, I myself find that going beyond the academic metaphor and into casual conversation about *Harry Potter* reveals a personal side to me that transcends age and position. It also models intellectual inquiry in everyday life.

Student-teacher relationships, curriculum development, teaching styles and learning styles are all topics relevant to the world of Hogwarts and to the university classroom today. What do students learn about the role of the professor from reading *Harry Potter*? What can professors learn about relating to students by exploring *Pottermore*? What academic subjects seem to be most successful at drawing on Potter for inspiration? This chapter will address the practical application of and professional scholarship about teaching *Harry Potter* to reveal the lasting effect Hogwarts has had on students and teachers in the twenty-first century.

Just a few years ago, it seemed that *Harry Potter* had to be defended as a topic for a college class. Today, *Harry Potter* Studies as a scholarly field is developing a critical mass of support in academe. A growing literature has emerged which addresses the intersection of Harry and pedagogy. In fact, using *Harry Potter* in college classes has also become the subject of entire books. While some seem to be for a popular audience, there are many gems in this category. In addition, while scores of courses or faculty may use *Harry Potter* as metaphor or as a "hook" for another subject altogether, I wish to contemplate the larger effect of *Harry Potter*, beyond metaphor and into both curriculum and campus culture. I will also review syllabi for courses on *Harry Potter* and will analyze the various ways that the text is used in diverse disciplines and curricula. I will conclude with a discussion of the usefulness of *Harry Potter* in teaching history and honors classes at my own regional state university.

In 2011, the volume *Teaching Harry Potter* appeared, combining both the serious study of the Potter texts as a world unto themselves and the interpretation and application of pedagogy in and through the series. The volume addresses such topics as multiculturalism, history of science, and curriculum development. Lest one think that talking about science in *Harry Potter* is unusual, the National Library of Medicine has a fantastic traveling exhibit called "Renaissance Science, Magic and Medicine." The lessons available online are designed specifically for university students. For instance, one section is titled "How Magic became Science," and teaches about, among other things, the history of alchemy, a subject familiar to *Potter* readers. In my own Western Civilization class, I have begun to assign Agrippa. Students may recognize him from the Chocolate Frog cards. It is he who said, "Magic comprises the most profound contemplation of the most secret things, their nature, power, quality, substance, and virtues, as well as the knowledge of their whole nature" (NLM, 2013).

The *Harry Potter* books offer a model for both contemplating secrets and plotting subversive acts, perhaps the best response to a school environment which values testing over critical thinking. In the classroom environment the books "serve as an opportunity to move beyond the standard canon" (Belcher and Stephenson, 2011, p. 60). Faculty face the daunting task of taking on the "sleeping dragons" of the educational system in the United States, and of including students in the re-imagination of school.

The Anti-Institutional Character of *Harry Potter*

The independent, risk-taking, premise-challenging themes in the series pit Harry and his allies against, not teachers or the school, but the

Ministry of Magic. Best demonstrated in *OotP* and *DH*, the Ministry controls, condones, or ignores such internal school matters as curriculum, discipline, admission, and examinations. The Ministry moves from being a nonthreatening entity, easily ignored by the headmaster Dumbledore, to a frightened, conspiracy-driven organization seeking to limit student engagement but not yet academically compromised. This is evident in *OotP* when outside examiners were empowered to test students in the practical application of Defense Against the Dark Arts, for instance. By the final book, the Ministry itself has fallen to totalitarian control and the school teaches only the ideology of the state in a militaristic, sadistic, and restrictive way. This is the moment in which Muggle-borns are excluded from school, stripped of their "citizenship," their wands, their professions. They become fair game for persecution. Rowling's direct references to the Nazi Germany experience, with Muggles in the place of Jews, is very evident, as is the warning that the path to thought control is guarded or abandoned by educators and policy makers who influence education.

The goal of the book *Teaching Harry Potter* is "based upon subverting the current movement toward a singular form of educational accountability in favor of one that privileges agency and decisions-making power (choice)— on the part of both teachers and students—in our schools." Belcher and Stephenson argue that by incorporating relevant popular culture into classes, educators open up a "powerful symbolic system that reflects and is reflected in everyday life" (Belcher and Stephenson, 2011, p. 62). Upon integrating elements of pop culture into the classroom, teachers accomplish two goals. First, they establish a rapport with students about a nonthreatening topic. The students find their previous knowledge gives them power. They become the experts and the teacher the learner. Secondly, using pop culture breaks down barriers to learning if a student population is unfamiliar with a "high culture" literary canon or tunes out tropes they consider irrelevant to their lives.

Teaching Harry Potter even argues that, because the books introduce an unfamiliar school world, one completely different from the home environment, bicultural students can find ways to identify with Harry's difference, despite his status as a typical white, male, middle class student. Conversely, race and class can be inaccessible concepts for students at a regional and rural institution such as my own. It may seem obvious, but explanations about race, specifically references to blood and purity, are clarified for students when Voldemort is referenced. A student may have muddled feelings about his or her own relationship to race, or be suspect of a faculty member who mentions class, but the fictionality of *Harry Potter* allows the subject to be approached both more familiarly and from a distance. Thus, the very act of teaching about or through *Harry Potter* challenges the norm.

Kansas State Leads The Way

The Kansas State *Harry Potter* program, along with Yale's Religious Studies course, has been credited with leading the way toward integrating *Harry Potter* into the college curriculum. K-State even boasts a "Harry Potter Room" in the library. With its cathedral ceiling and heavy wooden tables, this quiet study room reportedly makes students feel smarter. Kansas State uses Philip Nel's course as part of its admissions promotion. As a literature professor, he has a quick response to those who consider *Harry Potter* to be less valuable for study than Shakespeare or Tolstoy, "Children's literature is literature. Indeed, great children's books and great 'adult' books succeed for the same reasons: they tell good stories, and they reward rereading" (Kansas State, 2014). Nel requires more than a familiarity with the seven *Harry Potter* books in his course. He also expects students to revisit other children's literature classics they may have read previously, such as works by C.S. Lewis, Roald Dahl, and Philip Pullman. The course description could belong to almost any literature course which has as its core purpose the task of placing a work or author in historical context and measuring its literary weight, while applying critical perspectives to each text. Students take quizzes, participate in discussion and debate, and write a paper, all academic tasks completed in an academic context. Nel does not teach the *Harry Potter* course alone. It is also supported by Dr. Karin Westman, head of the English department and co-editor of the prestigious children's literature journal, *The Lion and the Unicorn*. In addition to the elective course "Harry Potter's Library," Westman, a specialist in modern British literature, also offers graduate-level course featuring Rowling's work, "*Harry Potter* and Literary History." Her iteration of the "Harry Potter's Library" course includes Melissa Anelli's *Harry, a History*, which traces Anelli's path from fan to fandoms to fan royalty. It is an essential work for any student of *Harry Potter* who wishes to understand the Potter Phenomenon. She also assigns *Emma*, by Jane Austen, a work Rowling herself cites as one of her favorite books of all time.

The Kansas State English department has an entire "FAQ" for their *Harry Potter's Library* curriculum. The content is revealing. Not only does Nel explain when he will next teach the class, but he also seems to feel he must explain *why* he and the department can only teach a certain number of sections of the elective. He states quite firmly that the expectation for the course is that students have already read the first two books in the series before the term begins. As for my own honors course, described below, students were expected to begin the fall term having recently read all seven books. In each case, it is clear, that for serious academic study of *Harry Potter*, understanding the story arc is essential to studying the Potter Phenomenon. Often, students have not returned to the text since adolescence and simply the act of re-reading the books is a useful and transformative experience. Even for college students, "Harry encourages people … to read." Harry offers students a "meeting space … to elaborate on traditional academic experiences" (Belcher and Stephenson, 2011, pp. 1–6).

Harry Potter and Theology

In addition to offering students an accessible way to make test-to-self, text-to-text and test-to-world connections, *Harry Potter* can be a gateway to civic engagement and advocacy. The themes of subversion, resistance and anti-authority behavior seem to be antithetical to an educational mission of training for professions or hitting marks on certification exams, but they are perfect for opening a discussion of underground resistance movements or identifying patterns of totalitarianism. When students identify with Dumbledore's Army, they identify with that experience and understand its worth.

One environment for exploring the ethical and philosophical values in *Harry Potter* is in religious studies. For those whose concern would primarily be whether *Harry Potter* might be unsuitable for study due to inappropriate content, one need look no further than the many works of John Granger, a *Potter* Pundit extraordinaire whom *Time* has called the "Dean" of *Harry Potter* studies, and the core inspiration of the Hogwarts Professor website. Granger's extensive training in the Classics and concentrated examination of the *Potter* series combine to produce a fascinating set of observations ranging from *Potter* as postmodern to Rowling's Ring cycle. But his first encounter with *Harry Potter* came as a response to concern that the books might not be appropriate reading for his children, being raised in an Orthodox Christian family. In *How Harry Cast His Spell*, Granger observes that Rowling's stories resonate with readers, especially Western readers, because they are familiar. Peter Dendle also argues that, in the end, despite the presentation of unusual and marginalized, even paranormal, ideas in *Harry Potter*, "Dumbledore's experience and Hermione's common sense are necessary counterweights for evaluating the reliability of institutionally disseminated knowledge." That is, that although diversity and difference are tolerated, even admired, there are limits to such as the fringe beliefs of Xenophilius Lovegood (Dendle, 2011, p. 421). Truth still exists, and the Wizarding World holds universal truths for the reader.

Yale University offers *Harry Potter* as a theme for a theology course. Danielle Elizabeth Tumminio is an acknowledged pathbreaker for this curriculum, and she has published a book about her experiences, *God and Harry Potter at Yale: Teaching Faith and Fantasy Fiction in an Ivy League Classroom*. In 2009, when the class first appeared on the books, it was packed. She subsequently offered it at Tufts, as well as Yale, to great acclaim. As an academic new to podcasts and iTunes in general, I remember well encountering Tumminio and Granger for the first time on *Pottercast* and being impressed that the discussion of *Harry Potter* could move so quickly from fan conversations trying to predict the end of the story halfway through the series into legitimate and engaging intellectual curiosity. In her syllabus, Tumminio states clearly that the course investigates the debate about whether the *Harry Potter* series violates Christian principles or reinforces them. She posits that, by reading Rowling's work, students can approach larger questions of faith, questions about the existence of evil in the world, or the value of sacrifice. Her required reading list includes two works of theology and all seven *Harry Potter* books. Additional readings and articles are primarily theological. Thus, she places *Potter* at the center of the discussion, but the driving ideologies are from her discipline. Tumminio is not the only theologian using Rowling's works, but she can be credited with being one of the first, and most public. Today, courses can be found at other schools, like Lee Jefferson's course "The Theology of *Harry Potter*" at Centre College in Kentucky. Jefferson's course has prerequisites in the religion department. Duke offers a wizard-inspired ethics course, as does Bridgewater State. Caroll College, a private Catholic school in Montana, offers a sophomore level course called "The Gospel According to *Harry Potter*" in the Theology department and LaSalle has a course in the Philosophy department titled "*Harry Potter* and Philosophy: Wizardry and Wisdom." The Wizarding World has proved itself worthy of spiritual and philosophical contemplation.

Breaking Ground in England: Durham University

The main characters of the books are students, while teachers are leaders, adversaries, and co-conspirators. Six of the seven books are set almost entirely in school, with daily life in dormitories, the cafeteria, in classrooms and in extra-curricular clubs. What could be a better topic for an education course? As Renee Dickinson has argued, studying how teaching is practiced at Hogwarts has many pitfalls. She herself understands this, as an assistant professor of English at Radford in Virginia.

Nevertheless, great hopes blossomed when Durham University pioneered an education course called "*Harry Potter* and the Age of Illusion." Enrolling upwards of eighty students the first time it was offered in 2010, it was the first university course of its kind in the United Kingdom (*Guardian*, "Durham," 2010), though preceded by a summer course at Edinburgh. The students in the module studied not only the educational system in the Wizarding World, but also the relevance of *Harry Potter* in contemporary educational settings. One of the most interesting goals of the course was to ponder "explicit connections between *Harry Potter* and citizenship education" (Durham, 2010). The link with Durham is a long one for *Harry Potter*. Durham hosted film crews several times and local schoolchildren can be spied in *Harry Potter* movie scenes.

Dr. Martin Richardson, head of the education department, designed the class for future teachers, in response to growing demand from students. Richardson considered the overall relevance of *Harry Potter* in England an important subject of study, as well as the specific educational context of the story. Course content explored everything from bullying and prejudice at school to magic/illusion/enchantment as educational examples. References to citizenship reveal the extent to which the course might actually identify and reinforce traditional norms in British education. Examples include a unit called "My station and its duties: *Harry Potter* and the good citizen," or an exploration of Rowling's moral universe that references both the colonial values of Rudyard Kipling and the postmodern grittiness of Grange Hill. The Durham syllabus lists learning outcomes like "Subject-specific Knowledge," "Key Skills," and "Subject-specific Skills." These reveal that a teacher in England is expected to consider the relevance of the course content to social, moral, spiritual and cultural values, to hone skills in interpreting a text (fictional) and analyzing how it has influenced culture or educational policy, as well as that a teacher should be able to make an argument using theory and backed by solid research skills in primary and secondary sources. Thus, Durham University has pioneered *Harry Potter* as a course that was more than just a textual study, but an analytical examination of a cultural phenomenon with the potential to influence social systems for generations to come. The course intentionally "eschew[s] textual analysis; instead it will use the text and films to shed light on contemporary society and look at the wider moral universe of the school environment" (Nine Worlds, 2014). Its lasting effect can be seen in continued course offerings, related seminars and conferences, undergraduate dissertations, and graduate studies on the subject, inspired by the "Age of Illusion" course.

Teaching about Teaching

Another element to understanding *Harry Potter* is to study the styles of teaching in Hogwarts. In the Wizarding World, students still engage with traditional learning practices (reading, writing tests, even copying answers from one another), but the teachers tend to practice "Annihilation of the Teacher," in which teachers facilitate rather than dictate learning. Renee Dickinson posits that measuring wizarding classroom pedagogies according to the tried and true measure of Bloom's Taxonomy yields a surprising result: few Hogwarts professors use the full range of techniques. Professor Binns lectures, but does not engage. Binns, Dickinson argues, is the last remaining practitioner of direct instruction, and his success is limited. Using Bloom's Taxonomy, Dickinson considers Binns to be using only the first level of learning: knowledge. Snape, she argues, "asks the students to move directly to application without the information [or] examples … necessary to get there" (Dickinson, 2006, p. 241). Professor Trelawney, in contrast, teaches a very amorphous subject, dependent on innate abilities and abstract results. This is in part a function of the subject, as the centaur Firenze also describes the subject as inaccessible to most. Thus, Dickinson argues, the second level of the Taxonomy is hard to reach: comprehension. Professor Snape's Potions class expects students to be able to apply knowledge, but he skips the two previous steps. Not only this, but he also interrupts any team-building learning communities with criticism and fear. Dickinson criticizes Professor McGonagall for skipping steps as well, arguing that her Transfiguration classes jump from introductory knowledge to application, to synthesis, but that she gives few examples or demonstrations. This is an unfair analysis, however, as the very first class Harry and Ron attend is Transfiguration and McGonagall transfigures herself from a cat into herself, doing this again later in lessons covering the topic of human transfiguration and Animagi. Charms is also a practice-based class, mostly consisting of "lab" hours, and quite noisy ones, making it a good class in which to chat, or plot. Defense Against the Dark Arts teaching methods vary since the teachers change so often, but students certainly spend time reading their textbook as well as viewing slide shows and observing dark creatures. In at least two years, students are even expected to practice forbidden spells (Year 4 and Year 7). And in one year, they are not allowed to use spells (Year 5), but set up a study group (DA) to learn them anyway. Dickinson argues that Hogwarts is not, therefore, an ideal model for a Muggle educational system, but still offers interesting insights into the consequences of certain teaching styles. By contrast, Belcher and Stephenson promote models of "effective, caring teaching ... and in Harry we see that it can be learned and nurtured through mentorship, engagement and experience" (Belcher and Stephenson, 2011, p. 12). This is the best kind of teaching, but it flies in the face of standardized lesson plans, testing, and yes, even institutional assessment.

As faculty, it seems nearly impossible to resist "sorting" one another, or being "sorted" by students, and one's teaching style is often the subject of discussion or introspection. Kerr Houston complains that, at Hogwarts, "[i]nformation is imparted, rather than discussed: quizzes and tests seem to involve regurgitation, rather than critical analysis. Furthermore, professors at Hogwarts don't anticipate or relish open conversation..." (Houston, 2011, p. 3).

The best teaching seems to be done outside the classroom by Remus Lupin and Albus Dumbledore himself, who were willing to demonstrate and explain magic, evaluate Harry's performance, and admit fault. Lupin serves as an example of a teacher who was willing to let a student try, and fail, an advanced type of learning. By establishing a practical learning environment in a familiar classroom, and building on known factors, in this case a boggart, Lupin let Harry practice a new skill under controlled conditions. He anticipated that Harry would need continued practice and even showed sympathy to the boggart they would use in the lesson, saying, "I can store him in my office when we're not using him; there's a cupboard under my desk he'll like" (*PoA*, p. 236). As Philip Nel of Kansas State accurately notes, Lupin is a favorite among Muggle teachers, because he is a favorite among Hogwarts students.

The headmaster in the story teaches Harry about specific magical objects, like the Pensieve, but he rarely reveals all he knows, such as his suspicions about the actual nature of Harry's Invisibility Cloak. Dumbledore also seems, throughout the series, to be willing to allow Harry to get himself into terrible scrapes. Perhaps he was confident Harry would recover, or perhaps he was testing whether Harry was really the Chosen One, but Dumbledore, for all his sympathy, seems to be experimenting on Harry as much as teaching him. He realized too late that asking Professor Snape to supervise Occlumency lessons and failing to reveal the importance of these lessons to Harry was a mistake, with the dire consequence of Sirius Black's death: "If I had been open with you, Harry, as I should have been, you would have known a long time ago that Voldemort might try and lure you into the Department of Mysteries, and you would never have been tricked into going there tonight" (*OotP*, pp. 825–826).

Dumbledore also admits when he is guessing, an important element of research. "I told you everything I know. From this point forth, we shall be leaving the firm foundation of fact and journeying together through the murky marshes of memory into thickets of wildest guesswork" (*HBP*, p. 197). By modeling exploring the fringes of knowledge, Dumbledore provided Harry with an important learning experience. Lupin allowed Harry to experiment safely. Dumbledore treated Harry like an equal partner in his search for knowledge.

In the end, scenes in classrooms function to move the plot forward by defining relationships, introducing spells the students use later, or putting the magical world in context. Hermione's success, whether described as "books" and "cleverness" reveals that she teaches herself, as must all the students (*PS*, p. 208). Terry Boot, a member of Dumbledore's Army, wondered about Hermione, with her excellent skills and book knowledge, and questioned whether she really belonged in Gryffindor. "You can do a Protean Charm? ... But that's ... that's N.E.W.T. standard, that is,... How come you're not in Ravenclaw? ... With brains like yours?" (*OotP*, pp. 398–399). In demonstrating how students learned at Hogwarts, both in class and outside class, "Rowling creates a school in which self-teaching is encouraged and succeeds" (Dickinson, 2006, p. 243). As a student leader and more teacher than tutor, Harry himself models good teaching: a great laboratory (the Room of Requirement), a good library (books he owns and books the Room provides), demonstrations and practice in *OotP*. Accounts of the film design for *OotP* report that Daniel Radcliffe, who played Harry, suggested that his costuming for Dumbledore's Army reflect Harry's respect for Professor Lupin's style of teaching Defense Against the Dark Arts (DADA), thus explaining the cardigan Harry wears in DA scenes (Mugglenet, p. 96, 2014).

It seems that the magic which manifests itself in untrained children is a trait they must learn to control as they mature, as much emotion as skill. When Harry doubts he is even a wizard, Hagrid asks him "Never made things something happen when you was scared, or angry?" (*PS*, p. 47). And Neville's wizard family kept testing him to see if he might be Muggle, "My great-uncle Algie kept trying to catch me off my guard and force some magic out of me..." (*PS*, p. 93). When it comes to the classroom, the *Potter* tale is less about the "How" of magic (and as much as we might wish for it, how could one get more specific?) than about the "What" and the "Why." Teachers, subjects, tests and rules introduce the reader to types of magic and to issues relevant to the plot, such as trust, exploration, empowerment, and "more important things—friendship and bravery" (*PS*, p. 208).

In Defense of a *Harry Potter* Curriculum

For any *Harry Potter* course, there comes a moment when an instructor must face the accusation that the course is "light" on content. This is a pitfall for any pop culture or film course, and is doubly dangerous for a course featuring books typically read by the twelve year old set. Nevertheless, by any standard, the foundational texts for a *Harry Potter* course are momentous: 4,224 pages of reading and 1,180 minutes of film, not counting outtakes and extras. Every college course listed above presumed a preexisting familiarity with the books, or the films, or both. Thus, reading the books a second time involves higher level analysis, reading together through themes in the course, and comparing "canon" discrepancies between the books and films or games. Even learning the concept of a canon, and the centrality of that idea to any textual analysis, is a significant leap for college students, especially if they are in the hard sciences or applied disciplines. Plenty of Potter defenders believe the subject to be of sufficient rigor. Martin Hughes of *TheUniversityBlog* puts words to the fear, "some people will now think lazy students are going to spend three years doing nothing but reading J.K. Rowling's books and perhaps writing the odd essay about what they've read. If they can be bothered. Bloody students…" (Hughes, *Blog*, 2010). The British tabloid *The Daily Star* lost no time in trumpeting about a "*Harry Potter* degree," even though the Durham offering was a "module." The *Daily Star* was not the only critic. Lighthearted mocking also showed up in the *Daily Telegraph*. Nevertheless, this can all be set aside in light of the positive response to the Durham course by *Times Higher Education*, a weekly magazine on higher education published out of London, and well known for its *Times Higher Education World University Rankings*. "It is only fitting that a university such as Durham responds to new developments in our academic and wider social and cultural environment to develop new modules such as this. Surely, higher education must explore issues relevant to today's society. Some of the universal themes covered in the works of J.K. Rowling certainly bear analysis, whether in English departments or outside" (*THE*, "Idea," 2010).

Martin Hughes agrees, making an impassioned case for including pop culture in the humanities and social sciences. It is relevant, provides a route into sophisticated cultural insight, and ought not be criticized as lacking the gravitas of older texts that have "stood the test of time." "The study of something that has made a significant difference to many people," he argues, "must be a good thing" (Hughes, *Blog*, 2010).

The question of how to get a *Harry Potter* course into a curriculum is a legitimate one. Certainly the texts belong in a Children's Literature course. Potentially a course on comparative British Literature would include reference to the resurgence of youth fiction spurred by Rowling. Any course on the modern novel might ponder the importance of *Potter* to transforming the *New York Times* bestseller rankings. But an entire course on *Potter* requires imagination, intellectual rigor, and a not inconsiderable amount of pre-existing goodwill toward the faculty proposing the course. The Durham course was approved at the highest university levels, going through a committee approval process before being offered. When courses are offered as an individual readings seminar, as a special topics class, or within a particular program, such as an honors college, this reveals that faculty may consider Rowling a useful, but temporary, phenomenon, putting it alongside other pop culture "fads" like *Twilight*/vampires or *The Walking Dead*/zombies. Others consider the Rowling books a lasting contribution to youth culture, and expect it to have the staying power of C.S. Lewis, Lewis Carroll, Roald Dahl or, at the risk of sounding sacrilegious, J.R.R. Tolkien.

Teaching History with Harry

Ask a student what the purpose of studying history might be, and you will get one of two replies: to understand one's own past and to learn from mistakes. Historians are a tough audience. Notoriously fussy, historians are fond of tradition. In the humanities, history is still predominantly male, and more conservative than similar disciplines like literature. Historians are less theory driven and still a bit romantic about the possibility of discovering truth in facts and sources. I myself am a trained diplomatic historian, a venerable field. Nevertheless, *Harry Potter* has transformed my teaching of history: using the books as the primary sources in courses built around the wizarding world, using the series as accessible metaphor in teaching about history (e.g., Blood/race/Nazi Germany), and by breaking down walls between faculty and student by referencing a common, loved text. When college level curricula use or reference J.K. Rowling's series, there is more to history, and to Harry, than meets the eye.

Multiple avenues are available to the historian who wishes to incorporate *Harry Potter* studies into a course. All of the elements essential to a successful history course are present: Research Methods, Biography, Chronology, Causality, Context/Culture, Artifacts, and Analysis. These are used by the characters (predominantly Harry, Hermione and Ron) to discover new information, enrich everyday life, solve problems, and predict and interpret events. In addition to the actions taken by the characters, the Potter series offers theoretical insights useful for historians in analyzing the broader social implications of race, gender, or memory.

It has not gone unnoticed, however, that the means for learning history is depicted in the story as the ultimate stereotype, the dull lecture. Even Professor Binns himself is ancient, disengaged, and seemingly irrelevant. After all, he is a ghost. Professor Binns, not Professor McGonagall (as in the film), responds to Hermione's question about Slytherin's monster supposedly living in the castle. Rather than demonstrate any capacity for imagination, Binns reiterates the nineteenth century ideology that history, as Ranke put it, should help one to understand *"wie es eigentlich gewesen"/* "as it actually was." He claims he only deals in facts, not myths. Nevertheless, one can still trace how the threesome use information gleaned from this dusty classroom as they pursue their adventures. History classes can teach students to rely on known authorities. For instance, if Ron and Harry had made themselves more familiar with their textbook *A History of Magic,* the trio might have been quicker to understand that magical historian Bathilda Bagshot might hold the key to understanding Dumbledore's past and his intentions for Harry. Instead, of course, she held a curse, but in the end, it is a children's story, not a textbook on historical methods. Despite its negative reputation, a history lecture, therefore, is also a potentially useful learning environment for students who must navigate the Wizarding World in context. The *Harry Potter* series definitely offers historians rich material for investigating the methods and usefulness of history.

Understanding One's Past

As an historian of early twentieth century European history, my own research often analyses how nations and individuals remember and commemorate past trauma. This theme is easily traced in the *Potter* series, and the topic of memory is a useful one for teaching history students. Whether asking Lupin questions about his father's school days or visiting one of Dumbledore's memories through the Pensieve, Harry confronts his own personal past. History students often begin with an interest in a subject because of a family connection, perhaps a grandparent is a Vietnam War veteran or perhaps they live in a community like White Deer or West Texas where Poles and Czechs settled. Genealogy is an important theme and easy to trace in the *Potter* series. It also reveals cultural and historical information beyond the immediate plotline.

For instance, American students at my regional state university may have read *Harry Potter*, but they seldom approach the books with any sense of British history or tradition. One thing I work very hard to do with my students is to help them at least begin to identify how a *British* audience would read the texts or see the film, as well as the American audience. Such straightforward references as the Protestant/Catholic/English/Irish/nobility/impoverished gentry/Malfoy/Weasley construction introduces them to the idea that race or class might be part of how children or societies understand themselves or seek to be understood. In a recent film course about children in the world, students seemed stunned when asked to ponder the glaring references to class and religion in comparing the Malfoys and the Weasleys. In that class, I asked students to write "cultural take-away" essays about each film, an assignment which asked them to explain the importance of some cultural element to the culture/country of origin for each film (e.g., *Whale Rider, Princess Mononoke, Children of Heaven, Sorcerer's Stone*). They overwhelmingly chose the race/class assignment (as opposed to gender, religion, geography or history) in this case. Students were faced, perhaps for the first time, with interpreting the historical and cultural context that shaped a beloved film, and they sought a means to do so.

Avoiding Past Mistakes

Students who seek to study history in order to avoid future mistakes often cite World War II as an example of clear divisions between right and wrong. In such a course, the metaphors in *Harry Potter* are easy for students to understand. A serious student of *Harry Potter* will also quickly catch on to the idea that the conflict over Grindelwald can be interpreted as World War I, a war not ever quite lost and which resurfaces in the racial war and depraved ideology of Voldemort. During the Grindelwald conflict the slogan he and Dumbledore developed while they were still friends and allies was "For the Greater Good" (*DH*, p. 353). Much like the infamous phrase on the gates of numerous Nazi concentration camps *"Arbeit Macht Frei,"* or "Work makes you free/work liberates," the phrase "the Greater Good" seems to be positive, but instead reflects a sinister intent, not to liberate, but to enslave, in this case Muggles. The most effective scene from the series I have used in my Nazi Germany course focuses not only on the differentiation between non-magical Muggles and magical Wizards, but also on the biological and familial ramifications for diverging from the totalitarian norm. For instance, multiple references to genealogies or family trees emphasize the link between old Wizarding families and the old English aristocracy. The struggle to maintain purity, and with that, power, was at the heart of weakness. In *DH*, the general dislike of Muggles takes a very personal turn when Voldemort refers to Bellatrix "pruning the family tree," meaning eliminating the line which intermarried with Muggles, that is, the Tonks family. Certainly her aunt Walburga Black, Sirius' mother, symbolically purified the family by burning holes in the Black family tapestry where their names were listed.

Even the names Grindelwald and Voldemort carry a Continental flavor—sounding Germanic or French, conjuring up manors and privilege, rather than solid Englishness or everyday/common folk. Grindelwald is actually the name of a Swiss mountain in the Alps, and the character attended the wizarding school Durmstrang, known for its dark magic tendencies and also vaguely Continental or Scandinavian. This is reinforced by the arrival by ship of the Durmstrang students who participated in the Triwizard Cup in *GoF.* His fortress, Nurmengard, also has a Germanic/Scandinavian tone, also conjuring up Adolf Hitler's favorite city, Nuremberg. Rowling demonstrates that she was not writing an exact reification of the European wars by blending the metaphors. The suffix "berg" in German means "mountain," but "burg" means fortress, much like "grad" in Russian. It would be easy for a European student or a student of European history to hear the similarity.

The Dumbledore-Grindelwald dynamic is a classic example for learning from past mistakes. Of all the authority figures the trio encounters, Dumbledore is really the only one who models self-criticism or introspection. Readers learn in *HBP* and in *DH* that Dumbledore had regrets: he should have revealed information to Harry sooner. He should have guarded his family closer. He should have considered whether he could destroy a Horcrux on his own.

Learning from the past requires engaging with original sources. For students learning *how* to do history, *Beedle the Bard* is a particularly fascinating source. Rowling has, in fact, provided an original source, a primary source. She has offered it translated by a character, including marginalia from a professor, modeling medieval modes of learning, right down to the original copy handwritten by herself. The Horcruxes reveal the importance of getting into the mind of the subject of one's research. The Horcruxes each represent something important to Riddle, so understanding Tom Riddle's personal history, values and presumptions contributes to solving the mystery, the puzzle of the series.

Once a student is made aware of the intentional use of history, and of patterns in the *Harry Potter* story, it can be very rewarding to continue to delve into external material. In this situation, I do in fact encourage students to explore web and print sources beyond the seven books. Sources produced by Rowling, like *Pottermore* (www.Pottermore.com) or *Tales of Beedle the Bard*, and those completely ancillary to Rowling's work, like the *Harry Potter* wiki (harrypotter.wikia.com) or the infamous but extremely useful *Harry Potter* Lexicon (www.hp-lexicon.org) are equally useful.

Research Methods

Students in a university class must learn practical skills used in research, and for most disciplines, this means a combination of library skills and textual analysis. This takes practice, and is something an ordinary student must exercise. Answers do not always appear by accident, or a friend's obsessive reading, or someone being handed the answer by a professor who cheats. Work produces results. Kerr Houston, medievalist and art professor, frets that the library, while used in Hogwarts, seems to be a choice of last resort, where one futilely searches for an answer to the question of the Philosopher's Stone or the Triwizard egg. Kerr objects to accidental knowledge. For instance, when Hagrid lets information about the maker of the Sorcerer's Stone slip while defending Snape's actions during Harry's first Quidditch match, "I'm tellin' yeh, yer wrong! ... I don't know why Harry's broom acted like that, but Snape wouldn' try an' kill a student! Now, listen to me ... [y]ou forget that dog, an' you forget what it's guardin,' that's between Professor Dumbledore an' Nicolas Flamel." To his credit, Hagrid had the grace to be "furious with himself" for using Flamel's name (*SS*, p. 193). After this, the trio do actually spend a significant amount of time in the library, including trying to get at what an historian might call "classified" information in the "restricted section." Chance (and Rowling's fondness for the headmaster) puts a Chocolate Frog card in Harry's hand before he ever arrives at Hogwarts. Much like a baseball card, the prize lists facts about the featured wizard, in this case, Dumbledore including "his work on alchemy with his partner, Nicholas Flamel" (*SS*, p. 103). When Harry remembers this (it takes him to page 219), then Hermione's penchant for "light reading" and library books identifies the Sorcerer's Stone as an important artifact in the story.

Houston has an excellent point about the danger of using the *Harry Potter* stories as a model for serious learning, since coincidence seems to play a large role in the revelation of knowledge. Secret information comes Harry's way less often because he studies and more because he is affiliated with a team sport, which apparently gives him the right to occasionally be moving about the grounds unsupervised, since it is again after a Quidditch game that he hears Professor Snape say to Professor Quirrell, "Students aren't supposed to know about the Sorcerer's Stone, after all" (*SS*, pp. 226–227). Houston may be over-estimating the extent to which the library alone is part of historical research when he exclaims over the happenstances of collecting information in pubs, passages, and the cemetery. Happenstance is part of the research experience. History students, like anthropologists or sociologists, need to learn to be observant, to engage with living subjects and material culture as much as libraries or primary sources. For instance, it is completely acceptable to stroll through a cemetery looking for names, dates, mottos or symbols that tie one grave marker to another, and consider this as research. It is even appropriate to follow a random old woman back to her house to hear the local gossip, especially if you suspect she is a prominent historian, just so long as she is not harboring a Horcrux.

Sometimes faculty might hand a student an answer, rather than show how to find the information. This can be true in a lecture or in a research project. Certainly, the false Alastor "Mad Eye" Moody manipulated Harry and other students in order to influence the outcome of the Triwizard Tournament. He confessed this at the conclusion of the book *GoF*, even mocking Harry and his friends for trying to research a problem properly "all those hours in the library. Didn't you realize that the book you needed was in your dormitory all along? I planted it there early on, I gave it to the Longbottom boy, don't you remember? *Magical Mediterranean Water-Plants and Their Properties*. It would have told you all you needed about Gillyweed." This is the scenario used in the films, but in the book the false Moody went one step further, ensuring that Dobby would learn about the Gillyweed and steal it for Harry (*GoF*, pp. 587–588). Dumbledore and Snape also hand clues or artifacts over to Harry, like the Invisibility Cloak or the Sword of Gryffindor. Dumbledore demonstrates research techniques such as oral history by using the Pensieve, but often guides Harry to the answer he seeks in discussion. By the end of Book Seven, Harry chooses his destiny, and the fate of the Wizarding World, equipped with answers and guidance provided to him by Dumbledore and Snape. Faculty are still key to learning.

What Does History Have to Do with Harry?

Harry as an Honors Course

Professors Karen Wendling (Department of Chemistry) and Patrick McCauley, (Religious Studies) teach *Harry Potter* in the Interdisciplinary Honors Program at Chestnut Hill College, a small Catholic school in Pennsylvania. In fact the entire town of Chestnut Hill celebrates a *Harry Potter* festival each fall, and the now well established *Harry Potter* Conference offers both scholars and fans an opportunity to talk about *Potter* in a meaningful way. Inspired by the interdisciplinarity of such honors programs, and by the variety of fields represented in *Harry Potter* Studies, I turned from using *Harry Potter* as a means for studying history and broadened the course scope for an honors class at my own institution. I set all seven books as a prerequisite for the course. Arranging for John Granger to visit campus as a part of our Distinguished Lecturer series, I consulted with him about which of his books he might recommend the students read, and he suggested *Harry Potter's Bookshelf.* It was a good choice, challenging for students with little experience of a literary canon but readable for a general audience. Students especially enjoyed discussing *Harry Potter's* Gothic and Romantic themes. I added the Anelli book for a unit on fandom which included viewing the documentary *We Are Wizards* and also one of Christopher Bell's edited volumes on *Harry Potter* Studies, *Legilimens! Perspectives in Harry Potter Studies.* Bell also visited campus and met with the honors class for a rousing debate about whether Dumbledore "created" Voldemort. By requiring students to engage with the series at a critical level, but not requiring this diverse group of majors to all behave as if they were English majors, I hoped to spark interest in approaching and using *Harry Potter* from many angles. The class also included a travel component to the Wizarding World of *Harry Potter* at Universal Studios in Orlando, Florida. Students practiced social science methods and conducted informal polls among visitors. For their final projects, the honors students were expected to find ways of integrating their own academic interests, preferably their major, and *Harry Potter.* The result was an interesting and inspiring mix,

ranging from a study of Gringott's by an accounting major to an interpretation of the Hogwarts Houses as Learning Communities by a future
teacher who concluded, as might be expected, "sometimes we sort too soon."
Some students found the assignment daunting, even mind-bending, unsure
they could find a way to apply the methods of their own discipline within
the Wizarding world. A chemistry student performed a *Harry Potter*
themed magic show, while a pre-dentistry student offered a insightful
assessment of how facial aesthetics in series characters either revealed or
concealed the true self.

What Effect Will *Harry Potter* Continue to Have on the *HP* Generation?

As a history professor (and generally, as a professor in the Liberal Arts),
can I use *Harry Potter* as a means for communicating with Millennials? I
learn about teaching and learning through the series and alongside my students. Teaching an honors seminar with a *Harry Potter* theme has forced me
to consider how to combine the study of history with in-depth reading and
analysis of familiar books and films—for all majors. It is a challenge that
one might need Dumbledore to meet, but has been a wonderful adventure.

The *Potter* franchise contributes to literacy, literature, cultural under-
standing, and intellectual debate. There is room for an *HP* II generation.
Like the "JP II" generation which grew up under democratic systems (John
Paul II, was given credit for helping defeat Communism in Poland) in
Eastern Europe, the *HP* II generation can be the generation which grows
up, not with bit by bit introductions to Harry, but having Harry as part of
their worldview from the beginning. Kerr Houston has posited that the
Harry Potter Generation thinks about college life, from residential living
and to learning communities, in the context of Hogwarts. When college
tours reference Quidditch grounds when touring intramural fields, when
West Texas study abroad students exclaim over the Polish train that has
compartments like the Hogwarts Express, when Chestnut Hill offers schol-
arships to high school students who present research at the *Harry Potter*
Conference, or when students post reviews on ratemyprofessor.com that
compare faculty to Hogwarts professors, it seems self-evident that "like it
or not, Potter's experiences are a lens through which teenagers view college
life" (Houston, 2011, p. 2). There is room for *Harry Potter* studies among
academics, and there is room for Harry Potter in the university curriculum.
Move over, Professor Binns, there's a new history professor at Hogwarts!

References

Belcher, C., and B.H. Stephenson. (2011). *Teaching Harry Potter: The power of imagination in multicultural classrooms.* London: Palgrave.

Bell, C.E. (2013). *Legilimens! Perspectives in Harry Potter Studies.* Cambridge: Cambridge Scholars.

Columbus, C. (2001). *Harry Potter and the Philosopher's Stone* [motion picture]. Warner Bros. Pictures.

Columbus, C. (2002). *Harry Potter and the Chamber of Secrets* [motion picture]. Warner Bros. Pictures.

Cuaron, A. (2004). *Harry Potter and the Prisoner of Azkaban* [motion picture]. Warner Bros. Pictures.

Dendle, P. "Cryptozoology and the Paranormal in Harry Potter: Truth and Belief at the Borders of Consensus." *Children's Literature Association Quarterly* 36:4, 410–425.

Dickinson, R. (2006). "Harry Potter Pedagogy: What we learn about teaching and learning from J.K. Rowling." *The Clearing House: A Journal of Educational Strategies, Issues and Ideas* 79:6, 240–244.

"Durham University Students offered Harry Potter Course." (2010, August 18). *BBC News.* Retrieved from http://www.bbc.co.uk/news/uk-england-wear-11011279.

"EDUC 2381: Harry Potter and the Age of Illusion." (2010). *Faculty Handbook, Education Department.* Durham University. Retrieved from https://www.dur.ac.uk/faculty.handbook/archive/module_description/?year=2010&module_code=EDUC 2381.

Flood, A. (2010, August 19). "Harry Potter Course to be offered at Durham University." *The Guardian.* Retrieved from http://www.theguardian.com/books/2010/aug/19/harry-potter-course-durham-university.

Granger, John. (2008). *How Harry Cast His Spell: The Meaning behind the Mania for J.K. Rowling's Bestselling Books.* Carol Stream, IL: Tyndale.

Granger, John. 2009. *Harry Potter's Bookshelf: The great books behind the Hogwarts adventures.* New York: Berkley Books.

Harry Potter Academia, *Nine Worlds Geekfest 2014.* (2013). Retrieved from: https://nine worlds.co.uk/2013/track/harry-potter-academia.

A Harry Potter Degree. (2010, August 21). *Daily Star.* Retrieved from http://www.daily star.co.uk/news/latest-news/150071/A-Harry-Potter-degree.

Harry's Here: Hogwarts, the College Years. (2014). *Kansas State University Admissions.* Retrieved from: http://consider.k-state.edu/features/potter/.

Houston, K. (2011). "Teaching the Harry Potter Generation," *Networks: An On-line journal for teacher research* (13:2).

How Magic Became a Science. (2013). *Harry Potter's World: Renaissance Science, Magic and Medicine.* Retrieved from: http://www.nlm.nih.gov/exhibition/harrypotters world/education/highereducation/unit2.html.

Hughes, M. (2010, August 27). What's so Potty about a Harry Potter Course? *TheUniversityBlog.* Retrieved from: http://theuniversityblog.co.uk/2010/08/27/whats-so-potty-about-a-harry-potter-course/.

McDaniel, K. (2010). "Harry Potter and the Ghost Teacher: Resurrecting the Lost Art of Lecturing." *The History Teacher* 43:2, 289–295.

Mekado, M. (2009, July 14). "Potter's Magic Numbers." *New York Times*. Retrieved from http://artsbeat.blogs.nytimes.com/2009/07/14/potters-magic-numbers/?_r=0.

MuggleNet. (2014, August 9). "Podcast Episode 96. *Alohamora, Open the Dumbledore*. Podcast retrieved from http://alohomora.mugglenet.com/podcast-question-of-the-week-episode-96/.

Newell, M. (2005). *Harry Potter and the Goblet of Fire* [motion picture]. Warner Bros. Pictures.

Rowling, J.K. (1998). *Harry Potter and the Sorcerer's Stone*. New York: Arthur A. Levine.

Rowling, J.K. (1999). *Harry Potter and the Chamber of Secrets*. New York: Arthur A. Levine.

Rowling, J.K. (1999). *Harry Potter and the Prisoner of Azkaban*. New York: Arthur A. Levine.

Rowling, J.K. (2002). *Harry Potter and the Goblet of Fire*. New York: Scholastic.

Rowling, J.K. (2003). *Harry Potter and the Order of the Phoenix*. New York: Arthur A. Levine.

Rowling, J.K. (2005). *Harry Potter and the Half-Blood Prince*. New York: Arthur A. Levine.

Rowling, J.K. (2007). *Harry Potter and the Deathly Hallows*. New York: Arthur A. Levine.

Rowling, J.K. (2008). *Tales of Beedle the Bard*. New York: Arthur A. Levine.

Sanghani, R. (2014, January 30). "Beyoncé studies anyone? 8 other ridiculous university courses." *Daily Telegraph*. Retrieved from http://www.telegraph.co.uk/women/womens-life/10607390/Beyonce-studies-anyone-8-other-ridiculous-university-courses.html.

Schulten, K., and S. Doyne (2011). "Teaching Harry Potter with the *New York Times*." http://learning.blogs.nytimes.com/2011/07/12/teaching-harry-potter-with-the-new-york-times/?_r=0.

Tumminio, D.E. (2010). *God and Harry Potter at Yale: Teaching Faith and Fantasy Fiction in an Ivy League Classroom*. Unlocking Press.

Walburga Black. (2014). *Harry Potter Wiki*. Retrieved from http://harrypotter.wikia.com/wiki/Walburga_Black.

Westmin, K. (2014). Harry Potter's Library, syllabus. Retrieved from http://www.k-state.edu/english/westmank/.

What a Wizard Idea. (July 13, 2010). *Times Higher Education*. Retrieved from http://www.timeshighereducation.co.uk/news/what-a-wizard-idea/412504.article.

"It's a natural part of us!"
The *Potter* Generation Reflect on Their Ongoing Relationship with a Cultural Phenomenon

Bronwyn E. Beatty

According to Lizzy,[1] the *Harry Potter* books, films, marketing and merchandise—Pottermania in short—is "a natural part of us." "Us" refers to the *Potter* Generation and she made her claim during a group discussion with other fans of *Harry Potter*. Lizzy's assertion points to the strong impact all things *Harry Potter* have had on these particular representatives of the global *Potter* Generation, and they believe their life is the better for it. Being part of the *Potter* Generation is considered a privilege, they argue, with it being impossible to imagine another phenomenon, past or future, so thorough in its influence on everyday life.

Pottermania epitomizes the intense commodification of children's culture that has occurred over recent decades, raising the ire of children's advocates, while marketers and global media conglomerates defend their content. Concern for children's wellbeing is expressed in "popular publications, press reports and campaigns" (Buckingham & Tingstad, 2010, p. 1) with the objective of protecting vulnerable children from the global corporates. These corporates, campaigners proclaim, aim to groom young people into lifelong consumption practices: "by the time they are five or six, they've been pulled into the marketplace. They're on their way to becoming not citizens but consumers" (Denby, 1996, p. 51). Predictably, those representing the global corporates disagree. Their intentions are honorable toward the savvy children who choose, or not, to engage with their content or marketing. So when Coca Cola was accused of using their record-breaking sponsorship deal with the *Harry Potter* films to cash in on global interest in the franchise, spokesman Andrew Coker dismissed concerns as purposefully ignoring the good work the company does "supporting education projects around the world" (cited in Day, 2001b). He stated that "[Coca Cola's] intention is to spread the joy of reading and that is exactly what we are doing.... To characterize our involvement in any other way is missing the point for the sake of sensationalism" (cited in Day, 2001b).

The binary opposition these views represent also aligns with common theoretical positions, with children often regarded as either victims or agents (Buckingham & Tingstad, 2010, p. 2; Marshall, 2010, pp. 1–2; Zanker, 2011, pp. 631–632). But as with any binary opposition, the either/or argument distracts us from a more thorough understanding of what is necessarily a more complex issue than either position will allow. As Zanker writes, "the simple binary drawn between corporate strategic planning and audience agency and creativity is inadequate to describe the rich and complex relationships between audiences and producers of culture" (2011, p. 632).

Part of the issue with these divergent claims about children and their engagement with consumer culture is that they typically fail to incorporate the voices of those they proclaim to represent—the children themselves. Assumptions are made and children are spoken about and on behalf of, but not so often consulted. This research asks members of the *Potter* Generation for their perspective and draws on Cook's ideas about cultural enculturation to reflect on their insights. "Cultural enculturation," Cook writes,

> calls our attention to the multiple trajectories of children's participation in the world of goods and meanings, acknowledges the differences among children and the connections between children and adults, and accounts for change over time without predetermining the specific pathways, timing or direction of change. The focus centers on how "consumption" and "meaning," and thus culture, arise together through social contexts and processes of parenting and socializing with others. What and how children learn about consumption occurs in contexts that are already enmeshed in the consumer world [2010, p. 76].

This chapter will therefore consider some of the *Potter* Generation's memories of *Harry Potter*, how the stories continue to resonate for them, and how they use the text today. Observations and commentary are included from a group of first-year broadcasting students in Aotearoa/New Zealand in order to review the value of such a franchise to those who engaged most closely and fully with it. What did *Harry Potter* mean to them as they grew up and what do they recall of their use of the merchandise? Indeed, what does the text continue to mean for them and how do they continue to engage with the merchandise and associated paraphernalia?

While the students were unequivocal in their ongoing approval of the story itself, they varied in their desire for merchandise. Engagement with merchandise has modified as they have matured, with early goods reflected on nostalgically (such as *Harry Potter* dolls, Lego sets, and board games) although they no longer form a part of their everyday lives. What remains, however, is the residue—fond memories and a shared discourse centered on the *Harry Potter* franchise which the group asserts is very important to them.

The *Potter* Generation's recollections are first contextualized with a theoretical section on children and the commodified consumer culture in which they grow up. The final section reflects on their claims and memories in relation to the theory, noting their equivocal support for the merchandise and unequivocal support for Rowling's enduring stories.

The Commodification of Children's Culture and Pottermania

In 1998, Rowling signed a deal with Time Warner for two films and related merchandising (Waetjen & Gibson, 2007, p. 6). Although she was "insistent she [did] not want to taint the stories' magic and innocence with aggressive commercialization" (Day, 2001a), it was reported that by 2002

> the conglomerate has granted 46 licenses to all manner of memorabilia manufacturers: Mattel for board games and toys; Hasbro, for trading cards and candy; Electronic Arts, for video games and computer-based ancillaries; Lego for the eponymous building bricks; and the Character Group for plastic and porcelain figurines. Coca-Cola has also signed a $150 million sponsorship deal, while rumors of everything from Hogwarts theme parks to Harry Potter Happy Meals are circulating [Brown, 2002, p. 7].

The theme parks have since eventuated (although not the McDonald's Happy Meals due to Rowling's refusal to endorse the potential promotional activity [Gunelius, 2008, p. 95]) and the frenzied but focused marketing hype and merchandising that enveloped the stories post–1998 turned Rowling's grassroots hit (Waetjen & Gibson, 2007, p. 6) into an "industry" (Travers, 2001) better known as Pottermania.

Described as "the standard bearer of synergy and vertical integration in the modern digital age" and the largest media company in the world at the time (Colombia Journal Review, 2004) Time Warner was well positioned to exploit Rowling's text. Two divisions at Time Warner took responsibility for the films and merchandising, Warner Brothers Pictures and

Warner Brothers Consumer Products respectively (Waetjen & Gibson, 2007, pp. 16–17). The *Harry Potter* brand was therefore spread widely, via a vast array of interrelated magazines, television channels and an internet service to ultimately ensure that "a Time Warner property is never too far away from any consumer's fingertips" (Colombia Journalism Review, 2004).

The ensuing exponential commercial success of the *Harry Potter* franchise has been much recorded and dissected, as has the author's personal accrued wealth as a result of the commodification of her stories (Nel, 2005; Travers, 2001; Kapur, 2005; Turner-Vorbeck, 2008; Gunelius, 2008). Yet, the connection between children's media culture and merchandising is not new. The Walt Disney Company began trading in 1923 and is described by Gunelius as a "merchandising machine" (2008, p. 95) with "not a single Disney movie … released without a preformed merchandising strategy attached to it" (2008, p. 95) from its earliest days. Kinder documented the children's entertainment supersystems in 1991, noting that "even *before* children go to the cinema, they learn that movies make a vital contribution to an ever-expanding supersystem of entertainment, one marked by transmedia intertextuality" (1991, p. 1, italics in original). Further, commodifying children's culture is not solely the domain of the commercial cultural industries. Buckingham points out that the public broadcaster BBC has successfully leveraged some television shows such as *Dr. Who* through merchandise (2013, p. 158). Merchandising has become typical of children's cultural content, therefore giving the consumer a transmedia experience—an opportunity to explore a consistent and thoroughly imagined story world and its characters across a number of platforms—which has become a consumer expectation as well as a commercial given.

Undoubtedly, the ensuing Pottermania was both created and fostered by Time Warner (Turner-Vorbeck, 2008, p. 335; Kapur, 2005, p. 148). Therefore the wider cultural and economic context in which the *Potter* Generation read *Harry Potter*, anticipated the upcoming books and films and consumed them was that of a coherent and aggressive global marketing and merchandising strategy. Heavy marketing of *Harry Potter* included midnight releases of new books, websites (official and unofficial) where merchandise could be bought or the wizarding world engaged with, and innumerable paraphernalia such as necklaces, clothing, bedspreads, wands, Lego sets, PlayStation games, and board games. Such was the presence of *Harry Potter* across all marketing and merchandising platforms that Stephen Brown, Professor of Marketing of the University of Ulster, claimed that Harry's scar was on the way to achieving the same level of global brand recognition as "Nike's iconic swoosh, Coke's copperplate curlicues, and McDonald's golden arches" (2002, p. 11).

The commodification of children's culture, exemplified by the *Harry Potter* franchise, has long been debated, often in emotive and binary terms: the child as victim of an overwhelming and cynical commercial system focused on corporate greed or the child as an empowered and sophisticated consumer of corporate culture who self-selects cultural products they want rather than need (Buckingham, 2013, p. 148; Zanker, 2011, pp. 631–632). Child advocates find children to be susceptible to the marketing targeted at them while watching television (advertising and programming) and to the merchandising that is associated with stories they enjoy (*Pokémon* and *Pocahontas*, for example). They feel it is their responsibility to protect children from the damage that will ensue, primarily an engrained and lifelong need to consume in order to achieve identity and happiness. Alternatively, those who argue children are capable of negotiating corporate consumer culture oftentimes have a vested interest in this position, working in the corporate cultural industries. They therefore wish to project an image of the caring conglomerate that provides fun and engaging cultural products that the discerning child consumer wants.

These same positions have been taken up in relation to Pottermania. Unsurprisingly, the intense marketing and extensive range of *Harry Potter* merchandise has led to polarized opinions as to the value and implications of such a heavily commodified child consumer culture. Tammy Turner-Vorbeck exemplifies the child-as-victim position, arguing that "when children's identities and child culture are used as the means to the end of creating the consummate future consumer, one must begin to question seriously the proclaimed innocuousness of Pottermania" (2008, p. 333). Language and phrases such as "corporations imprinting and manipulating children and child culture" (p. 330), "authenticity of our lives" (p. 332), "obedient child shoppers" (p. 332), "corporate consumerism's full frontal attack on child culture" (p. 333), "blatant exploitation" (p. 334), "children's true interests" (p. 334), and "exercising control over the imaginations of children" (p. 336) are emotive and undefined. As Buckingham (2010; 2013) and others have repeatedly asked of child advocates, what constitutes "authenticity" or a child's "true interests" in a culture marked by consumerism? How, precisely, do items of merchandise manipulate a child, to what extent and over what period of time? Is such manipulation (if accepted) necessarily and always bad?

By contrast, those who uncritically endorse and defend Pottermania are exemplified by those who come from the industry. Jan Hall, Senior

Vice President Consumer Marketing, Coca-Cola North America defends her company's association with the franchise against claims of exploitation or promoting a sugary product to a purchased audience. Rather "Coca-Cola celebrates and embraces the ideals promoted through the stories of *Harry Potter*—friendship, love, self-reliance, the importance of the family, the magic of shared experiences and the value of diversity" (Warner Bros., 2006). But this argument, too, is problematic. Rather than defining the child as an innocent and therefore incapable of coping with the market-place, this point of view suggests they serve the child; the child is viewed as exerting an agency that has the corporate doing the child's cultural bidding, creating the entertainment products they want. Buckingham writes, "Children are characterized here as a sophisticated and demanding audience, who are difficult to reach and to satisfy. Far from being passive victims of commercial culture, children are seen as all-powerful, sovereign consumers" (2013, p. 148).

Turner-Vorbeck is undoubtedly correct in claiming that Time Warner have achieved an unprecedented level of commodification with Pottermania; however, the elitist position of the purportedly all-knowing adult reader distances the child from the debate. This position rarely talks with children, who are nevertheless central to their argument and on whose behalf they speak. It is not to say that either position in this divergent debate does not have valid points to make. Rather the problem with theoretical binary oppositions is that they close down potentially nuanced understandings of actual cultural practices which are, of necessity, embedded in a consumer culture. Buckingham (2013) and Cook (2010) rightly point out the obvious; that children in "wealthy, media-saturated societies" (Cook, 2010, p. 76) are growing up in a consumer culture; there is no other "authentic" culture in which children can express their "true identity" or engage in unspecified "traditional childhood past-times." Buckingham declares that

> Consumer culture is not simply a means of manipulating people's authentic needs, or indeed of creating false ones; but neither is it necessarily one of "subversion" or autonomous creativity, in which such needs are unproblematically expressed. The social and cultural needs that are manifested in our uses of material objects do not exist in some supposedly pure, non-commercial sphere. On the contrary, consumer culture is now the arena in which those very needs are defined, articulated and experienced [2013, p. 165].

Rather than either decrying or uncritically validating the commodification of children's culture, this research considers the views of the *Potter* Generation themselves. To this end, I conducted a group discussion with first year tertiary students who self-identify as the *Potter* Generation. How do they reflect on Pottermania? Do they feel like cultural dupes and lament a childhood wasted on a story that was forced upon them by aggressive marketing from a global conglomerate or feel they have been given exactly what they asked for by a friendly media corporate who understands their needs? Alternatively, are there a range of experiences and responses that more closely reflect Cook's idea of "commercial enculturation," in which "the multifaceted, multifarious aspects of commercial life and the active involvement of children in it [are acknowledged], without presupposing either the parameters of economic action or the nature and trajectory of children's participation" (2010, p. 76)?

How the discussion was conducted is detailed in the ensuing section, followed by the participants' views on their engagement with the *Harry Potter* franchise.

The Group Discussion

This research reflects on information obtained in November 2014 from fans of the *Harry Potter* franchise. A group discussion was held with 25 first year broadcasting students from Aotearoa/New Zealand. The discussion ran for 60 minutes and, as with a focus group interview, was designed to facilitate a friendly conversation, in this instance about *Harry Potter*. We met in a familiar setting (the television studio where lectures are typically held), sitting on the floor in a large circle around the microphone and the participants all knew each other. This familiarity and the students' enthusiasm for the topic made for a congenial and open examination of personal reflections on the *Harry Potter* franchise. The conversation was redirected or ideas probed by myself as moderator when necessary. The discussion was audio recorded and transcribed, with pseudonyms used for each participant.[2]

This particular cohort of broadcasting students ranged in age from 18 to 23 years. They each self-identified as being of the "*Potter* Generation" despite their ages not aligning exactly with those of the characters. They reveal the tendency of "aging up"—becoming older younger—within aspirant children's culture in which they recognize and engage with brands and media content from a very young age (Nairn, 2010, p. 97). Rowling's hero and his peers are aged eleven in 1997, while these students were between one and six years old when the first book was published, between 11 and 16 in 2007 when the much anticipated final book arrived on the shelves, and between 15 and 20 when the final film was released in 2011. As a result, their childhoods were entirely colored by the franchise.

More than a third of this first year broadcasting cohort volunteered for the discussion, indicating a continuing interest in the text and a willingness, even a desire, to talk about it. Of the self-selected group of 25 participants, 13 were female and 12 male. The convivial atmosphere, laughter, "confessions" and "thank you's" expressed at the close of the discussion suggest it was a pleasure for this group to give up spare time to talk about *Harry Potter*, which continued through a closed Facebook group discussion through to the end of January 2015.

What, then, do these particular Antipodean members of the global *Potter* Generation have to say about the phenomenon? What themes and ideas were recurrent in the discussion, where did their experiences differ and what does *Harry Potter* mean to them now as young adults?

Talking *Harry Potter*

To open the group discussion, each participant was invited to state what first came to mind when they heard the words "*Harry Potter*." The "social" aspect of their engagement with the *Harry Potter* franchise was prominent in each of their introductory comments and was mentioned repeatedly and variously in the discussion. Most participants were originally read the first two to three books by one or more parents, before they embarked on independent reading of the series. It was noted that a parent would put on voices for the different characters and most claimed with amusement that their reader had difficulty pronouncing "Hermione" until the name was clarified in the films. For some participants, sharing the books with a parent through being read to was extended to include being gifted the books by a grandparent or even reading the book after everyone else in the family had done so. Jason said, "every single *Harry Potter* book I read had already been through the rest of my family" and as a consequence he had difficulty avoiding "spoilers" from older siblings. Yet this was a positive element of his *Harry Potter* experience: "It became a really social family event." Similarly, Lizzy, Jane and Karl noted the familial experience as central to their memories of *Harry Potter*. For Lizzy it was centered on the books, for Jane it was going to the movies together, and for Karl it was long periods spent in the family car on holidays listening to the audio books. Familial relations continue to be fostered through *Harry Potter* as young adults, with Ben receiving a chocolate frog from his sister on her return from England soon after the group discussion took place (Facebook, 3 December 2014).

"Harry Potter," then, conjures up fond family-oriented memories for these participants. But the social aspect extends beyond the nuclear setting to engaging with peers through a shared regard for and knowledge of the stories. As children, the participants played with a neighbors' Weasley House play set (Christine), mixed leaves with friends in the garden which became the potions for their ensuing game (Beatrice), Jendy made wands to play with, and Rhonda tested all the spells in her *Harry Potter* spellbook. As young adults, *Harry Potter* continues to inform their communication and engagement with others. They tease a friend who shares the hero's first name and initials, Karl held a pumpkin pie party to celebrate the release of one of the films and Ben recounted how he and friends fill in spare time between classes by completing a test in which they identify as many character names from the series as they can recall. Vessie's flatmate brought home a *Harry Potter* PlayStation game for them to play (Facebook, 30 January 2015) and Lance was given a Polyjuice Potion hipflask for his 18th birthday, which provided light entertainment as he invited others to share his "potion."

Notably, there is a competitive element to the socializing that arises from this group's experiences with *Harry Potter*. Emphasis was placed on being first to get each book, the first to complete reading the books (whether it was the American or British version of the text), and how many times the books have been re-read. Karl read *DH* in 30 hours; Christine read the early books within a day or two. Simon has reread the series as often as ten times, and for Rosemary, rereading the books is an annual event. Similarly, what items of merchandise were possessed as children and now as young adults were noted within the group. Interestingly, their perceived quality was more important than how many. Status is therefore accrued to the individual within this social network through these cultural practices and commodities. As one example, Christine asserts that she was the first to get *Harry Potter* dolls amongst her childhood peers. When her mother brought them home for her after a trip overseas, Christine was indifferent; she had wanted a Barbie. But once the marketing hype began for the first movie, she appreciated the status the dolls brought her, as her peers were impressed by her toys and wanted to be her friend: "I was the cool kid [because] I had [the dolls] first."

Another way in which these fans extended the social aspect of *Harry Potter* in their childhood was through "seeing" or "finding" *Harry Potter* in real life. Paul identified one of his teachers as Professor Umbridge, who "wore pink and everything." For Angela, it was hard not to think of one of her teachers as Professor Sprout. The phrases "no offense" and "alas, earwax" gained currency through their networks, and others looked to emulate a favorite character; Hermione and Ron were popular choices, but Laurel wanted to be an owl since she couldn't have one as a pet and so flew around the garden crashing into trees playing as Ron's excitable owl, Pigwidgeon. According to Lizzy, *Harry Potter* resonates in their lives in everyday language and ideas to the extent that "we don't even realize." The franchise has been internalized to become a cultural means of interpreting the world, expressing ideas, and forging social connections. Rosemary believes that she could easily connect with people overseas through a shared knowledge of *Harry Potter*, adding further social value to the depth of her engagement.

These members of the *Potter* Generation believe they have experienced a unique and special phenomenon for three key reasons: (1) being a similar age to the characters means that their own growth and maturity is aligned with that of the characters. This strengthens their connection with the characters, when they see themselves or people they know "reflected" in the characters. Ben, for example, liked seeing a fellow red-head as a key character (Ron Weasley) and Angela's identification with Hermione led her to frizz her hair; (2) publication of the series was protracted. With seven books coming out over a long period of time (1997–2007) the evolving story was given a sense of "real time," adding a unique dimension to storytelling, especially when coupled with the fact that these readers felt close in age to the characters (that is, they were the intended reader); and (3) they had to wait for each book installment which (when combined with the 11 years over which the books were published) meant they had to engage deeply with the book (and from 2001, the films) to maintain momentum in the lulls—rereading, rewatching, discussing, playing. Having to wait was a good thing and a big contributor to the quality of their relationship with the franchise. Owen "really liked the hype" and Christine likewise fondly recalls, "the hype of it all. Getting really excited and reading all the books until the next book came out and being the first to have it and lining up for the movies."

Participants believed that their particular experience with the *Harry Potter* texts was unprecedented and cannot be replicated. Principally this was due to the powerful combination of their ages roughly aligning with those of the characters and the necessary delay between publications. For Owen "the best part [was] when you grew up it was like you were growing up with [the characters]." Maintaining the connection through age and associated behaviors and attitudes was further enhanced by the length of the series. Seven books ensured that the reader's entire young life was marked by the stories, tapping into "where they were" (Beatrice) in terms of maturity in each succeeding book. Jendy claims that she loved *Harry Potter* so much, it was her "whole childhood" and Christine observes that she can recall certain moments of her life according to the book or film releases. If the series had been shorter, the impact of *Harry Potter* on their lives would be lessened. This "enforced" sustained engagement and anticipation, all managed by clever marketing around the necessities of novel writing and film production, where no one knew what would happen in the next book, gives *Harry Potter* "the competitive edge" (Jason) over trilogies such as *The Hunger Games*. Further, they noted that contemporary readers can "binge"; with all the books now published, they can read them sequentially without break, which fundamentally changes the reading experience. New readers therefore miss out on the depth of emotional engagement that occurred for the *Potter* Generation through rereadings while waiting on the next installment. "You had to be there as it unfolded" (Christine) was the consensus.

In terms of the film adaptation of Rowling's books, the participants gave warm reviews. The books were assumed to be the "truth" of *Harry Potter* and differences were related back to these whether in terms of the film or merchandise. For example, it was claimed that early PlayStation games were best when they didn't follow the films but rather were "free" with their interpretation of the books, just as readers were (Karl). Some participants commended the films for being faithful adaptations (Beatrice) and for Jason, the *Harry Potter* film adaptations are "near perfect" and "one of the best book to movie translations" he's seen. Vessie deferred to the films as you "finally got to see what the wands really looked like." Nevertheless, it was also recognized that it isn't possible to incorporate everything from the books into the films; Rosemary believes "they chose what to leave out and what to put in really well. They didn't miss out any of the story ... with Harry Potter they lifted the perfect amount [from the book]." Details were discussed about what was included and what was excluded, with discussion focusing mostly on the first few films. The omission of Peeves from *PS* was most remarked upon. As budding broadcasters, this group understood the rationale for omitting some of the book from the film version. For Vessie, omissions are a positive; "If you go back and read the books you get that added extra ... like an Easter egg at the end of a movie, it's kind of the same if you read the books again." They were less understanding of the breakout of *DH* into two movies. Paul is firm: if there isn't enough content "DON'T do it!" He infers the book could have been realized in just the one film, that there was an element of exploiting fans here for corporate profit.

Other issues raised in relation to the adaptations were the way that films impact on personal readings and the increasing "darkness" in them. Lance noted the impact the films had on personal interpretations of the books: "having the books come out first, not that the films ruined it in any way … when you read it it's how your imagination takes it and I guarantee you that if we asked around this circle everybody would see Hogwarts differently before the films came out." Lance observes that independent visions of the stories were closed out with the first film's release. It was felt that the first three films were "light," but the ensuing films became progressively dark in tone and aesthetic. Paul asserted the later films were "freaking depressing" but "depressing is good" while Imogen found the stories much darker in the theater than in the book and recalls being terrified. Lizzy's younger brother had nightmares from watching the films, although he persisted as he was "in love with the world" (Lizzy). The films remain much-loved in young adulthood. Rosemary enjoys movie marathons, and Vessie noted the frequent broadcast of the films on television. Lance caught one of these screenings: "Turn TV2 on and see Emma Watson. Nothing better than some surprise HP on ya Tuesday evening!!" (Lance, Facebook, 16 December 2014). Although "the ads are painful" he found he was picking up yet more detail: "Subtle things like I never noticed how intense Harry's visions of what Voldemort was seeing were" (Lance, Facebook, 16 December 2014). Lizzy, too, was tuned into TV2, replying to Lance's post, "Agreed Lance! I'm enjoying it muchly."

Overall, the participants valued the merchandise they chose to engage with. Ryan's first thought when recalling *Harry Potter* in the discussion was of the associated food—Bertie Bott's Every Flavor Beans and the chocolate frogs with their collectible holographic cards. This low cost merchandise is an easy way to participate in the *Harry Potter* universe. Other merchandise mentioned included the PlayStation games, Cluedo, spellbooks, dolls, Weasley Family house set, Deathly Hallows necklace, Lego, a cutlery set, or as Ryan noted, "you can get *Harry Potter* everything!" Some of the merchandise was important to them as children, but is now no longer played with; the dolls, Lego and spellbooks, for example. Yet they remain an important signifier of their love for *Harry Potter*—then and now. Other merchandise, more recently acquired, is modest but indicative of their willingness to engage with the paraphernalia of *Harry Potter* as an outward expression of their enjoyment in the series. Lance's Polyjuice Potion hipflask would be in this category, as would the gift of a Rowena Ravenclaw chocolate frog for Ben and Angela's Deathly Hallows necklace. That these items were gifts reinforces these participants' memories and claims of *Harry Potter* as being part of their social cultural practice; the gift giver acknowledges and shares the recipient's pleasure in the stories and franchise thereby enhancing their real life relationship.

Only Vessie demonstrated an ongoing engagement with the *Harry Potter* merchandise that reflects "traditional" fandom. In the group discussion she described in detail a purchase she made after the last movie was released in 2011 when she would have been 19 years old, all the while hinting at the shape and size of the goods with her hands:

> After the last movie I was waiting [because] I knew that they were going to release all the movies in some shape or form … and then they announced they were going to do this Wizard Collection and I thought "Sweet! I'll be in on that no matter what it costs and it might be 5[00] or 600 dollars." I got it from Mighty Ape, pre-ordered it and it's just this huge box and I got it and took it out and inside the box is another box and then there's all these secret places. So you open up one bit and there might be a couple of discs and then you open up another bit and there might be a locket and there's a map. But I haven't taken [the map] out of the plastic. It's still in there. There's just all this really cool stuff and down the bottom there's this certificate of authenticity which has got a stamp on it and all the codes for the digital copies and I haven't used anything except the codes because you have to use the code before it expires. But everything else in the box I've kept in the box and not really touched it because it's quite expensive.

Vessie's clear passion for the objects denoting *Harry Potter* indicates a different type of fandom from that of her peers. The objects are not necessarily bought items; when she dressed up for the final movie she combined branded goods with homemade pieces:

> For the final movie I dressed up. My nana made me a robe and I had a Slytherin badge on and she stuffed a hand puppet owl and put Velcro on it so it would stay on my shoulder which was really cool. That was awesome.

For Henry, his fandom is expressed through his willingness to purchase the hard copies of the films rather than following his usual practice of streaming films: "Any other movie and I'd be happy to watch and just see the film, but this was something that I really wanted: to have it there, the physical copy of it." Ben's youthful fandom extended to participating in a *Harry Potter* Secret Club during his last two years at high school (aged 17–18). He describes himself as a "rugby [union] macho boy" but unknown to his teammates, Ben would "dress up" and attend these meetings every second Thursday at lunchtime where they talked about and quizzed themselves on all things *Harry Potter*. "We'd go on the Internet and to Wikipedia and go down like wormholes of *Harry Potter* and that sort of thing … none of the lads knew what I was up to…. It was just great fun." In the group discussion Ben laughed that he was "coming out about something," that this was his "dirty little secret." There was much pleasure in being able to reveal the story about his younger self's passion for *Harry Potter* to his current peer group ("Everyone knows now!"), especially when he revealed that there were only two boys in this secret group and 20 girls!

Different levels of engagement with the film-related merchandise were therefore expressed in the discussion, from aversion (Simon) to passionate enjoyment (Vessie). Irrespective, all seemed to have been online at some point to visit *Harry Potter* websites such as Pottermore.com. They have been sorted into houses and assigned wands ("my wand is elder with a unicorn hair" [Ben]). They sought information online as the books and films were coming out, but this activity has waned as the books and films have all been published or released and they have matured, entering their late teens and early twenties. Ben used to visit the *Pottermore* site frequently, but "I don't go on it so much anymore but it's a good thing to do when you've got some downtime." For most of the participants, their current primary engagement with *Harry Potter* as young adults seems to be centered on the books, the films and social interaction. There is limited sense that the marketing or merchandise undermined the *Harry Potter* experience for them. As described, for many the merchandise was social—a means to commune with family or friends, or to project status. Yet, Simon advised:

> my whole group still loves harry potter [*sic*] but none of us bought much if any merchandise, like i have the books and between us i think we have all the dvd's, and we'll quote the things all the time and it's a big deal, but id kinda see the merchandise as being cheap and not anywhere near as nice as the actual works [Simon, Facebook, 15 December 2014].

Although there was merchandise available, heavily marketed to Simon and his friends, they chose not to engage with it beyond the films themselves. Rather, it is the familiarity with the text itself and the ability this knowledge gives to entrench friendships that is important, as indicated by Simon's claim that to quote *Harry Potter* was a "big deal."

This case study of a small group of Aotearoa/New Zealand members of the global *Potter* Generation indicates an ongoing and warm relationship with the *Harry Potter* franchise. In various ways they continue to engage with the stories; through the books, the films, the merchandise, through their social relations. *Harry Potter* even infiltrates their studies, with one group re-enacting *Harry Potter* as part of a class presentation. How, then, do their experiences align with or differ from theoretical assumptions about their relationship with the *Harry Potter* franchise?

Unpacking Pottermania

From the information above it is possible to identify three key points about the participants' particular experiences of Pottermania: the sociability that arises out of engaging with the franchise; the importance of the merchandise; and varying expressions of fandom. Overarching all of these ideas, and irrespective of the level of engagement with the *Harry Potter* series, is the unquestionable pleasure derived from their experiences.

Sociability

Throughout the group discussion, directly and indirectly, participants noted the social value of *Harry Potter* in their lives. Gifts, games, shared reading experiences, movie marathons, a shared discourse and fond memories all reveal the various ways in which these individuals encountered *Harry Potter*. Grandparents, parents and friends become an integral part of the cultural experience through their association with the books, films, games and paraphernalia. Owen thought it was "pretty cool" that his grandmother bought him each book on its release and friendships were cemented when pretending to make a potion from leaves and rose petals. As these members of the *Potter* Generation mature the sociability of the franchise persists; being read to by parents gives way to quizzes on *Harry Potter* minutiae during lunch breaks, and coveting a childhood friend's Lego set is forgotten in favor of sharing personal recollections about running like Hermione as a youngster and laughing about it with newly-made friends. Even being part of a group discussion on *Harry Potter* for research purposes extends the franchise's interpersonal aspect. Although this group had studied together for eleven months, they learned still more about each other in regards to their fandom and, through the intimacy of a shared text, deepened those ties that come with being part of a community.

The examples the participants shared point to what Buckingham & Sefton-Green describe as the "portability and flexibility" (2004, p. 22) of fandom. Their exemplar is *Pokémon,* but the ideas translate to the *Harry Potter* phenomenon too. The pleasure of the text lies in its complex detail. Fans search for clues and connections within and across the books, identify omissions in the film adaptations and engage with the *Potter* universe online. All of this potential for rewarding engagement with the franchise leads to longevity—the franchise satisfies continual investment and consequently fans commit, ensuring the franchise doesn't decline into a passing fad. In turn, the knowledge collected and committed to memory can be used to connect with a community of like-minded people. The different platforms (for example, toys, books, films, websites, and PlayStation games) and types of content (Rowling's books, film adaptations, wikis online, interpersonal discourse) give the franchise portability and flexibility which enables the fan to use the material variously; for short or long periods of time, with or without companions, fitting it into their everyday lives (Buckingham & Sefton-Green, 2004, p. 23). This integration into the fabric of everyday life over a long period of time has made *Harry Potter* a "natural part" of the *Potter* Generation's lives.

Cook's concept of enculturation is helpful here to further tease out the social value of *Harry Potter* to this group. He argues that as participating members of a consumer society, children are influenced in their responses to consumption by a number of public and private structures and not solely "the media" as conservative child advocates imply; "Born into and required to engage with ongoing social, economic and cultural practices and institutions, children forge understandings and meanings with the materials they have at hand, and they do so in concert with, in opposition to or in the presence of others" (Cook, 2010, p. 74). One of the understandings these members of the *Potter* Generation learned was about "consumption symbolism" (Young, 2010, p. 124), that social status that can be accrued through goods. They noted the way their peers responded to them according to the perceived symbolic value of *Harry Potter* products they possessed. This particularly occurred around early consumption (owning a *Harry Potter* doll, for example) and reading books first, thereby "possessing" the knowledge other fans were yet to discover. Toys and knowledge might have elevated their status temporarily, but they remained part of the peer group they desired to be in. That is, they did not use *Harry Potter* to distance themselves from others through "brand bullying" (Nairn, 2010, p. 97) but to ingratiate themselves within their peer group through popularity.

It is pertinent to note two factors about this use of goods: the goods were bought *for* them at this stage of their engagement with *Harry Potter* by family members, and the potential for status enhancement was not experienced uniformly. Although collectively the children's market is regarded as valuable both in terms of financial return and potential future earnings (creating loyal consumers for the future) (Marshall, 2010, p. 6) these members of the *Potter* Generation recall their childhood consumption as managed within social relations, hence there was variability in their attitude toward the goods. From his account, Simon did not possess *Harry Potter* merchandise, nor does he now. What mattered most to his group was the knowledge of Rowling's story. Alternatively, the majority of participants in the group discussion owned some merchandise and continue to engage with certain goods that they deem fits with their maturity as young adults. Of the group, only Vessie indulged in the merchandise consistently from childhood into adulthood, reflecting a fandom that was beyond the comprehension of the others: "who has $500 to spend on *Harry Potter*?" (Beatrice).

Irrespective of these distinctions, though, overwhelmingly their reflections indicate that their social relations through *Harry Potter* were positive and inclusive rather than antisocial. While Pottermania is arguably the epitome of recent hyper-commercialism in children's culture and the focus of anxiety regarding unfettered consumption leading to an unhealthy value system (Turner-Vorbeck, 2008; Kapur, 2005), these Potterphiles emphasize its value to them as a social tool.

The Merchandise

As the participants' discussion indicates, marketing and merchandise are central to the *Harry Potter* franchise. These members of the *Potter* Generation find Rowling's books to be the "core text," but the film adaptation and concomitant "*Harry Potter* stuff" (Vessie, Facebook, 15 January 2015) are intrinsic to the concept of Pottermania. Their observations, memories and descriptions of their engagement with *Harry Potter*, therefore, frequently invoke the hype, goods and online websites. All participants had seen the films, a few had not read the books, only one disliked the merchandise, but all enjoyed the feverish publicity that proclaimed and ensured the franchise's success.

Key to the marketing and merchandising "wizardry" by Time Warner was the decision to ignore Rowling's Muggle world and only produce products that come from and are positioned in the magical world. This decision is outlined in a rule from Warner Brothers Consumer Products' style guide; "take people into Harry's world. Don't put Harry into our world" (cited in Waetjen & Gibson, 2007, p. 18). To ensure that all activities related to *Harry Potter* project the consumer into the magical world makes sense, as this is the environment that most captures the audience: "This would be my ultimate dream to be a wizard!" (Beatrice). More than this, though, Waetjen and Gibson argue that this commercial decision enables fans "to consume exactly as Harry does" (Waetjen & Gibson, 2007, p. 18) resulting in the "verisimilitude" (Waetjen & Gibson, 2007, p. 18) of all *Harry Potter* merchandise.

Heavy marketing, merchandise marked by verisimilitude and a simplified story for the film adaptation that emphasizes consumption, combine to encourage young fans to purchase or engage with *Harry Potter* branded products (Waetjen & Gibson, 2007). Understood in this context, the symbolic value of the goods is heightened. Bertie Bott's Every Flavored Beans, for example, are a minor item from the wizarding world, yet at a relatively low cost the fan can immerse in their favorite story by consuming them, significantly, just as Harry, Ron and Hermione might. The symbolic value of other products is more mundane, or "of this world"; Lego, for example, combines the *Harry Potter* brand with its own longstanding reputation for producing popular toy sets for other franchises such as *Star Wars*. The value consumed when playing with a *Harry Potter* Lego set relies on agreeing that both brands are worth investing in.

The participants' comments indicate that the symbolic value of different elements of Pottermania can change as they mature. Their investment in *Harry Potter* is irrefutable; however, the various components that make up that franchise are subject to individual scrutiny and assessment, suggesting some agency in their consumption. For example, what they valued as a child may now be regarded fondly but no long played with or else kept as a memento. Rhonda, for instance, no longer refers to her *Harry Potter* spellbook in her spare time, but the play it inspired for her as a child makes for a good memory that can be shared with others to witness her identification as being part of the Potter Generation. Still other goods have retained favor from childhood into adulthood with differing levels of value attached to them; the candies are a cheap and easy way to engage with the *Harry Potter* brand, while the PlayStation games reward increasing competency and are valued by both younger and older audiences.

For a franchise to enjoy longevity, there needs to be a range of goods that allow for ongoing engagement that accommodate changing expectations as the individual matures. The *Harry Potter* franchise has achieved this "kind of progression" (Buckingham & Sefton-Green, 2004, p. 16), with Vessie noting "you get them hooked young and you've got them for life." Once enamored by a franchise as a child, the individual will ideally pursue this interest into adulthood, so long as the merchandise appeals to their demographic.

Supplying the market with an ongoing series of goods can be considered manipulation. The corporate provides endless branded products that distract the individual from citizenry as they satisfy "false needs" with soft toys, key chains and online trivia and so are inculcated as consumers. "The tendency in late capitalism," Turner-Vorbeck writes, "is that human thinking becomes mechanized as the mind begins to correspond to a machine" (p. 338). As "a segmented and degraded instrument that has lost its capacity for aesthetic creation and critical thought" (p. 338), the human mind is unable to envisage another way of being and thus is caught in the web of capitalism, in which consumption is a pivotal, even obligatory, practice. Yet, while acknowledging the importance of merchandising to most of these Potterphiles' engagement with *Harry Potter*, it is also pertinent to note they were mostly modest with their consumption and petals and stuffed owls were adequate for fantasy play. This observation fits with Kapur's claim that "there is a limit to how many *Harry Potter* objects a child wants to buy" (2005, p. 159) with shelves being cleared of unpurchased goods at Wal-Mart and Barnes and Noble indicating some consumer discretion (2005, p. 159).

Again, the usefulness of the merchandise for negotiating social and cultural needs of the individual living within consumer culture should be noted within this broader and legitimate concern about the glut of merchandise. Nairn writes that "brands can play a constructive part in children's everyday lives in terms of acting as tools for forging identities and social roles" (2010, p. 107). Vessie suggests the merchandise might deepen the heroic values in the stories, arguing:

> I don't think the toys necessarily undermine any of the messages. For example if a kid or adult wanted to dress up as a wizard, it means they can be a hero in their mind. Perhaps when it feels more of a reality, the values are more real [Vessie, Facebook, 15 December 2014].

As broadcasting students, they would object to the determination that they have no capacity for intellectual rigor or creativity as a result of being from the *Potter* Generation. Indeed, Simon suggests that his career choice could be at least in part attributed to Pottermania; "I'd say it definitely had a lot to do with it—sparking imagination as a child probably has an effect on trying to be interesting and creative later on" (Facebook, 5 January 2015).

Variability of Fandom

The group discussion demonstrates the participants' shared love of *Harry Potter* was similar but not identical, lending credence to the argument that how an individual experiences and is influenced by media and consumer content is complex and multifaceted. Attitudes towards the merchandise has been considered above; here the focus is on the idea that fandom as a concept can differ between individuals. Within this group three types of fans can be discerned: those who dismiss the merchandise and focus their fandom on the books and films; those who enjoy one or both of the books and films but also engage with the merchandise as part of their fandom to foster play and friendships; and those who relish all elements of Pottermania and treat some merchandise reverentially. This final group most closely resemble "traditional" fandom.

Simon reflects the first group. He revealed that he loves the books and films but feels the merchandise cheapens the story. He and his peers didn't spend pocket money on the attendant paraphernalia or receive *Harry Potter* gifts. For Simon, the intellectual capital is more important than the merchandise. He rereads the books and watches the films again to fuel his fandom. He possesses intimate knowledge of the story and this detail fosters friendships and satisfies his personal interests. Vessie is no less knowledgeable about *Harry Potter*. She watches the films, plays the games on PlayStation with her flatmate and thereby incorporates *Harry Potter* into her everyday life, but for her the collectibles and homemade pieces are an important facet of her fandom and so she embodies the third type of fan. She lovingly describes the Wizard Collection purchased at significant cost, smiles as she recalls the stuffed owl her grandmother velcroed to her wizard's robe to wear to *DH2* and is bemused as to why she hasn't bought the Slytherin scarf she has always coveted. The other participants in the group discussion constitute the second "type" and account for the majority of those involved. They enjoyed the merchandise they had access to as children and the related games they play as adults (quizzes, PlayStation), but no one expressed particular concern about not possessing certain items. On the whole there was a sense that the goods were purposeful (to play games, assert status, to become part of a particular community) rather than the objects being of intrinsic value in and of themselves.

The various social and cultural practices these fans of *Harry Potter* record reflect the behavior Henry Jenkins suggests cultural content producers are looking for; they range across platforms, they enjoy the detail, and they communicate and socialize through the *Harry Potter* brand (2007, pp. 359–60). The *Potter* Generation reveal the increasing normality of all types of "fannish" behavior—passionate and deep engagement with a text— that a digitized and participatory culture facilitates. As Jenkins asks, "as fandom becomes such an elastic category, one starts to wonder—who isn't a fan?" (2007, p. 364). Lance's "fans and superfans" might roughly correlate to the participatory behavior and traditional fandom above but where does that leave the first group, represented by Simon? He would consider himself no less a fan than Vessie, irrespective of their different approach to the phenomenon. And if we consider Simon a cynical consumer, uncoerced by a global corporate to consume beyond the film adaptation, is this to suggest that Vessie is a victim of those same pressures? To make such a claim is simplistic and fails to accommodate the "messiness" of real life. It is also an unacceptable interpretation of Vessie's fandom, rehashing as it does dated attitudes towards fandom (primarily psychologizing the individual) that have since been exposed as theoretically unhelpful (Jenkins, 2007, p. 361). There is no reconciling the category of fandom for these participants. As Jenkins states, fandom is in flux at present with traditional fandom becoming mainstream and participation the norm.

Irrespective of the inability to categorically define fandom, one can argue that these participants convey hegemony at work; they are complicit in their own subjugation, reveling in and determining their ongoing imaginative constraints. There is some credibility to this argument as we are always and everywhere subject to social, political, economic and cultural systems to which successful acculturation requires us to submit to rules and values that necessarily contain the individual for the "good" of the social group. Yet, hegemony also allows for some means of escape from complete domination. These participants were not literally bombarded by an "avalanche of crud" (Denby, 1996); the crud was there—Rowling herself vetoed a Moaning Myrtle lavatory seat alarm and advised interviewer Jeremy Paxton that the only way to have prevented the merchandise would have been to kill off her eponymous hero (2003)—but they and their parents, in recollection at least, were selective and the goods used to socialize. It would be anathema to the *Potter* Generation, therefore, to suggest that their childhood and ongoing identity was in some way damaged by Pottermania.

Conclusion

This essay has documented a specific audiences' ongoing engagement with a cultural phenomenon that defined their generation. Recurrent themes in the discussion included the sociability the text accorded them, the differing value attributed to the merchandise and varying expressions of fandom. These members of the *Potter* Generation indicate commonalities and distinctions in their experiences with *Harry Potter*, suggesting there is no one way to account for how each individual responds to and engages with cultural content. Their reflections indicate family and peers were significant in their experiences with *Harry Potter* alongside the global corporates' incitements to purchase, confirming that "their engagement with the commercial world is part of their everyday social experience and is very much mediated by other social relationships with family and friends" (Department for Children, Schools and Families, 2009, p. 9).

By reflecting on their younger selves, these members of the *Potter* Generation reveal the pleasures of consuming *Harry Potter*. These pleasures certainly include the heavily marketed merchandise, but no less important were the non-commercial objects, the fantasy play and the intellectual capital that underpinned ongoing social interaction. Their examples and reflections also confirm that Pottermania, and by extension merchandising in general, does not act on an "isolated child" (de la Ville & Tartar, 2010, p. 32) but on an individual who consumes within a socio-cultural context; "between a child and an adult, a child and a more experienced child, or within a small group" (de la Ville & Tartar, 2010, p. 32). This broader understanding of how and in what circumstances consumption of commodified culture occurs indicates the complexity of the interaction, rather than limiting the activity to a reductive conception of victimhood or agency.

Legitimate concerns are raised by child advocates about the level of marketing and merchandising directed at young people, but the reflections of this group from the *Potter* Generation would indicate that these concerns need to be considered within the "messy context of their everyday lives" (Nairn, 2010, p. 100). Ben's claim that he has had "a lot of fun experiences with *Harry Potter*" should not be dismissed as corporate manipulation of a vulnerable individual. But nor should the financial imperative of global corporations be obfuscated as servitude to a demanding and canny children's demographic. The "truth" of each individual's experience will likely lie somewhere on a continuum between the two claims, dependent on a variety of factors such as the social, educational, political and cultural institutions that influence the particular individual. For Ben, his good times with *Harry Potter* suggest a balance of material goods and social interaction with family, confirming that "children's consumption practices cannot be reduced to a mere purchase decision: educational, social and institutional dimensions are at the core of the long process allowing children to take part in the consumer world" (de la Ville & Tartar, 2010, p. 34).

These Potterphiles confirm, then, that they enjoyed a unique cultural experience for which they feel privileged. Growing up with *Harry Potter*—as novel, film and phenomena—has thoroughly infiltrated their lives, and they wouldn't have it any other way.

Notes

1. Quotations which invoke only a name refer to comments made during the group discussion conducted 28 November 2014, e.g., (Lizzy). References to comments made

through Facebook will be clearly identified as such, e.g., (Vessie, Facebook, 4 December 2014).

2. The author would like to acknowledge the assistance of Isaac Spedding and Dr. Ruth Zanker in this process. Isaac provided clean audio-recorded data despite the larger than expected numbers participating in the discussion and Ruth was note-taker extra-ordinaire, ensuring that it was possible to identify who said what when transcribing.

References

Brown, S. (2002). "Marketing for Muggles: The Harry Potter way to higher profits." *Business Horizons 45*(1), 6–15.

Buckingham, D. (2013). *After the death of childhood*. Hoboken, N.J.: Wiley.

Buckingham, D., & Sefton-Green, J. (2004). "Gotta catch 'em all: Structure, agency and pedagogy in children's media culture." In J. Tobin, ed., *Nintentionality: Pikachu's global adventure* (pp. 12–33). Durham: Duke University Press.

Buckingham, D., & Tingstad, V. (2010). Introduction. In Buckingham, D., & Tingstad, V., eds., *Childhood and consumer culture* (pp. 1–14). London: Palgrave Macmillan.

Colombia Journalism Review. (2004). "Who Owns What: Time Warner." Retrieved from http://libertyparkusafd.org/lp/hancock/reports/Who%20Owns%20What%20%20--%20Time%20Warner.htm.

Cook, D.T. (2010). "Commercial enculturation: Moving beyond consumer socialization." In Buckingham, D. & Tingstad, V., eds., *Childhood and consumer culture* (pp. 63–79). London: Palgrave Macmillan.

Day, J. (2001a, 20 February). "Coke to cash in on Harry Potter." *The Guardian*. Retrieved from http://www.theguardian.com.

Day, J. (2001b, 18 October). "Harry Potter fans oppose Coke deal." *The Guardian*. Retrieved from http://www.theguardian.com.

de la Ville, V.I., & Tartas, V. (2010). "Developing as consumers." In David Marshall, ed., *Understanding children as consumers* (pp. 23–40). London: Sage.

Denby, D. (1996, 15 July). "Buried alive: Our children and the avalanche of crud." *The New Yorker*, pp. 48–58.

Department for Children, Schools and Families & the Department for Culture, Media and Sport. (2009). *The impact of the commercial world on children's wellbeing: Report of an independent assessment* [website]. Retrieved 7 January 2015, from http://web archive.nationalarchives.gov.uk/20130401151715/http://www.education.gov.uk/publications/eOrderingDownload/00669–2009DOM-EN.pdf.

Gunelius, S. (2008). *Harry Potter: The story of a global business phenomenon*. New York: Palgrave Macmillan.

Jenkins, H. (2007). "Afterword: The future of fandom." In C. Harrington, J. Gray, & C. Sandvoss, eds., *Fandom: Identities and communities in a mediated world* (pp. 357–364). New York: New York University Press.

Kapur, J. (2005). *Coining for capital: Movies, marketing, and the transformation of childhood*. New Brunswick: Rutgers University Press.

Kinder, M. (1991). *Playing with power in movies, television and video games: From Muppet Babies to Teenage Mutant Ninja Turtles*. Berkeley: University of California Press.

Marshall, D. (2010). Introduction. In David Marshall, ed., *Understanding children as consumers* (pp. 1–20). London: Sage.

Nairn, A. (2010). "Children and brands." In David Marshall, ed., *Understanding children as consumers* (pp. 96–114). London: Sage.

Nel, P. (2005). "Is there a text in this advertising campaign? Literature, marketing and Harry Potter." *The Lion and the Unicorn*, 29(2), 236–267.

Rowling, J.K. (2003, 19 June). Interview with Jeremy Paxton. *BBC News*. Retrieved from http://news.bbc.co.uk.

Travers, P. (2001, 6 December). "Harry Potter and the art of packaging." *Rolling Stone*. Retrieved from http://www.rollingstone.com.

Turner-Vorbeck, T. (2008). "Pottermania: Good, clean fun or cultural hegemony?" In Elizabeth Heinman, ed., *Critical perspectives on Harry Potter* (pp. 329–341.). Hoboken, N.J.: Taylor and Francis.

Waetjen, J., & Gibson, T. (2007). "Harry Potter and the commodity fetish: Activating corporate readings in the journey from text to commercial intertext." *Communication and Critical/Cultural Studies* 4(1), 3–26. DOI: 10.1080/14791420601151289.

Warner Bros. (2006, 15 February). "The Coca-Cola Company and Warner Bros. Pictures to Share the Magical Experience of Reading with Harry Potter and the Sorcerer's Stone." [press release]. Warner Bros. http://movies.warnerbros.com/pub/movie/releases/cokehp.htm.

Young, B. (2010). "Children and advertising." In David Marshall, ed., *Understanding children as consumers* (pp. 115–131). London: Sage.

Zanker, R. (2011). "Child audiences becoming interactive 'viewers': New Zealand children's responses to websites attached to local children's television programmes." *Participations: Journal of Audience and Reception Studies* 8(2), 629–652.

Ministry of Misinformation:
Harry Potter and Propaganda

CHRISTINE KLINGBIEL

"The *Prophet*? You deserve to be lied to if you're still reading that muck, Dirk. You want the facts, try the *Quibbler*," says Ted Tonks in J.K. Rowling's *DH* (p. 299). In the *Harry Potter* series, there are many things that are not what they seem; even when the facts are uncovered people choose to believe something else. Sometimes the reader is misled as well, as in the case of Sirius Black in *PoA*. Other times, the reader knows the truth along with the protagonist. Harry is not Slytherin's heir, Voldemort has returned, Dumbledore has not lost his mind. And that is when readers feel most frustrated with the citizens of the wizarding world. Why are they so blind, dumb, gullible, and willing to be misled? J.K. Rowling, in her *Harry Potter* books, offers up a few explanations as well as numerous examples of how rhetoric works. As a rhetorician, a writing instructor, and an average citizen who has to negotiate a world filled with people, political parties and corporations trying to get me to behave in a certain way (buy X, vote for Y, do Z) I am interested in how language works to influence my thinking.

When the word "propaganda" is mentioned, we often think about the prime examples of World War II and Nazi Germany. Elsewhere, other writers have noted the similarities between the Nazi regime and the Ministry of Magic, so I will not discuss that here. Rather, I am interested in the everyday propaganda. The obvious and subtle ways we are influenced. In today's world, where journalism is rapidly changing, consumerism is the air we breathe, and PR firms make millions, we need to be aware of how we are being manipulated for the good or bad. As Wendell Potter (2010) put it in his insightful book *Deadly Spin: An Insurance Company Insider Speaks Out on How Corporate PR is Killing Healthcare and Deceiving Americans*, you need "to understand why you believe some of the things you believe and do some of the things you do" (p. 45). As the *Harry Potter* books teach us, words have power. But it's not just the magic words. It's the everyday words, whether they are coming from Rita Skeeter, that master spin doctor, or Harry himself, "the way an object is described and the manner in which a course of action is presented direct our thoughts and channel our cognitive responses concerning the communication" say Anthony Pratkanis and Elliot Aronson (1991) in their book, *Age of Propaganda: The Everyday Use and Abuse of Persuasion* (p. 44). Propaganda will not disappear. If anything, it is more prodigious in the media saturated modern world. The wizarding world can help us spot it, thereby helping us choose consciously if we want to be persuaded or not. As Mad-eye Moody says, "constant vigilance!"

The Elixir of Life

"How can I speak a language without knowing I can?" asks Harry (*CoS*, p. 196). Language is how we communicate ideas and feelings to other humans. But it is never just a jumble of impartial facts and we cannot include everything. (This paper may, in fact, be critiqued by what I left out as well as what was included.) The first way we shape what comes out as language, is by what we take in. According to Newman Birk and Genevieve Birk (1977) in "Selection, Slanting and Charged Language," "what we know or observe depends on what we notice; that is, what we select, consciously or unconsciously, as worthy of notice or attention" (p. 4). So, what we notice or remember about a personal experience, or what we have been told, depends upon numerous things, including our background and our purpose or intent. Birk and Birk give the example of three people, a lumberjack, an artist and a tree surgeon each looking at a tree. Each of these people will observe the tree differently because of their background training or what they intend to do. This is like the difference in how Professor Snape views Harry upon first meeting him versus other teachers. When Harry finally re-enters the wizarding world (after his ten year exile with the Dursleys) most people treat him well, even with some reverence. In *SS*, the patrons of the Leaky Cauldron jump up to greet Harry saying, "Can't believe I'm meeting you at last. So proud, Mr. Potter, I'm just so proud. Always wanted to shake your hand—I'm all of a flutter" (p. 69). This, of course, is only based upon what they already have heard about of Harry: he defeated You-Know-Who. Snape, however, takes an instant dislike. After his first lesson with Professor Snape, "Harry's mind was racing and his spirits were low.

He'd lost two points for Gryffindor in his very first week—*why* did Snape hate him so much?" (*SS,* p. 139). This seems most unfair to readers, and it is because, as we find out later, entirely based upon Snape's past experience with Harry's father which colors his view of Harry. In the final book, *DH,* we flash back to the same time and Snape describing Harry to Dumbledore as "mediocre, arrogant as his father, a determined rule-breaker, delighted to find himself famous, attention-seeking and impertinent" (p. 679). What Dumbledore says in reply is quite insightful: "You see what you expect to see, Severus ... other teachers report that the boy is modest, likable, and reasonably talented" (p. 679). This example is also evidence of Birk and Birk's next term: slanting. Because of what he chose to see about Harry, Snape's description of him is slanted. Birk and Birk write: "Slanting may be defined as the process of selecting (1) knowledge—factual and attitudinal; (2) words; and (3) emphasis, to achieve the intention of the communicator. Slanting is present in some degree in all communication: one may slant for (favorable slanting), slant against (unfavorable slanting), or slant both ways (balanced slanting)" (p. 6). A perfect example that shows the contrast of slanting for and against is the difference between Elphias Doge's obituary of Albus Dumbledore and Rita Skeeter's biography in *DH.*

In Doge's article he describes Dumbledore as an "outsider ... the most brilliant student ... generous and never proud or vain; he could find something to value in anyone, however apparently insignificant or wretched, and I believe that his early losses endowed him with great humanity and sympathy" (*DH,* pp. 16–20). On the other hand, Rita Skeeter calls Dumbledore a "flawed genius" with a "disturbed childhood, the lawless youth, the life-long feuds, and the guilty secrets" (*DH,* p. 22). In these two articles, many of the facts both are describing are the same, but notice how the words change their impression—for example the difference between "most brilliant" and "flawed genius." Separated only by a page and a half, it is my belief that JK Rowling wanted readers to notice the contrast. Although readers already knew Dumbledore was an admired wizard and one of the "good guys," Rita Skeeter's version comes off all the more slanted by comparison. Or was Doge's slanted? Harry begins to question not only the facts, but where they are coming from and the point of view of the author or speaker. Harry already knows Rita Skeeter cannot be trusted, but was Doge too easy on Dumbledore because he liked and admired him? Readers can notice how words are chosen to create two very different impressions. This is a great lesson in rhetoric: be aware of it.

Rhetoric "emerged as a discipline in the 5th Century B.C. in Greece" according to Richard Leo Enos (1993) in *Greek Rhetoric Before Aristotle,* "it was an evolving, developing consciousness about the relationship between thought and expression" (p. ix). Scholars agree that while people no doubt used persuasive tactics before this, the Greeks decided to study it and raise it up as an art form. Crassus said, "there is to my mind no more excellent thing than the power, by means of oratory, to get a hold on assemblies of men, win their good will, direct their inclinations wherever the speaker wishes, or divert them from whatever he wishes" (Enos, 1993, p. 23). With the rise of democracy, came the need to influence groups of people.

In *Aristotle on Rhetoric: A Theory of Civil Discourse*, translated by George A. Kennedy (1991), Aristotle defines rhetoric as "to see the available means of persuasion in each case" (p. 35). So the rest of the book reads, not like a manual, but a list of techniques, what to try to persuade your audience, which he gathered by observing what the most effective speakers did and labeling it. One of the most enduring labels, known to many college freshmen via their Comp & Rhet handbooks, is the Three Greek Appeals: ethos logos and pathos. Let's examine these techniques of persuasion using the example of Dumbledore.

First, ethos is often called the ethical appeal. It persuades audiences by relying on the credibility or trustworthiness of the speaker or writer (in other words their character). If that person is already known and deemed trustworthy, audiences are more likely to agree with him/her. If s/he is not known, s/he needs to establish credibility; this happens often by someone citing his or her authority, "I'm an expert on … I've studied … I've experienced…" and so on. Dumbledore is well known and he can usually rely on his good reputation. As the chocolate frog card establishes: he is "considered by many the greatest wizard of modern times" (SS, p. 102). Yet, in the occasional arguments with people, he does tend to remind them, as with Harry in *HBP* when he says, "Blessed as I am with extraordinary brainpower, I understood everything you told me … I think you might even consider the possibility that I understood more than you did" (p. 359). Of course, it's not just having knowledge that makes one trustworthy, it depends upon the situation and what is being argued. We trust people also because they have been trustworthy; in the past or people we know endorse them. Dumbledore trusts Snape, so Harry should too, argues both Hermione and Lupin.

Logos is an appeal to logical reasoning best demonstrated by Dumbledore in *OotP* during Harry's hearing. After some back and forth between Cornelius Fudge, Dolores Umbridge, and Dumbledore, Dumbledore says: "If it is true that the dementors are taking orders only from the Ministry of Magic, and it is also true that two dementors attacked Harry and his cousin a week ago, then it follows logically that somebody at the Ministry might have ordered the attacks" (p. 147). Logos is about facts, reasoning, and order. Finally, pathos is an appeal to the audience's emotions or beliefs and values. Towards the end of *GoF*, Dumbledore memorializes Cedric, but at the same time makes a very political speech. He uses the audience's feelings of grief to exhort listeners to come together, to cooperate and to fight against Voldemort. He says: "Remember Cedric. Remember, if the time should come when you have to make a choice between what is right and what is easy, remember what happened to a boy who was good, and kind, and brave because he strayed across the path of Lord Voldemort. Remember Cedric Diggory" (*GoF*, p. 724). Pathos is often dismissed in academia where facts and evidence take precedence over emotion (which can be illogical), yet pathos can move people very effectively. I would say beware of any argument that relies only on pathos, but at the same time, all three appeals can be used for good or ill.

When does ordinary rhetoric cross the line and become spin or propaganda? One can argue that every spoken or written communication is meant to persuade, if only to persuade the audience to accept it, to listen to it, and yeah, maybe to believe it. Is it the difference between truth and lies? Intent? Sincerity? Garth Jowett and Victoria O'Donell (1992) discuss the difference between ordinary rhetoric and propaganda in their book, *Propaganda and Persuasion* where they say, "propaganda, in the most neutral sense, means to disseminate or promote particular ideas. In Latin, it means 'to propagate' or 'to sow'" (p. 2). It lost its neutrality, however, when the Roman Catholic Church used that term; their intention was to spread their ideology, while opposing others (Protestantism). However, just having an ideology is not enough to make one a propagandist. Dumbledore has an ideology. In order to fight evil, he believes wizards must come together. He also thinks muggles, as well as goblins and house elves, should be treated equally and fairly. In our world, Michael Moore is a controversial film maker. Those opposing his documentary films often say it's because "he has a point of view," as if that negates anything he has to say. To answer "yes, he does" does not mean, however, that one has won the argument. The faulty warrant (underlying assumption) in this argument is that documentary films are neutral; that they just show what is happening, i.e., reality. But that never has been the case. Just like with language, the filmmaker carefully selects (edits, shapes), therefore slants. Patricia Aufderheide (2007) in her book *Documentary Film: A Very Short Introduction* uses the example of one of the first documentary films, *Nanook of the North*, which was meant to depict the life of Inuit who "assumed roles at filmmaker

Robert Flaherty's direction, much like actors in a fiction film. Flaherty asked them to do things they no longer did, such as hunt for walrus with a spear, and he showed them as ignorant about things they understood" (p. 2). At the same time, he "built his story from his own experience of years living with the Inuit" (Aufderheide, 2007, p. 2). Now if the opponents of Michael More would take their argument further and claim that the filmmaker is arguing for his point of view with false or misleading evidence, then we may have a legitimate claim that could be either supported or refuted. (That debate has been waged elsewhere and won't be included here.)

Just because someone has a point of view, just because she or he is making an argument, the argument is not necessarily propaganda. But this where it gets tricky. Jowette and O'Donnell mention that "words frequently used as synonyms for propaganda are lies, distortion, deceit, manipulation, mind control, psychological warfare, brainwashing, and palaver" (p. 2). Even these words should carry a caution sign. As we have seen, we could also call regular ol' rhetoric manipulation. For a class I once taught, we read Martin Luther King's "Letter from Birmingham Jail." Not only is it an important historical document and a powerful civil rights statement, it is great writing where the Three Greek Appeals are used effectively. Some students were loath to analyze it rhetorically because they didn't want to see it as manipulative. Manipulate can mean "to manage or utilize skillfully," according to Merriam-Webster Online Dictionary—again, like "ideology," a neutral term. We need to look at the *way* it is done and the purpose. The second definition in the dictionary adds the adjectives "unfairly" and "insidious," which gives "manipulation" its negative spin.

Psychologists Anthony Pratkanis and Elliot Aronson regarded propaganda as the *abuse* (not just use) of language, the abuse of persuasion as the title of their book suggests. Jawett and O'Donnell, as they define propaganda mention it uses "strategies of questionable ethics" (p. 4). This suggests there is a right way and a wrong way of using persuasion. Turning again to the Three Greek Appeals, we can contrast the above example of Dumbledore with that of Gilderoy Lockhart. First with ethos. In *CoS*, Lockhart is employed at Hogwarts to teach Defense Against the Dark Arts classes, but we soon understand that his favorite subject is really himself. Lockhart's character can be seen in this passage: "he reached forward, picked up Neville Longbottom's copy of *Travels with Trolls*, and held it up to show his own, winking portrait on the front. 'Me,' he said, pointing at it and winking as well. 'Gilderoy Lockhart, Order of Merlin, Third Class, Honorary Member of the Dark Force Defense League, and five-time winner of Witch Weekly's Most-Charming-Smile Award'" (p. 99). Gilderoy establishes credibility through the rank, honors and publications he has, which is the usual way to do so, but he also includes the "Most-Charming-Smile Award" which really doesn't tell us anything other than he is handsome. Most people are impressed with his publications, especially Hermione. When he is questioned by Harry and Ron she says, "You've read his books—look at all those amazing things he's done" (*CoS*, p. 103). Although Ron remains skeptical: "'He says he's done,' Ron muttered" (*CoS*, p. 103). Ron, it turns out, was right, because towards the end of the book, we find out that Lockhart used unethical means to write the books. Other people actually accomplished the things he writes about, such as defeating evil creatures, but Lockhart steals their memories. When admitting to it, he says, "My books wouldn't have sold half as well if people didn't think I'd done all those things" (*CoS*, p. 297). Lockhart is also not very logical. He likes to give Harry advice such as "Celebrity is as celebrity does, remember that" (*CoS*, p. 120). This statement resembles familiar truisms in tone—for instance, "look before you leap" and "winners never quit, and quitters never win"—and sometimes when things *sound* logical, people are persuaded. But looking closer at this, it doesn't make sense. One should always ask "What does that really mean?" What Lockhart wants most is fame. He wants people to like him, to admire him. The way he tries to evoke this emotional response in his audience (pathos) is through his good looks and charm; in other words, his image. I will go further into the use of images as a propaganda strategy later. As we see in *CoS*, Lockhart has spent a good deal of time and energy on carefully crafting his image through personal grooming (even his portraits wear curlers) as well as his illicit activities. As he says: "there was work involved. I had to track these people down. Ask them exactly how they managed to do what they did. Then I had to put a Memory Charm on them so they wouldn't remember doing it … no, it's been a lot of work … if you want fame, you have to be prepared for a long hard slog" (*CoS*, pp. 297–298). It is clear that Dumbledore's use of persuasion is ethical, but Lockhart's is not.

So does that mean manipulating with truth is okay, but lying is not? We might be getting nearer when we talk about lies. Yes, propaganda often can use outright lies. Promoting cigarettes as healthy is a lie. Sirius Black was framed as a murderer so expertly by Peter Pettigrew (a.k.a. Wormtail) that the whole wizarding world believed it. If propaganda was just lies, however, it would be so much easier to recognize and fight against. The real, sneaky propaganda often uses a bit of truth, but slants or distorts it so much that it becomes very close to fabrication—but the propagandist can say, "No, this is true." Political spin doctors do this a lot. During the 2012 U.S. election, a big deal was made about Mitt Romney's criticism of the Olympics. Yes, he did say two things that he would have done differently, but if you watch that full interview, you can see he was asked his opinion and gave it with some reluctance and the criticisms were mild (Walshe and Friedman, 2012). Likewise, in 2008, the phrase "lipstick on a pig" blew up. Yes, Obama said it, but in reference to the policies McCain was saying he would be promoting as president (as in "this is the same old stuff just dressed up differently") and not about McCain's running mate, Sarah Palin, as the opposition accused. In an interview on *The View*, McCain deflected criticism of this spin by repeating "but he said it." In *GoF*, yes, Harry's scar gives him pain, and yes, he walked out of Divination class, but from that, Rita Skeeter writes an article claiming he is "unstable and possibly dangerous" (p. 611). Fudge, who does not want to believe Voldemort is back, uses this article as proof Harry and Dumbledore are lying: "You admit that he has been having these pains then?" (p. 705). This is also a favorite technique of propagandists: just get your opponent to say "yes," to agree with anything you have to say (whether it be a minor point or even unrelated), and it will seem like (to those not paying close attention) they agree with you and you have won the argument.

Even if the propaganda is an outright lie, there is a theory that says if a lie is repeated often enough, people believe it is true. Pratkanis and Aronson say, "According to Nazi propaganda theory, one effective way to persuade the masses is to develop and repeat falsehoods" (p. 72). Also, there is research that says even if the lie is found out and it is established it is NOT true, some people will still believe it. Prakanis and Aronson mention "in one experiment, Saul Kassin and his colleagues found that the credibility of an expert trial witness could be damaged merely by asking accusatory questions, such as, 'Isn't it true that your work is poorly regarded by your colleagues?' The expert's credibility was damaged regardless of whether the accusation was denied or withdrawn" (p. 73). In *CoS,* Harry can deny that he has anything to do with opening the Chamber, but the other students don't believe him. He even starts to doubt himself!

The final ingredient in our propaganda potion is purpose. If the purpose of the writer or speaker is to deceive, we can pretty much call it propaganda. Jawett and O'Donell say, "When the use of propaganda emphasizes purpose, the term is associated with control and is regarded as a deliberate attempt to alter or maintain a balance of power that is advantageous to the propagandist. Deliberate attempt is linked with a clear institutional ideology and objective" (p. 2). We can use again the example of Dumbledore vs.

Lockhart. Dumbledore's intention is not to deceive his audience, but Lockhart's whole personae is based upon deception. This also requires some scrutiny because some propagandists will try to seem very sincere. Even when caught in deception, they might act like they did not know it was false. When Rick Santorum was running for president in 2012, he made the false claim that "10 percent of all deaths in the Netherlands are from euthanasia—half of which are involuntarily" (Heil, 2012). When his PR spokesperson, Alice Stewart, was confronted by a Dutch reporter about Santorum's lie, she did not acknowledge it; rather, she insisted "it's a matter of what's in his heart" (Heil, 2012). Gilderoy Lockhart also very sincerely believed he had done just as much work as the people he stole the memories from. It seems sincerity can also be faked. Watch out for this.

It would be impossible to cover every propaganda technique in this essay and some of them may fall into a few different categories, but here are a few more examples:

The Propaganist's Spellbook

How do propagandists fool us? Like with a spell, they choose the right words or conjure up convincing images.

LABELS. As seen above, just by the words you use, you can influence how people view something. People often make decisions based on a name or the adjectives that surround the name. A great example of this was on the TV show *Jimmy Kimmel Live*. They asked people on the street which they preferred, the "Affordable Care Act" or "Obamacare," and all of the people they showed said they would support the ACA, but not Obamacare, not realizing they are the same thing. The crafters of bills are very crafty when it comes to naming them. Pratkanis and Aronson say, "Through the labels we use to describe an object or event, we can define it in such a way that the recipient of our message accepts our definition of the situation and is thus pre-persuaded even before we seriously begin to argue" (p. 44). The "Affordable Care Act" sounds much better because as one of the people interviewed said, "it's affordable." Companies carefully consider their names and the names given to the products they sell. This is what marketing companies call branding. Tom Riddle did his own kind of branding when he changed his "foul, common muggle" name to Lord Voldemort, as he says, "a name I knew wizards everywhere would one day fear to speak" (*CoS*, p. 314). A lord is definitely not a common person and "Voldemort" contains the word "morte," French for death. It did indeed become a name wizards and witches feared. Just saying the name brings out an emotional response (pathos) in listeners. Throughout the series, wizards and witches are so afraid they flinch, jump, yelp, fall and drop things when the name is spoken. Harry is also given labels: "The Boy Who Lived," and later on, "The Chosen One," marking him out as special. The Ministry calls him "Undesirable Number One" in *DH*, when they want to turn public opinion against him. This label marks him as the enemy, while "The Chosen One" makes him the people's savior.

GLITTERING GENERALITIES are "attractive sounding but vague terms" (Jackson and Jamieson, 2007, p. 39). Sometimes these are also called "purr words"(Pratkanis and Aronson, 1991, p. 45). These words work because they sound good and they are so vague they can mean anything; that leaves it up to the listener to apply their own meaning. Politicians often say: "Stand up for America!" Many companies make products or sell services "for a brighter future."The word "freedom"is used for so many things, however, lately it has been the go-to purr word for political front groups who actually might want laws that restrict some freedom. In *OotP*, Dolores Umbridge, Senior Under-secretary to the Minister, comes to Hogwarts and gives a speech that includes: "Let us move forward, then, into a new era of openness, effectiveness, and accountability, intent on preserving what ought to be preserved, perfecting what needs to be perfected, and pruning wherever we find practices that ought to be prohibited" (pp. 213–214). Harry finds her speech loaded with "waffle." And most of the other students' eyes glaze over and they cannot follow what she says. It is only Hermione who is able to sift through the generalities to see that the Ministry intends to interfere in the school.

WEASEL WORDS "suck the meaning out of a phrase or sentence, the way that weasels supposedly suck the contents out of an egg, leaving only a hollow shell" (Jackson and Jamieson, 2007, p. 49). Stores do this all the time. There is an advertised sale "up to 50 percent off."That's half off, most people think. The weasel words here are "up to." There could be one item for 50 percent off, the rest could be 10 percent, and the store would technically be telling the truth (Jackson and Jamieson, 2007, p. 49). Orange juice "made with real orange flavor" doesn't have to contain a single orange, the weasel word being "flavor." When Rita Skeeter writes her article entitled, "Harry Potter 'Disturbed and Dangerous,'" she gets others to do some weaseling for her. She writes, "It is possible, say top experts at St. Mungo's Hospital for Magical Maladies and Injuries, that Potter's brain was affected by the attack ... he might even be pretending ... this could be a plea for attention" (*GoF*, p. 612). While these "top experts" sound like credible sources, none have examined Harry, and they use words like "it is possible," "might" and "could" to not make any claim at all, yet it still sounds like they are. Also, just who are these experts? What are they experts in? For all we know, they could work in the hospital cafeteria and make a mean treacle tart.

IMPLIED FALSEHOOD. Even though we have seen lately that propagandists don't mind lying because getting caught doesn't seem to affect their reputations much, there are still some who do not want to come right out and say a lie. In these cases, they imply. As Jackson and Jamieson say, "Advertisers often try to imply what they can't legally say" (p. 61). The phrase on the badges Malfoy makes and distributes on *GoF* say, "Support Cedric Diggory—the real Hogwarts champion!" and imply that Harry is not a "real" champion. What if Harry's name had come out of the goblet first, second or third? Would he have been seen as a real champion? (Not to Malfoy, of course.)

The real master of implication is Rita Skeeter. In her *Witch Weekly* article about Hermione, Skeeter writes: "'She's really ugly,' says Pansy Parkinson '… but she'd be well up to making a Love Potion, she's quite brainy. I think that's how she's doing it.'"(*GoF*, p. 512). Skeeter continues, "Love potions are, of course, banned at Hogwarts, and no doubt Albus Dumbledore will want to investigate these claims" (*GoF*, p. 512). Once again, we see Skeeter using questionable sources to do the dirty work for her. The implication is that Hermione is using a love potion on Harry (it also further implies the lie that Harry loves Hermione) yet Pansy only says "she'd be well up to" it and Skeeter simply says that Dumbledore should investigate. Jackson and Jamieson have some good advice when they say, "When you see or hear something being strongly implied but not stated outright, ask yourself, 'Why do they have to lay it between the lines like that? Why don't they just come out and say it?' Often there's a very good reason: what the speaker wants you to believe isn't true" (p. 62).

FUD FACTOR. FUD, according to Jackson and Jamieson, stands for "fear, uncertainty, and doubt" (p. 26). Playing upon an audience's fear is also a technique linked to pathos. Advertisers do this all the time. You might lose friends or people will not want to be around you if you do not use our brand of deodorant or breath mints! Is your family safe from germs? Buy our anti-bacterial wipes and be sure! "If it's scary, be wary," Jackson and Jamieson say (p. 26). In the *Harry Potter* series, Voldemort epitomizes the FUD factor technique. He instills fear to get what he wants. Sirius says, "In the old days he had huge numbers at his command; witches and wizards he'd bullied or bewitched into following him" (*OotP*, p. 5). When Harry asks why everyone was afraid of the dark mark that was sent into the sky at the Quidditch World Cup, Mr. Weasley answers, "You-Know-Who and his followers sent the Dark Mark into the air whenever they killed ... the terror it inspired ... you have no idea, you're too young. Just picture coming home and finding the Dark Mark hovering over your house, and knowing what you're about to find inside ... everyone's worst fear ... the very worst" (*GoF*, p. 9). And when Voldemort finally does take over the Ministry, Lupin says he "is playing a very clever game. Declaring himself might have provoked open rebellion: Remaining masked has created confusion, uncertainty, and fear" *(DH,* p. 208). Wendell Potter, in his book *Deadly Spin* states, "organizations with the most to lose are most likely to resort to fear mongering. Their information may mention the loss of jobs, a threat to public health, or a general decline in social values, standard of living, or individual rights. It may also vilify a specific cause or even a specific person in order to create the desired point of view" (p. 52). Voldemort and other Pure-blood families vilify muggles and muggle-born wizards and witches and say they are responsible for a decline in standards in the wizarding world. Jackson and Jamieson also call this propaganda technique "the blame game," pointing a finger at an unpopular group and hoping to divert attention from the weakness of his own evidence (p. 37). Sirius says about his family: "they thought Voldemort had the right idea, they were all for the purification of the Wizarding race, getting rid of Muggle-borns and having purebloods in charge" (*OotP*, p. 112).

IMAGES. We are not just persuaded with words but images also shape how we think. Lockhart knew a winning smile would get him what he wanted. A lot goes into the marketing of a product—not only what the product looks like, but the images associated with it. This is why beer commercials have sexy models or depict a fun party atmosphere or why trucks in commercials are covered in mud or drive through the rugged country side. They say a picture is worth a thousand words, and they are an effective way of implying something without saying it. Politicians often use pictures. He or she might be seen visiting a local factory with his or her jacket off and shirt sleeves rolled up, implying the candidate is ready to work hard for their constituents. Symbols are used in their photographs and ads; the American flag is often in the background. The Ministry of Magic uses symbolic images to shape what people think. Rowling draws our attention to the fountain at Ministry headquarters a couple times. First, in the *OotP*, the statues in the fountain are described as "a noble-looking wizard with his wand pointing straight up in the air. Grouped around him were a beautiful witch, a centaur, a goblin, and a house-elf. The last three were all looking adoringly up at the witch and wizard" (p. 127). Dumbledore recognizes it as propaganda when he says, "The fountain we destroyed tonight told a lie. We wizards have mistreated and abused our fellows for too long" (p. 834). The statues were destroyed when Dumbledore dueled with Voldemort in *OotP*, and what replaces it later in *DH*—a giant statue of black stone labeled "Magic is Might"—is even more slanted propaganda. To Harry, "what he had thought were decoratively carved thrones were actually mounds of carved humans: hundreds and hundreds of naked bodies, men, women, and children, all with rather stupid, ugly faces, twisted and pressed together to support the weight of the handsomely robed wizards" (p. 242). This is symbolic of wizards ruling over muggles. Why wizards are right to rule over muggles ties back to the FUD factor. It is rumored that they are stealing magic from wizards, or, as Voldemort suggests, they will somehow taint Pure-Bloods. (Notice also how "Pure-blood" and "Mudblood" are propaganda labels.) The pamphlet that Harry sees workers at the Ministry putting together is entitled, "MUDBLOODS and the Dangers They Pose to a Peaceful Pure-Blood Society"; it has "a picture of a red rose with a simpering face in the middle of its petals, being strangled by a green weed with fangs and a scowl" (*DH*, p. 249). As with most images crafted for propaganda purposes, the message is pretty obvious.

The Invisibility Ploy

Most people can identify advertising when it's in the usual places (TV, magazines, billboards), but we are sold in so many other ways. The TV or Internet commercial is just the tip of the iceberg—the part we can see. So much persuasion goes on that is invisible to us. In just one day of TV viewing, I saw a "news" story about the new flavor of Oreo that will soon be out about four times, on different programs. This "news" story was mostly likely a press release written by the PR department or company hired by Mondelēz International, Inc. To my earlier definitions of propaganda, let me add the terms "organized" and "systematic." This is why most books on propaganda usually focus on governments, but in this day and age of multinational corporations and lobbyists for hire, any organization that can afford PR and/or marketing firms can shape public opinion. As Wendell Potter says in his book *Deadly Spin*, "The 'spin-doctors' who shape much of what we see and read today are often shadowy figures in the multibillion dollar industry we call 'public relations'" (p. 45). Potter's primary example is the PR campaign against healthcare reform which goes back decades and uses many tried and true propaganda techniques. He talks about PR companies that write the script (sometimes called "talking points") that everyone from the CEO, to the lobbyists, to the politicians, to the media spokespeople follow. He mentions "astroturf" front groups, a group that looks like a grassroots effort (random group of concerned citizens fighting for a cause they believe in) but is really put together and paid for by one person or company. The general public often cannot see the money trail or where the strings are. We hear the rumor from a "whisper campaign" but we seldom trace its origins.

In the *Harry Potter* Series, readers get an insider view. Let's look at one rumor maker, Rita Skeeter. When we first meet her in *GoF*, she does things like this: "A ministry official emerged some time after the appearance of the Dark Mark alleging that nobody had been hurt, but refusing to give any more information. Whether this statement will be enough to quash the rumors that several bodies were removed from the woods an hour later, remains to be seen" (p. 147). Mr. Weasley responds: "Well, there certainly will be rumors now she's printed that" (p. 147). As Mrs. Weasley says, she just likes to stir up trouble. Her purpose it to get readers. And as Skeeter says to Hermione, the purpose of her newspaper is to "sell itself" (*OotP*, p. 567). This is Skeeter's main reason for reporting that Harry was having "funny turns." However, when Fudge and the Ministry don't want to believe Voldemort has returned, they begin an intentional, organized campaign to discredit both Dumbledore and Harry. Dumbledore is kicked off of official committees and demoted; in other words, stripped of his credentials that gives what he says authority. *The Prophet* pretty much comes under the control of the Ministry. They do not print a direct story accusing Harry of lying, rather as Hermione tells Harry: "they keep slipping in snide comments about you. If some far-fetched story appears they say something like 'a tale worthy of Harry Potter' and if anyone has a funny accident or anything it's 'let's hope he hasn't got a scar on his forehead or we'll be asked to worship him next'" (*OotP*, p. 74). Notice how this type of propaganda seems low-key, it can just slide right in and become what "everyone is saying" or as Skeeter says "the public mood" (*OotP*, p. 567). This propaganda campaign convinces nearly everyone in the wizarding world including Harry's close friend Seamus Finnigan.

Dirigible Plum or Why We Are Spun

"The mind is a very complex and many-layered thing," says Professor Snape in *OotP* (*OotP*, 330). "Have you ever wondered why other people are so unreasonable and hard to convince? Why is it that they disregard hard facts that prove you're right and they're wrong? The fact is, we humans aren't wired to think very rationally" say Jackson and Jamieson (p. 65). Director of the Skeptics Society, and publisher of *Skeptic* magazine, Michael Shermer (1997) makes the point in his book *Why People Believe Weird Things: Pseudoscience, Superstition, and other Confusions of Our Time* that "the modern, scientific way of thinking is a couple of hundred years old, whereas humanity has existed for a couple of hundred thousand years" (p. xxii). It could be than humans evolved to see patterns, make associations and quick judgments. Jackson and Jamison also acknowledge, "Our minds tend to take short cuts" (p. 69). Critical thinking is a skill that needs to be learned; it does not come naturally to us. We have all been spun at one time or another, even when we know better. In *GoF*, Mrs. Weasley admonishes Amos Diggory for being angry at Harry for something Rita Skeeter wrote. She says, "Rita Skeeter goes out of her way to cause trouble ... I would have thought you'd know that, working at the Ministry!" (p. 617). This is true. He knows Skeeter has misrepresented what he and other Ministry officials have done. Mrs. Weasley should know better also, yet she believes Skeeter's *Witch Weekly's* article about Hermione (*GoF*, p. 619).

Selection, as described earlier, is another reason we are spun. Jackson and Jamison say, "We embrace information that supports our beliefs and reject evidence that challenges them" (69). They call this *confirmation bias*. In *GoF*, Rita Skeeter's article about Hagrid makes him seem violent and malicious. Why do people believe it? Other than the fact that using a quote from a student (Draco Malfoy) gives the article the appearance of other professional journalism, like there's evidence from eye witnesses (that they might be biased is never questioned), also there's the established fact: giants are vicious and violent. Hagrid is a half-giant, therefore, he might be violent too. This confirms most wizards' and witches' view of the world.

It is also difficult to admit when we are wrong. "People find it easier to forgive others for being wrong than being right," Hermione quotes Dumbledore in *HBP* in reference to why Percy is still estranged from his family (p. 96). Jackson and Jamison say, "the discomfort at being confronted with evidence of error is a universal human emotion. It's just no fun to admit we've been wrong. So we strive to avoid that unpleasant feeling of psychological conflict—what Festinger calls cognitive dissonance—that occurs when deeply held beliefs are challenged by conflicting evidence" (p. 67).

"Constant vigilance!"

Do we have more propaganda today or just more mediums to deliver (and receive) it? James Combs and Dan Nimmo (1993) in *The New Propaganda: The Dictatorship of Palaver in Contemporary Politics* say, "propaganda today is complete. It surrounds us like the air we breathe. Propaganda is everywhere, is all pervasive and all penetrating. To live in contemporary times is to be showered with the seeds of suasive ideas, seeds encountered by chance, seeds planted in us, seeds scattered over us" (p. 15). The very reason why we need to be aware of it is also the reason it is so hard to distinguish. Fiction has long allowed us to examine our reality. It is easier to see the propaganda when it is not aimed at us. The *Harry Potter* series can show us how language and images can manipulate us especially when there is an organizing, intentionally deceitful effort behind it. Be aware of language. Ask yourself, why was it said that way and would it make a difference if it was said another way? Know yourself, and how your background shapes your thoughts and what biases you have, as we all have biases. Harry didn't just learn magic at Hogwarts; he learned more about himself. He was able to defeat Voldemort (a master at manipulation) not by having greater magical skills, but by knowing more. During their final duel in *DH*, Harry says, "I know things you don't know, Tom Riddle. I know lots of important things that you don't" (p. 738).

Fiction also allows us to see multiple perspectives. We have already seen the differing views on Dumbledore from Doge and Skeeter. There are also two views on death: Voldemort's and Dumbledore's. Voldemort declares in *OotP*, "There is nothing worse than death" (p. 814). Voldemort fears death so much that he willingly tore apart his soul to never die. Dumbledore, on the other hand, says, "to a well-organized mind, death is just the next great adventure" (*SS*, p. 297). Viewing things from multiple perspectives can help us avoid confirmation bias. That does not mean we will agree with every point of view, but knowing there are other views will help us see the spin. As Jackson and Jamison say, "look for general agreement among experts" which means more than one source is necessary (p. 159). A little bit of research goes a long way; so does a healthy dose of skepticism. Hermione is a great example of this. While I absolutely love Luna Lovegood as a character, Hermione proves to be right more often. Hermione weighs the facts. She asks the right questions, even when others don't like it, as was the case with Lavender Brown's rabbit. While most of the students take it as a sign of Trelawney's prognostication powers, Hermione says, "Well, look at it logically … Binky didn't even die today … and she can't have been dreading it, because it's come as a real shock" (*PoA*, p. 149). Hermione tries to caution Harry from believing Kreacher and running into a trap at the Ministry in *OotP*, and she slows them down enough so that Harry thinks twice about going after the Hallows in *DH*. So be skeptical, but not cynical. A cynic just gives up. "They're all crooks. They're all the same. I don't know who to believe," say a cynic. That just plays into the propagandist's hands. Negative campaigning, for instance, is often meant to keep people from voting at all. Or, if you give up on finding the facts, you are more likely to settle for confirmation bias. So as Mad-Eye Moody said in *GoF*, "you need to be prepared. You need to be alert and watchful" (p. 212). And remember that Mad-Eye Moody was an imposter, a death-eater in disguise.

References

Aufderheide, P. (2007). *Documentary Film: A very short introduction.* Oxford: Oxford University Press.

Birk, N.P., & Birk, G.B. (1977). "Selection, slanting, and charged language." In G. Goshgarian, ed., *Exploring language* (13th ed., pp. 4–11). Boston: Little, Brown.

Combs, J.E., & Nimmo, D. (1993). *The new propaganda: The dictatorship of palaver in contemporary politics.* New York: Longman.

Enos, R.L. (1993). *Greek rhetoric before Aristotle.* Prospect Heights, IL: Waveland Press.

Heil, E. (2012, March 12). "Rick Santorum spokeswoman's Dutch treat." *The Washington Post.* Retrieved January 31, 2015.

Jackson, B., & Hall Jamieson, K. (2007). *Unspun: Finding facts in a world of disinformation.* New York: Random House.

Jowett, G.S., & O'Donnell, V. (1992). *Propaganda and persuasion,* 2d ed. Newbury Park, CA: Sage.

Kennedy, G.A. (1991). *Aristotle on rhetoric: A theory of civil discourse.* New York: Oxford University Press.

Potter, W. (2010). *Deadly Spin: An insurance company insider speaks out on how corporate PR is killing health care and deceiving Americans.* New York: Bloomsbury Press.

Pratkanis, A.R., & Aronson, E. (1991). *Age of Propaganda: The everyday use and abuse of persuasion.* New York: W.H. Freeman.

Rowling, J.K. (1997). *Harry Potter and the sorcerer's stone.* New York: Scholastic.

Rowling, J.K. (1998). *Harry Potter and the chamber of secrets.* New York: Scholastic.

Rowling, J.K. (1999). *Harry Potter and the prisoner of Azkaban.* New York: Scholastic.

Rowling, J.K. (2000). *Harry Potter and the goblet of fire.* New York: Scholastic.

Rowling, J.K. (2003). *Harry Potter and the order of the phoenix.* New York: Scholastic.

Rowling, J.K. (2005). *Harry Potter and the half-blood prince.* New York: Scholastic.

Rowling, J.K. (2007). *Harry Potter and the deathly hallows.* New York: Scholastic.

Shermer, M. (1997). *Why people believe weird things: Pseudoscience, superstition, and other confusions of our time.* New York: W.H. Freeman.

Walshe, S., & Friedman, E. (2012, July 26). "Romney in London for Olympics: Candidate angers Brits." Retrieved from abcnews.go.com.

More Than Moving Images:
The Visual Culture of *Harry Potter*

Tolonda Henderson *and*
Amy M. Von Lintel

During Harry's first ride on the Hogwarts Express, he quickly discovers the magic of images in the wizarding world. When examining a Chocolate Frog card that features Professor Dumbledore, Harry registers surprise at the sudden disappearance of the headmaster's image from the frame (*SS*, p. 103). Ron responds to Harry's obvious confusion by noting that Harry shouldn't expect Dumbledore to hang around all day. Harry then summarizes for Ron—and for Rowling's readers—one key difference between the Muggle and wizard realms: people "just stay put" in Muggle pictures. Ron's shock in learning about this immobility, which he qualifies as "*weird*," underscores the expectation that wizarding images are magically animate.

Unlike our own "motion pictures," the movement in wizarding pictures is not based on the visual illusion of motion. What we experience as moving pictures are in fact still photographs projected in rapid sequence onto a screen, a technology descended from the Cinématographe invented by the French brothers Lumière in 1895 (Friedberg, 2006, pp. 87, 152). Rowling's magical images are, in contrast, animate in broader and less illusionary ways: they are not only visually mobile, they are also sentient, emotive, playful, opinionated, and independently responsive to the thoughts and actions of wizarding viewers, often acting as narrative characters themselves. Wizarding images reveal the emotional mood of a moment in the plot, not unlike the chorus in ancient Greek theater. For example, the Hogwarts portraits whisper and point at the incoming students, reflecting and adding to the anxiety of the novice witches and wizards (*SS*, p. 128). Magical pictures also add humorous anecdotes to the *Harry Potter* series: mirror images of Harry, for instance, poke fun at his physical appearance, telling him that fixing his hair is a "losing battle" (*PoA*, p. 55), while the portraits in Dumbledore's office hiss and make rude hand gestures at the hated Cornelius Fudge (*OotP*, p. 623). Additionally, images advance the action at pivotal points in the narrative, such as when Harry invokes the visual power of the Mirror of Erised to obtain the Sorcerer's Stone. In this instance, an animate image intervenes in the plot to help Harry overcome his enemy. The power Harry deploys here lies not just in seeing the image in the mirror, but also in knowing how to control and exploit its magic. Whether rendered or reflected, wizarding images function more like manipulable screens than like solid and fixed material objects. In so doing, they reflect important aspects of our own screen-saturated historical moment, even as they create a magical alternative realm for our entertainment.

Not all pictorial forms in the wizarding world possess such magical potency. Three-dimensional (3d) objects such as statues and suits of armor primarily "just stay put." Hermione, we are told, stands "still as a statue" when she is caught out of bed in the middle of the night (*SS*, p. 243). This phrase would make little sense if the statues magically moved. Young witches and wizards at Hogwarts continuously hide behind sculptural forms, and use them as landmarks in their castle navigations. Some are even tied to them as hostages during the second task of the Triwizard Tournament, further revealing the presumed stationary and inanimate status of these objects (*GoF*, p. 498). In an important moment of foreshadowing, Harry marks a hiding place in the Room of Requirement with a sculptural bust. This sculpture later becomes crucial for his ability to locate a Horcrux (*HBP*, p. 527; *DH*, pp. 620, 627–8). Harry and his friends rely on these 3d objects to remain solid, immobile, and essentially non-magical, at least until they are "bewitched," as in the Battle of Hogwarts when the statues and suits of armor are jinxed to help the witches and wizards in their fight (*DH*, pp. 599, 602). In contrast, the painted image of the Fat Lady guarding Gryffindor Tower hardly "stays put"; instead, she frequently disappears from her portrait at night to socialize with other painted figures, occasionally leaving students stranded outside of the tower. Flat or two-dimensional (2d) images in the *Harry Potter* books, especially those featuring human figures—including painted pictures, photographs, and newspaper illustrations—demonstrate a particularly screenic animation.

Recent scholarship on screens in visual culture has characterized the complex nature of these image-objects. As Wu Hung explores in *The Double Screen: Medium and Representation in Chinese Painting* (1996), painted screens have long been prevalent in Chinese culture. Chinese screens operate as both 3d architectural objects that delineate separate spaces—for instance, a screen would be placed in a room to section off a more private portion of the room—and as 2d visual images that feature painted surfaces and construct illusionary spaces for viewers. At times, these painted spaces on Chinese screens are literal and relatively realistic, such as when they depict a garden scene of socializing figures that invites viewers into imaginative participation. At other times, the images on Chinese screens are poetic and metaphorical, allowing viewers to project their own mental meanings onto abstracted forms. Painted screens even appear as smaller images within larger compositions on Chinese screens or scrolls. Such screen-within-screen modalities construct complex mediated pictorial spaces where imaginary realms are created on the surfaces of architectonic objects which themselves literally shape physical space.

This layering of screens in Chinese art—both pictorial and architectural—reflects the familiar screens we now confront on our many digital devices, as well as the multiple "windows" within each device's primary screen. Anne Friedberg's *The Virtual Window: From Alberti to Microsoft* (2006) examines this pervasive multiplicity of screens and windows in our own digital era. Such multiple screenic modalities also play out in the magical images of the *Harry Potter* series. The portrait of the Fat Lady, for example, is magically animate both as a 2d pictorial image and a 3d physical object, comparable to Chinese painted screens and their digital descendants. The Fat Lady's figure in her pink silk dress can transfer between other images when she exits her frame, and she leaves behind visual traces of her socializing presence, including empty bottles of chocolate liqueurs littering the bottom of her portrait or the wine bottles she drank in a painting of monks (*GoF*, p. 411; *HBP*, p. 351). The reader is left to wonder whether the liqueurs or wine will ever be magically replenished.

The Fat Lady can also physically manipulate her painting as a material object: its frame, canvas ground, wooden stretcher, and colored oil paint can all move together at her discretion. When she is given the correct verbal password, she swings her portrait outward like a door to reveal the Gryffindor Tower entrance. Part of the magic of this painting and other wizarding images is that they function simultaneously as 2d and 3d forms, as representational pictures and structural objects. Yet, as the scholarship on screens has demonstrated, the multi-dimensionality of such image-objects is actually quite quotidian in our own world and perhaps not that magical after all.

Both Rowling's images and our own screens deploy non-perspectival constructions of space. In images composed strictly through linear perspective, such as Leonardo da Vinci's *Last Supper*—an Italian Renaissance mural painting on a wall in a Milan monastery—the pictorial space is fixed and centered. All the orthogonal lines of the floor, ceiling, and table in *The Last Supper* converge on the head of Christ, emphasizing the religious significance of the painting through this centrally focused composition. According to Erwin Panofsky (1991), linear perspective functioned as a "symbolic form" in the Italian Renaissance, serving as a concrete expression of an epistemological or philosophical world view (p. 65). Panofsky explains that symbolic forms encapsulate the predominant spiritual and cultural values of an era (p. 41). Leonardo's wall mural is both literally and pictorially immobile, whereas Chinese screens are physically mobile and construct space variably, for they can be repositioned into a variety of spatial configurations. As painted surfaces, Chinese screens also tend to be more visually animated than Leonardo's static image. They frequently display multiple decentered spaces across their different wooden panels and on both sides of their 3d structures. These multiple spaces unfold across time rather than offering a single, pregnant, symbolic moment in time, such as the biblical scene of Jesus' final meal.

Pictorial images of screens embedded within Chinese paintings, especially in handscrolls such as Gu Hongzhong's *Night Entertainment of Han Xizai*—a 10th-century painting now lost but copied in a 12th-century version—further challenge strictly linear perspectival views (Wu, 1996, p. 31). In Gu's horizontal handscroll, painted screens punctuate the visual narrative as it unfolds, thereby creating what Wu Hung describes as "a coherent composition based on a complex spatial system." He goes on to describe the result as "a visual journey comprised of a series of episodes in four sections that are divided and also connected by a number of screens" (Wu, 1996, p. 49). In *Night Entertainment,* the depicted screens signal not only new spaces in the narrative but also new times, much like a modern comic strip employs different frames to show the passage of time and the changes in setting and action. The viewing of Chinese handscrolls activates "a moving picture, with shifting moments and loci," as the long horizontal format is unrolled and viewed in parts, over a period of time; it is a picture "characterized by well defined sub-frames on a moving picture plane" (Wu, 1996, pp. 59, 63). In other words, these handscrolls require an animate and filmic viewing that contrasts distinctly with stationary perspectival images seen ideally from one fixed point of view. Although he never says so directly, Wu Hung's characterizations of Chinese screens and the screenic perspective they concretize arguably make them a Panofskian "symbolic form."

Rowling likewise plays with such screenic and "moving picture" functions in her descriptions of magical images, highlighting their image-object hybridity as well as their mobility. Rowling deploys a semiotic decentering, playfully shifting pictorial signs and their meanings. As Roland Barthes reminds us, "all images are polysemous; they imply, underlying their signifiers, a 'floating chain' of signifieds" (Barthes, 2003, p. 117). Rowling's magical pictures highlight the fluid meanings of images in particularly evident ways. The portrait of the Fat Lady is not fixed and stationary but rather animated, playful, and semiotically complex like a Chinese screen. She moves independently and visually when she vacates her frame at her own leisure. Students out of bed after hours are therefore at the mercy of her off-duty wanderings. The portrait also moves independently, physically, and at the students' request when the Fat Lady and her viewers do share the same time-space so that she can receive their spoken password. Her physical and architectural movement when she swings her painting outward like a door reveals the Gryffindor Tower entrance. With this action, the Fat Lady's portrait functions like a Chinese screen; it simultaneously divides and connects two distinct spaces, specifically a relatively public from a more private space. The portrait engages its viewers both verbally and visually in exchanges of gazes and words that unfold across time; the portrait as an image-object is thus distinctly unfixed in time. Whereas Leonardo's *Last Supper* mural constructs a single, synchronic moment frozen and preserved for all viewers in all times—or as Panofsky writes, an "infinite, unchanging, and homogeneous" time-space (pp. 28–9)—wizarding images function diachronically, changing their meanings and positions across time and space. Comparable to Chinese screens and to the digital screens that have followed, magical images challenge traditional modes of viewing a picture from a fixed perspective as "a single whole" (Wu, 1996, p. 61). Rather than just adding an otherworldly ambiance to her stories, Rowling's magical images illuminate many tensions and potencies of our own digital screen culture from their unfixed and mobile status, to their 2d/3d hybridity, to their diachronic perspectives.

Rowling takes this diachronic viewing even further when she shows how deceased witches and wizards continue to be animate in their images. This is true in their portraits and photographs, as well as in the Mirror of Erised when it shows Harry his mother, father, and other family members who are no longer living (*SS*, pp. 208–10). These animated ancestors can engage directly with living people, a behavior that becomes especially evident when the house-elf Kreacher takes orders from his dead mistress, Mrs. Black, through her painted portrait (*OotP*, p. 110). In his study of the rhetoric of images, Barthes (2003) described how certain images, especially photographs, collapse the "here-now" with the "there-then," bringing the photographed past into the present of viewers (p. 120). Magical pictures in the *Harry Potter* series likewise enact this collapse as the "there-then" of a dead wizard confronts the "here-now" of a living wizard by way of an image. Pivotal to the plot is the portrait of the deceased Ariana Dumbledore in the Hog's Head Inn that opens onto the only remaining magical passageway into Hogwarts for Harry's final battle (*DH*, p. 570). When Ariana disappears into the depths of her portrait along a tunnel depicted in the distance of her painting instead of exiting laterally out of her frame like the figures in other magical portraits, she reveals her direct role in connecting two divergent spaces. We visually witness Ariana returning from the distance accompanied by the image of Neville Longbottom who then steps bodily out of the secret passage revealed when Ariana's portrait physically swings aside like "a little door" (*DH*, p. 570). In this scene, we are taken on a complex time-space journey between the 2d and the 3d, the screenic and the physical, the visual and the embodied, the illusionary and the "real." We learn from Rowling that it is indeed the "real" Neville who traversed the "real" tunnel, and not just Neville's painted image. This distinction further underscores the difference between pictorial and physical realities, even in the magical world of Harry Potter.

Moreover, we can describe the experiences of viewing Rowling's magical images as both virtual and phenomenological. We use the term "virtual" following Friedberg (2006): "The virtual is a substitute—'acting without agency of matter'—an immaterial proxy for the material" (p. 8). Friedberg goes on to define the virtual as either functionally or effectively, but not formally, "of the same materiality as what it represents. Virtual images have a materiality and a reality but of a different kind, a second-order materiality, liminally immaterial" (p. 11). The Fat Lady, Ariana, and the pictorial Neville are not of the same physical materiality as their wizarding viewers, but are nonetheless functionally and effectively material for the narrative of the series. These images engage people directly and purposefully. They define a liminal physicality, being unquestionably and magically real but not bodily real. Their images serve as uniquely liminal screens between two spaces: the castle hallway and the Gryffindor Tower, or the Hog's Head Inn and the Room of Requirement. The notion of "screen" here operates as both noun and verb (Friedberg, 2006, p. 17). The magical portraits function like screens on which figures can appear and disappear, while also effectively and physically "screening" portals into new spaces.

Phenomenologically, these portraits engage more than just the eyes of their viewers. When the Fat Lady is present in her portrait to receive the password prompt, young Gryffindors can crawl physically and bodily through the portal she controls. Similarly, Neville appears first in the image with Ariana, and then walks physically out of the passageway she guards. Characters engage with these portraits mentally, visually, verbally, and physically. These modes of engagement demonstrate embodied, multisensory, and therefore phenomenological experiences. The scholarship on phenomenological aesthetics is extensive (Kaelin, 1970; Butler, 1989; Sobchack, 1992; Johnson, 1993; and Jones, 1998 and 2003), but most relevant for our discussion is the work of Maurice Merleau-Ponty. According to Merleau-Ponty (1981), the philosophy of phenomenology deals with the human body's relationship to objects in the world: thought, perception, and the construction of meaning are all part of an embodied experience. The body is not a subservient surface or container for the mind, but instead a system intertwined with the mind to produce meanings. We see this embodied production of meanings when Harry invokes the power of the Mirror of Erised both visually and mentally and then gains the physical and tactile possession of the Sorcerer's Stone in his pocket (*SS*, pp. 292, 300). The success of Harry's magic is affirmed by the weight of the material object of the stone against his body. Another revealing example occurs when students must physically tickle a pear in a still life painting in order to gain entrance to the kitchens at Hogwarts (*GoF*, pp. 366, 375). Here we see that multisensory exchanges can occur between images and characters even when the images lack human figures. Moreover, the people in the pictures at Hogwarts possess their own sensory perceptions, as when the portraits mutter and wince at the pain of being scrubbed clean in preparation for Triwizard Tournament guests (*GoF*, p. 236). Humans and magical images thus share the same time-space, unlike the separate and universalized time-space constructed by Leonardo's *Last Supper*. This perspectival mural functions like a window to divide earthly from heavenly space, allowing human viewers to gaze into the saintly realm, but not engage it directly or bodily. Alternatively, functioning as richly phenomenological images, wizarding pictures invite dialectic and multisensory experiences with their viewing witches or wizards, reaching out to them through visual, auditory, mental, and physical exchanges.

    With Friedberg's *Virtual Window* (2006), the scholarship on screens extends into our own 21st-century digital age:

> [S]creens are now everywhere—on our wrists, in our hands, on our dashboards and in our backseats, on the bicycles and treadmills at the gym, on the seats of airplanes and buses, on buildings and billboards. Our position is no longer fixed in relation to the virtual elsewheres and elsewhens seen on a screen [p. 87].

Pervasive screens connect us instantaneously to those "elsewheres and else-whens" that we access through their surfaces. Perhaps our most common contact with images today—our "vernacular system of visuality" (Friedberg, 2006, p. 3)—is through screen views that are non-perspectival, unfixed, multiple, and manipulable. They require many of the same complex and multisensory manipulations that we witness with Rowling's magical images. Tickling that pear to open the Hogwarts kitchens is strikingly like swiping or tapping the touch screen of our phones or tablets to "wake them up" or "open" their applications. The voice command function on our devices, which allows us to dial a number or text a message through an oral expression, reminds us of speaking a password to spring the Fat Lady's image into physical action. With our own screen-based technologies, the boundaries between past and present, between the virtual and the material, are increasingly fluid and blurred, just as they are in Rowling's magical images. We watch YouTube videos or DVR recordings that were digitally captured in the past as if they were continuously happening in our present moment, especially when we pause them, rewind them, and restart them. We also connect to living people sharing our same moments in time, although not our same physical space, through Skype or FaceTime chat. As Friedberg (2006) explains, "On the computer, we can be two (or more) places at once, in two (or more) time frames, in two (or more) modes of identity, in a fractured post–Cartesian cyberspace, cybertime" (p. 235). Rowling's magical shifts between times and spaces begin to resonate less as science-fiction or fantasy imaginings of the author and more as familiar forms of communication in our own screenic and digital age.

Rowling describes how Muggles in her series enjoy several screen-based entertainments that her readers will recognize. Just after we meet the Dursleys, Dudley receives a new video camera and VCR for his birthday (SS, p. 22). He later complains that he needs his television set so that he can watch his favorite shows (SS, p. 43). Rowling also informs us that Muggle screens are housed within non-animate, material formats easily controlled and even destroyed by their Muggle owners: Dudley breaks his new video camera shortly after he receives it and puts his foot through his television set when his favorite program is cancelled (SS, pp. 31, 37). In the wizarding world, however, there is little evidence of such screen-based distractions. No witch or wizard is ever caught watching TV, playing video games, or viewing a movie. There is no differentiation for wizards between still photography and motion pictures. Every magical image is internally animated without the necessity of electrical power, technological trickery, or digital coding. Martin Jay (1993; 1998) employs the notion of the "scopic regime" to describe the historical and cultural relativity of vision: cultures in different times and places select, employ, and expect distinct visual perspectives. In these terms, the "scopic regime" of the wizarding world centers upon animate imagery; as Ron summarizes, one cannot "expect" a magical image to "stay put" (*SS*, p. 103).

The dominant visual regime in the *Harry Potter* books also presupposes that witches and wizards will have less control over magical images than Muggles have over non-magical images. As with any use of magic, wizarding students must learn to control the magical powers of images psychologically rather than relying on the brute force Dudley uses on his video camera and TV set. Magical control over images occurs mainly through mental invocation or direct verbal dialogue. Characters must often persuade images into performing tasks for them. For instance, Harry and Hermione cajole the painted figure of Phineas Nigellus from Grimmauld Place to disclose information about the sword of Gryffindor that hangs adjacent to his companion portrait at Hogwarts (*DH*, pp. 301–4, 314). They ask him direct questions, engage him in conversation, and obtain information from him as from a living witness rather than an inanimate object. In another telling scene, Alastor "Mad-Eye" Moody gruffly tells the figures in a group portrait to scoot around so that Harry can view his parents; Moody cannot force the movement of these figures, but must prompt them and then wait for them to perform the task on their own (*OotP*, pp. 173–4).

This equitable power relationship between wizards and images highlights the complicated functions of "the gaze," or the power and politics at work in a visual exchange. The power of the human gaze is traditionally understood as being held by the viewer rather than the person or object being viewed: a viewer actively looks at a passive, objectified image (Mulvey, 2004; Berger, 1972). The relationships between viewers and viewed objects in the *Harry Potter* stories, however, are more intersubjective, by which we mean that the viewer and the object of the gaze share a more equitable subjectivity (Jones, 1998, pp. 5, 40–41; Friedberg, 2006, p. 17). As we learn from the many scenes involving the portrait of the Fat Lady (and there are dozens), painted figures in wizarding pictures hold some power and control over the experience of viewing them; the Fat Lady plays a subjective role in the story as an active and sentient being. Those wishing to enter Gryffindor Tower must engage her subjectivity before she will perform her useful purpose; they cannot physically force her as they might with an inanimate or non-magical object. She is a protective figure but also a trickster, often playfully conversing with her wizarding viewers. This pushback of power held by an image reminds us that the politics of the gaze in our own world is rarely simply unidirectional and that a viewed image can withhold information or trick the viewer in ways that maintain a more dispersed and dialectical control within the visual exchange. Photographs and paintings are, of course, not exact reflections of reality. Instead, they shape their own representational realities, a status we cannot miss in the examples of Rowling's active images.

The fact that the relationships between wizarding folk and images are neither truly voyeuristic nor fetishistic in Rowling's novels further complicates theories of the gaze. A voyeuristic gaze would imply that the witches and wizards peer at images without the images' awareness, as if looking at them secretly through a keyhole (Mulvey, 2004, p. 839). Wizarding portraits, photographs, and mirrors are generally aware of being viewed, and often actively look back at their viewers, thus undermining any presumed voyeurism. Also, a voyeuristic gaze is often a gendered gaze, yet Rowling's magical images complicate any presumed gendering of these gazes. As Laura Mulvey (2004) argues, "in a world ordered by sexual imbalance, pleasure in looking has been split between active/male and passive/female" (p. 841). Mulvey's now seminal study, first published in 1975, which examines the female characters and gendered structures in classic Hollywood narrative film, concludes that the cinematic codes in these films created a gendered gaze based on male desire. When the Fat Lady and Ariana Dumbledore show themselves to be magically animate, however, they essentially come to life and cease to be passive objects of admiration. Their magical animation upsets the traditional gendering of the visual exchange between active/masculine viewer and passive/feminine art object while dissolving the presumed boundaries between art and life. Wu Hung (1996) describes a similar alternative gendering of the gaze: "once a painted woman comes to life, she ceases to be a passive object of admiration and acts according to her own wishes" (p. 122). Here, he references the Greek myth of Pygmalion and similar Chinese legends in which an artistically created woman comes to life for the artist and/or viewer. Painted portraits in the *Harry Potter* books are magically both subject and object, both art and life. Rowling plays upon the deep human desire for art to become life, but in so doing, she also removes the important societal role of the human artist as creator. Wizarding images seem to need no identified creator either to come into existence or to become animate. Magic is their creator. For instance, Dumbledore's portrait appears in the headmaster's office the very night he dies, without indication of anyone having painted, framed, or hung it (*HPB*, p. 626). Harry Potter's world has a much clearer "destroyer"—Voldemort—than a recognized creator.

A fetishistic gaze, in turn, implies that a viewer excessively values an image beyond its functional purpose (Mulvey, 2004; Marx, 1906; Marx, 2004; Metz, 2003). According to William Pietz (2003), a fetish is "an object of irrational fascination, something whose power, desirability, or significance a person passionately overvalues, even though that same person may know very well intellectually that such feelings are unjustifiably excessive" (p. 306). The witch or wizard who respects the magical powers of an image does not fetishize that image but rather values it rightly. This lack of fetishization of images by wizarding folk is underscored when Hermione alters the painted portrait of Phineas Nigellus by magically adding a painted blindfold to protect Harry and his friends from the portrait's spying gaze (*DH*, p. 301). Even when Phineas Nigellus accuses her of "ruining a great work of art" by adding to his canvas—an action that would clearly constitute destruction of property or graffiti in our world—the accusation bothers Hermione very little. In matters of life and death for the characters of Rowling's novels, the preciousness of art objects is far less valued than control over their magical functions. Defacing the portrait is a worthy activity if it means protection against enemy spies and the requisition of information necessary for Harry's quest.

The best example of fetishization of art objects in the novels comes from the goblin characters. Rowling describes goblins as virtuoso metal workers who have forged everything from armor to the sword of Gryffindor to the tiara that Fleur Delacour borrows from Auntie Muriel for her wedding to Bill Weasley. On the one hand, the goblins' valuation of these objects comes from an understandable artistic pride in their personal craftsmanship. On the other hand, Rowling characterizes the goblins as greedy and jealous; they claim perpetual ownership of objects even when these objects are possessed by those who paid for them or their descendants. The goblin Griphook shows himself willing to double-cross Harry to (re)possess the sword of Gryffindor, a betrayal that nearly gets Harry killed in the bowels of Gringotts (*DH*, p. 540). Rowling casts the artistic and creative powers of goblins in an overtly negative light, which positions both artists and art-making as distinctly associated with powers of evil in her books.

Beyond the goblins, a few wizarding images-makers do appear in the *Harry Potter* books. For example, Rowling describes photographers operating magical cameras, such as the man from the *Daily Prophet* who takes Gilderoy Lockhart's picture with a "large black camera that emitted puffs of purple smoke with every blinding flash" (*CoS*, p. 59). Colin Creevey appears to use an ordinary Muggle camera for his photography; but we learn that he can "develop the film in the right potion" to create magically animate images (*CoS*, p. 96). While Rowling never tells us whether the magic of wizarding photographs is created more in the mechanics of the camera or in the chemistry of the developing process, she clearly de-emphasizes the human artistry of these photographers. They function more as recorders of reality than as creators of photographic art. In other instances, a witch or wizard has acted as the artist for drawings (Dean Thomas draws some banners: *SS*, p. 184; *GoF*, p. 365), decorative arts and crafts (Mrs. Weasley knits a dragon onto a Christmas sweater: *GoF*, p. 410), paintings (Dobby the house elf makes a pitiful Christmas painting for Harry; Luna Lovegood paints a ceiling mural in her bedroom: *OotP*, p. 502; *DH*, p. 417), and sculptures (Xenophilius Lovegood sculpts a replica of the bust of Rowena Ravenclaw: *DH*, pp. 403–4). The examples concerning the Lovegoods are perhaps most revealing. Rowling makes the point to inform us that both of the Lovegoods' creative endeavors fall short of a successful production of truly magical images. Xenophilius's bust is repeatedly ridiculed for its silliness, and though Luna's mural seems to have a "certain magic" of its own—the figures appear to Harry to be breathing—it lacks the full animation of proper wizarding images. The most successful creation of magical objects, aside from goblin metalwork, seems to be Voldemort's production of Horcruxes when he imparts his fractured but sentient soul into numerous objects. Ultimately, though, destruction supersedes creation in the narrative: Harry and his accomplices systematically destroy each Horcrux Voldemort has created, thereby saving the world from his reign. It appears that magical and artistic powers are at odds in the wizarding world, and that artistry is at best insignificant and silly, and at worst, pure evil.

Returning to the politics of images and vision, there are moments when magical images in the *Harry Potter* series possess powers of regulatory surveillance over witches and wizards. For instance, Phineas Nigellus comments with a "sly voice" from beyond his portrait's frame in Grimmauld Place, observing signs of madness in Harry and showing that he can see Harry without being seen (*OotP*, p. 178). Michel Foucault (1977) theorizes the role of vision in surveillance and control in his discussion of the Panopticon, a circular prison with a central viewing tower where prisoners can be seen without seeing their surveyors, a structure that, for Foucault, embodies the power relationships inherent in the visual exchange. The Panopticon's prisoners, Foucault argues, would continuously monitor their own behavior because they never knew when they were being watched. Such visual control is evident in the video surveillance and CCTV cameras now pervasive in our own modern society. However, Rowling's magical images fall far short of having the total viewing power of the Panopticon watchtower. The characters in the series are generally aware of when they are being viewed by images. The monitoring portraits also directly confront witches and wizards about their behavior, showing their role to be more like a hovering parent than like a hidden spy. Harry and his companions are also aware of times when they are not being viewed by images. For example, portraits are repeatedly observed sleeping—and even snoring—in their frames in the headmaster's office. At other times, characters prevent surveillance by images, such as when Hermione stuffs the painting of Phineas Nigellus into her beaded bag so that he cannot spy on them (*DH*, p. 228). Surveillance can be further thwarted by magical intervention, as when Hermione adds the painted blindfold to Phineas Nigellus (*DH*, p. 301), or when the Fat Lady cannot tell that Harry is in front of her because of his invisibility cloak (*SS*, p. 205).

Along with the ubiquitous but restricted viewing powers of magical pictures, the power of eyes as viewing organs also forms a central theme in the *Harry Potter* series. For instance, the enchanted mirror fragment that Harry carries with him after the death of Sirius Black repeatedly displays the image of a single blue eye. This eye turns out to be the protective view of Aberforth Dumbledore. After his brother's death, Aberforth watches out for Harry and his friends. As Rowling puns for her readers' amusement, he literally keeps an "eye out for" them (*DH*, p. 560). Through this mirror fragment, Aberforth witnesses Harry and his friends' imprisonment at Malfoy Manor and summons Dobby the house-elf to rescue them. Another significant magical eye is that of Alastor Moody, whose biological eye was lost in the enactment of his protective role as Auror. After Mad-Eye's death, his famous magical eye becomes the means for Dolores Umbridge to spy on her workers at the Ministry of Magic (*DH*, pp. 249–51). The disembodied eye motif resurfaces yet again when Harry and Ron open Voldemort's locket–Horcrux to see a single "living eye" belonging to Tom Riddle staring back at them from each interior glass pane (*DH*, p. 375). These moments of surveillance by an eye-without-a-body remind us once again of Foucault's Panopticon and its controlling power of vision, just as they recall that "eye in the sky" at a Vegas casino or even the god's-eye view of a single, all-seeing, all-knowing presence. Such a god's-eye view appears, for instance, on the back of the American dollar bill in the single human eye at the peak of the pyramid. Panofsky (1991) linked this god's-eye-view with the perspectival focus of Leonardo's *The Last Supper*, where the ultimate power and control is focused symbolically on the monotheistic, omniscient, and omnipotent figure of Jesus. However, Rowling decidedly undermines such universal and unified control in her novels. Only Voldemort seeks the god's-eye-view of totalitarian power, and the power he does amass is democratically destroyed by Harry and his supporters.

Unlike the fixed, centralized viewing of the Panopticon watchtower or the immobile and static figure of Jesus in *The Last Supper*, wizarding images are not bound by their frames and their return gaze is as mobile as their visual forms. Rowling uses the word "frame" continually to describe how this physical boundary does not delimit magical images; the figures most often "exit their frames" rather than leaving their paintings. However, in a few instances, the painted figures collide with or hide beneath their frames, suggesting that the frame is at least a solid obstacle if not a fixed barrier to magical images. For example, the blindfolded Phineas Nigellus shrieks with pain when he bumps into his frame, blending the senses of sight and sound for his viewers (*DH*, p. 301). Friedberg (2006) argues that the frame of a moving image must be present to show relative movement; something must "stay put" in order to show mobility (p. 84). Rowling deploys the notion of the framed picture or mirror to make this contrast; it is only through the stationary or the non-magical frame that the magical animation of images can be demonstrated.

Much like the television set that Dudley puts his foot through, Rowling informs us that the materiality of wizarding images is at times vulnerable to damage. The most vivid example is when the Fat Lady's canvas is slashed by Sirius Black (*PoA*, pp. 160–1). Yet, the slashed portrait only serves to scare the students and require repair; the Fat Lady's persona remains intact because she flees her portrait. Other portrait figures likewise exit their frames before harm befalls them. For example, when Harry aims a jinx at fleeing enemies and instead hits some "bewigged witches" in a portrait, they run "screeching" into nearby paintings (*HPB*, p. 600). The magical power and animation of these portraits is apparently never really at risk. While the Fat Lady's canvas is being repaired, guardianship of the Gryffindor Tower is transferred to another magical portrait. The depicted human figure, Sir Cadogan, can likewise directly dialogue with the young witches and wizards and is equally prone to independent thought and action, such as when he challenges the students to duels and designs overly complicated passwords (*PoA*, pp. 165–7). At the same time, the emotional trauma that coincides with the physical damage of their structures is apparently very real for magical images; among the many portrait figures at Hogwarts, only Sir Cadogan is willing to accept the temporary job of replacing the Fat Lady while Sirius Black is on the loose.

Images play a key role in Rowling's novels when they possess information crucial to the plot. Sometimes this knowledge is accessed in traditional ways, such as simply viewing a photograph or reading a book. For instance, Harry uses photographs and book illustrations to identify the pivotal character of Grindelwald (*DH,* pp. 336–7, 352–3). But just as often, the information held in Rowling's pictures can only be accessed through nonlinear, indirect, and even physically embodied methods. The magical images in the *Harry Potter* series thus reflect a familiar means of accessing information in the digital age. The knowledge held by the animate image is often embedded within the image's consciousness as with digital data embedded in code rather than merely apparent on its surface. We are now highly accustomed to hypertextual and hyperlinked connections on screens that archive information through digital networks rather than through fixed, linear, physical formats. Friedberg (2006) explains that the computer screen's "overlay of 'windows'—open to different applications for word-processing, Web browsing, emailing, downloading—transforms the screen surface into a page with a deep virtual reach to archives and databases, indexed and accessible with barely the stroke of a finger" (p. 19). This deepness and archival reach corresponds to the intelligence held by magical images that wizarding folk can access only through intersubjective dialogues, manipulation, and a mature understanding of the magic therein. The deepness of image-knowledge is made clear, for example, when Harry discovers how the diary of Tom Riddle works and is prompted verbally by Riddle to enter his memory. Rather than inviting Harry to read the diary linearly, Riddle promises to "show" Harry the past. The page of the diary turns into "a minuscule television screen," against which Harry presses his eye, making physical contact with the diary-screen. He then pitches magically and bodily through the portal in the page (*CoS,* p. 242). In this instance, a screenic image connects and collapses two different times and spaces, allowing Harry to travel mentally and physically into another wizard's life.

In addition to providing witches and wizards with much needed knowledge by giving them passage across times and spaces, images can also directly protect them from harmful magic. For instance, the basilisk's killing power is thwarted through mediating images. Colin Creevey is saved from death when he sees the monster's eyes through the lens of his camera, just as Hermione was petrified but not killed when she glimpses the image of the basilisk in a mirror (*CoS,* pp. 180, 257, 291). This function of images as protective mediators recalls the Greek mythological story of Medusa and Perseus, where Perseus uses his reflective shield to view Medusa indirectly thereby avoiding being frozen by the sight of her. It also reflects the differences between images—even the magical ones in the world of Harry Potter—and reality. Our own digital screens often serve as protective and distancing mediators between ourselves and others, for better or for worse. The potentially harmful direct gaze of another person is easier to control with the mediation of a screen; we can seemingly present ourselves as controlled images through digitized social media more comfortably than when we participate directly in living conversations.

Like wizarding folk with their magical images, we must constantly negotiate the relationships between the virtual images on our digital screens and the material realities that exist beyond these framed screens. Whether it is the humans with whom we interact by way of their digital effigies, the physical goods advertised for our purchase and consumption, the bills of currency converted into virtual money when we buy and sell and bank online, or the famous works of art and architecture and the natural wonders we are called upon to visit as tourists, these virtual digitized proxies presumably correspond to embodied, physical objects and realities that exist somewhere in the world, but in a time and/or space separate from our own. On the other hand, they appear to us as disembodied visual forms that we cannot physically feel or bodily consume. Just as Harry puts his hands on the Mirror of Erised but feels only the cold metal surface that separates him from the warm loving embrace of the family that he just sees visually, we are likewise restricted by our digital screens and forced to accept the visual image as a mere surrogate for physical reality (*SS*, p. 209). We might do well to heed Dumbledore's advice regarding Harry's growing obsession with the Mirror of Erised: one should not "dwell on dreams and forget to live" (*SS*, p. 214). This statement reminds us how the dream world of virtual images on screens can never truly replace the living world of physical forms.

Rowling continually highlights the difference between images and reality in her books. Given the many magical photographs that depict Gilderoy Lockhart, for instance, Rowling specifically informs us when we are seeing the "real" Lockhart or that the "real magical" Lockhart will teach at Hogwarts (*CoS*, pp. 59–60). We learn that Harry is pleased with his "photographic self" for putting up a fight against appearing in an image with Lockhart (*CoS*, p. 106). Apparently Harry's image-double acts in ways that the "real" Harry was also feeling, but Harry's pleasure in discovering this correspondence suggests that such similarities are not expected. Phineas Nigellus outlines for us how the depicted figures in Hogwarts portraits, which can freely transfer between pictures within the castle, can only leave Hogwarts by way of painted portraits of themselves existing elsewhere. They are networked across time and space but only by way of their own image (*DH*, p. 303). These depicted surrogates are thus not one and the same as the "real" witches and wizards they resemble, but are confined to and bound by their virtual image networks. Even for wizarding folk, there is a clear difference between the living self and its pictorial representations. As Harry observes regarding the image of Neville that appears in Ariana's portrait, the real Neville must emerge into the wizarding world before he is his true self again.

Neville's immersion into a magical image is an exception to Rowling's distinction between image and reality that is both dramatic and unique (*DH*, p. 570). When Neville appears in Ariana's painting, we wonder exactly how he has united with this image. Does the portrait simply become like a transparent window showing us Neville as he approaches from the distance through the tunnel hidden behind the portrait? If so, why does he appear to share the same pictorial space of the portrait with the painted figure of Ariana? How does the living wizard commune with the dead witch? Also, we never hear about a portrait of Ariana on the other end of the tunnel in the Room of Requirement with which she can network according to Phineas Nigellus's rules of portrait transfer into and out of Hogwarts. In many ways, Rowling breaks her own rules for magical images with Ariana's portrait. But what is perhaps most important with this pivotal scene is how Rowling once again positions an image as central to a climactic moment of the plot. Here, image and wizard work together in symbiosis, neither controlling the other but both operating in cooperation and equal subjectivity. In this instance, the fluidity and porousness of the boundaries between the real and the pictorial become most pronounced. The "real" Neville becomes pictorial, and the pictorial Ariana becomes functionally real, moving the plot forward in vital ways. This example can illuminate how fluid and symbiotic our own relations with images have become, and how we must maintain a complex understanding of the power of images rather than believing them easy to control. Perhaps the magical images of the *Harry Potter* series can become yet another Panofskian "symbolic form" for our own image-culture today: rather than a far-fetched fantasy, these images seem to embody the very modes of viewing and vision that predominate in our digital, screen-oriented world. The significance of images in Rowling's books is not simply that they move, but how they are profoundly "moving," advancing Rowling's plot while also reflecting back on our own visual culture. Instead of the dystopic allegories of Plato's cave or the 1999 film *The Matrix*, where humans are completely fooled by images that create all-encompassing but entirely false realities, we might turn to the more utopic visions of Rowling as inspiration to strive for mature and informed relationships with the images which are part of our everyday reality.

References

Barthes, R. (2003). "Rhetoric of the image." In L. Wells, ed., *The photography reader* (pp. 114–25). New York: Routledge.

Berger, J. (1972). *Ways of seeing.* Reprint, 2003. London: Penguin.

Bielstein, S. (2006). *Permissions, a survival guide: Blunt talk about art as intellectual property.* Chicago: University of Chicago Press.

Butler, J. (1989). "Sexual ideology and phenomenological description: A feminist critique of Merleau-Ponty's *Phenomenology of perception.*" In J. Allen and I. Young, eds., *The thinking muse: Feminism and modern French philosophy* (pp. 85–100). Bloomington: Indiana University Press.

Foucault, M. (1977). "Panopticism." In *Discipline and punish* (A. Sheridan, Trans., pp. 195–228). New York: Pantheon.

Friedberg, A. (2006). *The virtual window: From Alberti to Microsoft.* Cambridge: MIT Press.

Jay, M. (1993). *Downcast eyes: The denigration of vision in twentieth-century French thought.* Berkeley: University of California Press.

_____. (1998). "Scopic regimes of modernity." In N. Mirzoeff, ed., *The visual culture reader* (pp. 66–69). New York: Routledge.

Johnson, G. (1993). *The Merleau-Ponty aesthetics reader: Philosophy and painting.* Evanston, IL: Northwestern University Press, 1993.

Jones, A. (1998). *Body art: Performing the subject.* Minneapolis: University of Minnesota Press.

_____. (2003). "Body." In R. Nelson and R. Shiff, eds., *Critical terms for art history,* 2d ed. (pp. 251–66). Chicago: University of Chicago Press.

Kaelin, E. (1970). *Art and existence: A phenomenological aesthetics.* Lewisburg, PA: Bucknell University Press.

Marx, K. (1906). "The fetishism of the commodity and its secret." In *Capital: A critique of political economy,* vol. 1 (pp. 81–96). New York: Charles H. Kerr.

_____. (2004). "Commodities and money." In V. Schwartz and J. Przyblyski, eds., *The nineteenth-century visual culture reader* (pp. 42–7). New York: Routledge.

Merleau-Ponty, M. (1981). *Phenomenology of perception.* C. Smith, trans. London: Routledge.

Metz, C. (2003). "Photography and fetish." In L. Wells, ed., *The photography reader* (pp. 138–45). New York: Routledge.

Mulvey, L. (2004). "Visual pleasure and narrative cinema." In L. Braudy and M. Cohen, eds., *Film theory and criticism,* 6th ed. (pp. 837–48). New York: Oxford University Press.

Panofsky, E. (1991). *Perspective as symbolic form.* C. Wood, trans. New York: Zone Books.

Pietz, W. (2003). "Fetish." In R. Nelson and R. Shiff, eds., *Critical terms for art history,* 2d ed. (pp. 306–17). Chicago: University of Chicago Press.

Rowling, J. (1997). *Harry Potter and the Sorcerer's Stone.* New York: Scholastic.

_____. (1999). *Harry Potter and the Chamber of Secrets.* New York: Scholastic.

_____. (1999). *Harry Potter and the Prisoner of Azkaban.* New York: Scholastic.

_____. (2000). *Harry Potter and the Goblet of Fire.* New York: Scholastic.

_____. (2003). *Harry Potter and the Order of the Phoenix.* New York: Scholastic.

_____. (2005). *Harry Potter and the Half-Blood Prince.* New York: Scholastic.

_____. (2007). *Harry Potter and the Deathly Hallows.* New York: Scholastic.

Sobchack, V. (1992). *The address of the eye: A phenomenology of film experience.* Princeton: Princeton University Press.

Wu, H. (1996). *The double screen: Medium and representation in Chinese painting.* Chicago: University of Chicago Press.

Unplottable: Subversive Books and Radical Reading in *Harry Potter*

Tracy L. Bealer

"Books are places"

When discussing his life as a reader, Neil Gaiman offered the above cartographical definition of books (Gaiman and Holdengräber, 2014). Experiencing texts as places radically reconfigures not only the conventional understanding of a book as a discrete and static object, but also demands a reconceptualization of the act of reading. If a book is a place, a reader is a traveler, surrounded by and immersed in a world he or she cannot completely master—a world that both responds to and is shaped by the reader's presence. Calling a book a place means that texts have histories, futures, and even something we might call lives that are distinct from, but related to, each individual reader. Following this definition, learning how to read is not (merely) a matter of translating a series of symbols into decipherable language, nor is it limited to "comprehension" of information or plot. Learning how to read in this meaningful way implies learning how *not* to read—how to avoid treating texts like static objects that contain discrete and mimetic representations of life readymade for instrumentalization. It means not just a willingness but an expectation to be transported and transfigured by words on a page. It means you have to believe in magic.

Vladimir Nabokov, in "Good Readers and Good Writers" (1980), employs the vocabulary of magic to explain effective reading and writing. He explains, "a great writer is always a great enchanter," and good readers therefore must look for "the individual magic of his genius" (p. 5) when studying texts. Nabokov describes reading as a physical process of empathetic connection, where the body of the story meets the body of the reader to produce a mysterious act of transfiguration:

The magic of art may be present in the very bones of the story, in the very marrow of thought…. In order to bask in that magic a wise reader reads the book of genius not with his heart, not so much with his brain, but with his spine…. Then with a pleasure which is both sensual and intellectual we shall watch the artist build his castle of cards and watch the castle of cards become a castle of beautiful steel and glass [Nabokov, 1980, pp. 5–6].

Nabokov describes reading as participating in a magic trick, but not one that frivolously or cynically exploits the audience. Rather, when the "wise" reader encounters a book with her "spine,"—the part of the body that connects the mind with the senses (and, it must be noted, the pages of a book with its cover)—the "magic" of narrative is activated, transforming a two-dimensional object into an aesthetically exquisite and structurally sound space for the reader to inhabit. But what does it mean to read with both your mind and your body? Does the "magic of art" have a dark side? Is this description a poetic metaphor or an applicable theory of critical reading? It seems there is no better place to further explore the nature and mechanisms of the magic of deep reading than a series of fantasy novels about a boy attending a school for witchcraft and wizardry.

As J.K. Rowling's *Harry Potter* series takes its shape and setting from the rhythms of the school year, it's not a surprise that books and reading play a large role in its universe. Because the students begin Hogwarts at the age of eleven, they are all capable of reading. However, they are not necessarily prepared to encounter books in the way Gaiman and Nabokov describe and prescribe. Therefore, though our primary protagonists Harry, Ron Weasley, and Hermione Granger are literate, they might have not yet learned how to read. Rowling's novels position the activity of deep, engaged, critical reading as central not merely to Harry's and his friends' educations, but also to the development of their ability to engage productively with the increasingly complicated and threatening world surrounding them, and their development as self-actualized and curious individuals. Interestingly, their intellectual and emotional growth as critically engaged readers occurs simultaneously with their wizarding education, but takes place largely outside the walls of the classroom through extra-curricular texts.

As Lisa Hopkins (2003) notes, "Lack of access to technological, commodified versions of knowledge … means that for Harry Potter, knowledge, which is crucial to his survival, must always be acquired slowly, painfully, and over a period of time" (p. 25). For many readers, this is an all too accurate description of the process of assimilating information from books. Though the pain quotient varies depending on the text, Harry, Ron, and Hermione frequently rely upon the written word to supplement their experiential knowledge of the wizarding world, and often come across and seek out texts that have nothing to do with their classes in order to acquire the knowledge Hopkins identifies as crucial to the trio's survival. The three discover and discuss not only textbooks, but also newspapers, magazines, how-to manuals, histories of Quidditch and Quidditch teams, comic books, and guides to dating. In some ways, these extra-curricular texts are even more demanding of, and rewarding for, their readers than the spell guides and transfiguration manuals the trio reference and memorize for their end of term exams.[1] Hopkins describes such extra-curricular books in the Potterverse as "dynamic and transformative" (2003, p. 29). Accurate though it is, this two-word description is meant to cover such diverse texts as Tom Riddle's diary-*cum*-Horcrux, the restricted spellbook *Moste Potente Potions*, and an advanced textbook on the magical properties of Mediterranean water flora. Surely these volumes, along with the many other books the trio encounters outside of the approved curriculum, are distinctive both in their dynamism and their capacity to change and develop their readers.

In "Cruel Heroes and Treacherous Texts: Educating the Reader in Moral Complexity and Critical Reading in J.K. Rowling's *Harry Potter* Books" (2003), Veronica Schanoes also addresses the centrality of books and reading in the series. She reads texts in the novels as Rowling's meta-commentary on the unreliability of the written word, and writers in particular. She claims that the way "official narratives, despite a pretense of accuracy, objectivity, and coherence, are revealed to be made of unreliable, arguable assumptions and manipulative misinterpretations" should cause the reader to be similarly suspicious of Rowling's own narratives, pointing towards the many instances when Rowling's plots might have led a reader to unfairly suspect Professor Snape, or unwisely trust the false Professor Moody (Schanoes, 2003, p. 138). Schanoes terms all published narratives in the series "treacherous texts" (2003, p. 143) and notes that "the *Harry Potter* books thus provide their reader with an education in the importance of alert, questioning reading" (2003, p. 142).

I agree with Hopkins and Schanoes that the series encourages critical reading, but not merely to secure knowledge necessary for survival, and not because all texts are uniformly deceitful. It seems unfair and unwise to treat Tom Riddle's diary, Professor Lockhart's fictionalized memoirs, the dangerously bewitched books in the restricted section of the Hogwarts library, and Harry's annotated copy of *Advanced Potion-Making* as if they all operate the same way, and have the same effect on heedless readers. The variety of extra-curricular textual worlds Harry, Ron, and Hermione encounter over the course of the seven books deserves more careful consideration. Rather than "treacherous," I call such difficult, demanding, and devious texts "subversive." These books undermine and overthrow assumptions about what books are and what they can do, and therefore complicate the traditional power dynamics of reading that situate a reader in a position of relative power over a text. By refusing to be "objective" accounts, these texts also challenge the conception of a book as an "object" that should (or can) be casually encountered and appropriated by readers, wizard and Muggle alike.

GoF (2000) introduces the magical designation of "unplottability"—the concealment of physical locations for their own and others' protection. This spell makes a place both there and not there, existing in an in-between space of language, but a concrete reality of experience. The spell's etymology connects a subversive place to a subversive text. Some books in the series are also "unplottable"—unable to be secured or stabilized in a traditional definition of narrative or genre, but available to be explored and assimilated by inquisitive witches and wizards. In order to "find" the value of these texts, Harry, Ron, and Hermione must become radical readers.

Subversive texts in the series expose the autonomy and power of textual worlds, demand a sensitive, brave, and engaged reader, and have the potential to seriously endanger a careless or compliant one. Harry, Ron, and Hermione are all guilty in different moments of the series of the latter type of passive reading, and all three suffer the consequences of underestimating subversive texts. In an opinion piece for the *New York Review of Books*, Tim Parks (2014) argues that passive reading is a form of submission to the written word that makes individuals improvidently compliant to the words (and worlds) they encounter. He charges, "we have too much respect for the printed word, too little awareness of the power words hold over us. We allow worlds to be conjured up for us with very little concern for the implications" ("Weapon"). Parks' language here resonates with an argument about modes of reading in a series about a wizarding school. He implies that without critical attentiveness, all books can become spellbooks, charming their enthralled readers into endorsing a certain perspective or version of events. Passive reading thus allows texts to become tyrannical monologues rather than spaces for constructive dialogue. Parks' solution equates critical reading with political activism, encouraging readers to engage in a constructive struggle with the writers they encounter if they are to grow not only as readers, but as human beings:

> But if writers are to entice us into their vision, let us make them work for it. Let us resist enchantment for a while, or at least for long enough to have some idea of what we are being drawn into. For the mindless, passive acceptance of other people's representations of the world can only enchain us and hamper our personal

growth, hamper the possibility of positive action.... Better to read a poor book with alert resistance, than devour a good one in mindless adoration [Parks, 2014, "Weapon"].

Parks endorses a model of reading that seeks to make visible, question, and undo the perception of books as cohesive and impervious artifacts, and the accompanying conception of writers as offering anything other than a worldview limited by their own perspective. Following Parks' politically charged language, I will call this active and engaged relationship to a text "radical reading," and explore the ways the failure to read radically places Harry, Ron, and Hermione in not just abstract, but also very real positions of submission to authors who seek domination not only in the world of the text but in the sociopolitical wizarding world as well.

Despite the persistent description of the Hogwarts librarian Madame Pince as a "vulture," books are not dead in the *Harry Potter* universe. In *CoS* (1998), and *HBP* (2005), Harry, Ron, and Hermione come upon texts that have the power not just to act upon, but interact *with* the readers who encounter them. Professor Lockhart's collected works, Tom Riddle's diary, and the marginalia of Professor Snape's Potions textbook are texts that are not only likely to be misunderstood, overlooked, or downright dangerous but in some cases *aim* to perplex and mislead their readers. These books are places, and they are not always hospitable ones. Harry, Ron, and Hermione must learn to treat these texts as spaces to be explored rather than objects to be consumed. In *DH* (2007), they are able to open up the subversive worlds of Albus Dumbledore's will, his unauthorized biography *The Life and Lies of Albus Dumbledore*, and his copy of *Tales of Beedle the Bard* as radical readers, and thereby unlock the capacity of these texts to aid them in their struggle against Lord Voldemort.

Part 1: "We're in the *Chamber of Secrets!*": A Book Is Not a Mirror

CoS (1998) is in part a meditation on the authorial production of books and the very real dangers of reading uncritically. The novel engages in several instances of wordplay, subtly signaling the subversive way books can intersect with the "real world," and the importance of encountering them with a wary and respectful eye. In the opening chapter of the novel, Dobby the House Elf warns Harry against returning to school because he knows of a "plot" to cause mischief and danger at Hogwarts (*CoS*, p. 16). And in fact, Lucius Malfoy indeed has a plan to reintroduce a piece of powerful dark magic, Tom Riddle's diary, into the Hogwarts environment. However, Dobby's words could also describe the "plot" of Rowling's novel itself—a story structure that uses the device of the diary to place Harry and the other students in danger. Similarly, Harry proclaims to Ginny Weasley at the book's climactic face-off with Tom Riddle: "We're in the *Chamber of Secrets*" (*CoS*, p. 309, italics Rowling's). They are indeed! The italic typeface that indicates the intensity of Harry's alarm also collapses the distinction between the space of the Chamber and the pages of the novel (italics being commonly used to denote book titles). This last clever turn of phrase points towards a Gaimanic understanding of books as spaces readers can inhabit. The plot, however, illustrates the way these textual spaces can be manipulated by their authors to mislead a too-trusting reader. *CoS* emphasizes the importance of learning to move within texts carefully and critically.

As authors, new Defense Against the Dark Arts Professor Gilderoy Lockhart and Tom Riddle[2] erase the line between personal writing and performance. The distinction between a writing self and the text that self produces is profoundly troubled by Lockhart's fictional memoirs and Riddle's misleading diary, to the extent that the more appropriate verb to describe their autobiographical writing process is "performing" rather than "relating" or "chronicling." And just like works of art, the texts they produce take on lives of their own. Lockhart and Riddle count on their readers *consuming* their texts unquestioningly, the way Harry's orally fixated cousin Dudley eats his enormous meals: quickly, and in one gulp. Both authors, for different, though similarly self-serving reasons, want their readers to consider their books as mirrors—material correlatives for and proof of a highly constructed and manipulative version of themselves.[3] In order to properly read Tom's diary, Harry must learn how *not* to read Lockhart's oeuvre. Harry's experience with both texts shows him the danger of assuming all books are honest narratives from trustworthy authors.

Professor Lockhart's syllabus is both a humorous manifestation of his vanity and an important marker in the novel for the gap between what nonfiction books promise and what they might deliver. Seven autobiographical memoirs authored by Lockhart comprise the textbook list for Defense Against the Dark Arts in Harry's second year. Because they are taught in a class, and because they are published, the books carry with them an imprimatur of reliability, an impression that Lockhart himself encourages actively and often. When establishing himself as an authority on dueling, the professor mentions his books as proof of his extensive history with the practice, noting the students should "see my published works" (*CoS*, p. 189) for detailed information about his purported adventures. He goes so far as to verbally and visually assert a one-to-one relationship between his books and his self on the first day of class, using the cover of one of his memoirs as a textual mirror. Using Neville Longbottom's textbook as a prop, he gestures towards the photograph of his winking face and emphasizes, "'Me' … pointing at it and winking as well" (*CoS*, p. 99). After Lockhart's alleged expertise in combating dark creatures is undercut by his inability to corral an impishly destructive but otherwise unthreatening horde of Cornish Pixies that he releases in his classroom (*CoS*, p. 102), his pedagogy becomes entirely performative. Lockhart retreats to the textual world he has created by planning lessons that consist of him reading aloud from his memoirs and at times reenacting the exploits recorded therein with Harry (*CoS*, p. 161).

It is Ron who first introduces the possibility of a phenomenological gap between nonfictional texts and the events they supposedly describe. In a squabble concerning Lockhart's ineptness, Hermione uses Lockhart's books as proof that, all evidence to the contrary, he must be a proficient wizard, snappishly reminding Ron that he's read Lockhart's work, and therefore knows about all the remarkable feats he's accomplished. Ron's cutting, if muted, response—"*says* he's done" (*CoS*, p. 103, emphasis Rowling's)—highlights the distance between writer and text that Lockhart's performances in class desperately endeavor to elide. The act of *saying* (or writing, which is afforded more authority because it is saying in print) creates the textual space for embellishment, obfuscation, or outright deception. By the end of the novel, both Lockhart and Riddle will be exposed for precisely these authorial offenses.

Lockhart explicates his fluid ethics of authorship and slippery definition of nonfiction when, in order to avoid helping Harry and Ron find the Chamber of Secrets and rescue Ron's sister Ginny, he reveals that he fabricated the nature of his role in the exploits his memoirs recount. Lockhart places the blame, though, not on his own mendacity but on the nature of texts themselves, explaining, "*Books* can be misleading" (*CoS*, p. 297, emphasis mine). Harry's protest that the confusion actually stems from Lockhart's claim to have authored the texts is not quite on the mark: Lockhart in fact has written the words that appear on the pages of his memoirs. The problem is, he framed the books as autobiography when they were really a mixture of performative fiction and reportage. Just as he acted out scenes from the books with Harry in class, when writing his books, he cast himself as the hero in real stories not his own in order to accumulate fame and wealth.

As if imparting knowledge on the only sort of subject he would actually be qualified to teach, public relations, Lockhart informs Harry that sales would have suffered if readers didn't assume the handsome author hadn't also been the heroic wizard (*CoS*, p. 297). Lisa Hopkins also concludes that Lockhart's robust sales are due to readers who hope to share in this manufactured aura of authenticity, noting that readers gain "access to something of the reflected glory of his glamorous image" (Hopkins, 2003, p. 29). This formulation reveals that trusting readers are similarly confounded when treating books as mirrors. Lockhart's books are more like theatres where Lockhart is always performing the starring role for an adoring and voyeuristic audience.

Lockhart's profoundly dishonest, though ultimately victimless, writing ethic is twinned in the novel with Tom Riddle's diary. Harry and his friends approach both texts as if they are like the other books they have encountered so far at Hogwarts: stable and reliable. When Hermione is speculating as to why someone tried to dispose of Riddle's diary where Harry and Ron found it, in the girls restroom, she assumes the person behind the attacks wouldn't want anyone else to discover the diary's valuable, and trustworthy, information.[4] She assumes the text would contain "everything" worth knowing about the Chamber—its location, its entrance, and its deadly inhabitant (*CoS*, p. 233). In fact, the diary isn't a manual for finding and defeating the Heir of Slytherin. It's another performance, like Lockhart's memoirs, designed to exploit and manipulate readers who expect books to be honest accounts from their authors.

The similarities between Riddle's diary and Lockhart's memoirs are numerous. Both are nonfictional texts that represent events that did actually happen, but do so though selective editing and misrepresentation of the authorial "hero" or "I" of the narrative. However, whereas Lockhart lied for personal financial gain and celebrity, Riddle created his diary to accumulate power at the expense of anyone who reads it. The diary (and the wizard who created it) consciously mimics the tropes of trustworthy texts (and authors) in order to communicate a misleading version of the past to readers, and in so doing, exploit and distort the relationship between reader and author so egregiously that the act of reading literally becomes a possession. The diary acts as both a time machine and interactive conversation with the author—this text makes metaphorical experiences that are possible through engaged reading magically and monstrously literal.

The diary gives readers the illusion that they are watching a moment from history, encouraging them to forget that they are only getting the perspective of the diarist.[5] The diary *becomes* a place its reader visits, but Tom is a highly selective tour guide. Harry describes the experience of "reading" an entry in the diary as a cross between watching a television program and attending a live theatrical performance. When he looks at a date in the diary, the page turns into a tiny live-action window that, when watched, immerses the reader completely in the sensory experiences of that day (*CoS*, p. 242). Once Harry is "in" the diary, he is able to see and hear the conversations and activities described by (and therefore, presumably, experienced by) Tom. Riddle's account of June thirteenth implicates Hagrid as the culprit behind the attacks on students at Hogwarts. His story is so convincing, and his personality is so engaging, that not only is Hagrid expelled from Hogwarts and his wand broken, Harry, one of Hagrid's dearest friends, also believes in his guilt (though Hagrid's caretaking of an Acromantula called Aragog doesn't help his case). Of course, Tom is covering for his own complicity in the attacks and death of a student; it was he who released and controlled the basilisk that resides within the Chamber of Secrets (*CoS*, pp. 311–312). The diary's capacity to produce a visual representation of events seduces readers, even more than in Lockhart's memoirs, into believing that the account that they're seeing, and the author they're communicating with, is trustworthy, and dissuades them from asking critical questions, or looking around blind corners.

In addition to providing highly edited and biased historical "recreations," the diary is a place that can not only epistemologically mislead but outright consume its readers. Confessional writing is a genre that historically encourages an emotional identification with the author.[6] Riddle's diary exploits that impulse by using a reader's empathy as an opening to insert his own consciousness and desires into a body capable of acting on them. Because Lord Voldemort's body was nearly annihilated by his failed attack on Harry, and then further compromised after being ejected from cohabiting in Professor Quirrell's skin at the conclusion of *SS*, he needs a physical body to further his plans to return to power. When Lucius Malfoy slips Riddle's diary into Ginny Weasley's stack of schoolbooks at the beginning of the term, he both acts as and provides Voldemort with that body. Unable to act upon others himself, Voldemort relies on his still-loyal Death Eaters to keep his influence alive. Once Malfoy passes on the diary, Ginny becomes Voldemort's thrall through the exploitation and perversion of an engaged reading relationship.

Rather than a model of conversation or mutual recognition, though, Riddle's diary ultimately enacts a model of occupation. Though Ginny thinks the diary is a sympathetic and portable confidante, who "*under-*

st[ands]" her, and who she grows to *"love" (CoS,* pp. 309–10, italics Rowling's)
through written communication with Tom, the version of himself Riddle
left behind in and as the diary only mimics human empathy, as it mimics
human conversation. What Tom really wants is an exchange not of ideas
or experiences or human emotion, but an *incorporation* of Ginny's body
and mind. As Tom explains to Harry:

> So Ginny poured out her soul to me, and her soul happened to be exactly what I
> wanted.... I grew stronger and stronger on a diet of her deepest fears, her darkest
> secrets. I grew powerful, far more powerful than little Miss Weasley. Powerful
> enough to start feeding Miss Weasley a few of *my* secrets, to start pouring a little
> of *my* soul back into *her* ... [*CoS,* p. 310, ellipses Rowling's].

By the time Harry finds Ginny in the Chamber, she and Tom are one body
living within the confines of the diary.[7] According to Tom, he is *eating*
Ginny's soul through communicating with her through writing. The "diet"
of her inner self makes his textual body more vigorous, until it has the control to "feed" Ginny his own dark desires and demands—the diary has
become her entire reality. Ginny performs physical actions Tom cannot
(vandalizing the school, slaughtering roosters) at his written command
(*CoS,* pp. 310–311). Tom is able to achieve independent physical form by
the end of the novel because he has drained Ginny of any physical or psy-
chic agency. His embodied apparition is killed by stabbing the "heart" of
the *diary* with a basilisk fang, causing the book to bleed ink until Riddle
disappears (*CoS,* p. 322). The unusual destruction of the diary illustrates
how this extra-curricular text subverts understanding a book as an object.
Though it bleeds, it is not a human body, but it is not exactly a book, either.
This ontological slipperiness is addressed in *HBP,* when Dumbledore
informs Harry that the diary was a Horcrux: a space created (in an object
or a being) by dark magic in which a wizard can hide a piece of his or her
soul (*HBP,* p. 500).

Arthur Weasley has the final cautionary word on Riddle's diary in
CoS when he upbraids his daughter for confiding in a subversive text,
reminding her to avoid trusting in or sympathizing with any sentient object
"if you can't see where it keeps its brain" (CoS, p. 329, emphasis Rowling's).
Mr. Weasley points out an important distinction between Riddle's diary
and Lockhart's memoirs—most books witches and wizards encounter in
their reading lives will not engage them in intelligent conversation. However, that doesn't mean they are safe, reliable, or passive objects. *HBP* (2005)
illustrates the way that the most sanctioned and authoritative books—textbooks—can also be claimed and made subversive.

Part 2: A Book Is Not a Magic Wand

HBP introduces Harry, Ron, and Hermione to a text that does not lie or manipulate, but nonetheless destabilizes their understanding of the relationship between book and reader. Due to late registration, Harry acquires a used textbook for his Advanced Potions course. He soon discovers the text's margins are covered, "graffitied" (p. 220), in Hermione's words, with notes from the mysteriously monikered former owner, the Half-Blood Prince. The additions to the approved spells quickly make Harry top Potions student, and provoke a furious and terrified response from Ginny, who is shocked that he would follow the instructions of a book that appears to be speaking just four years after she nearly died from doing the same with Riddle's diary (*HBP*, p. 192). Harry reassures her by pointing out the differences between his textbook and Riddle's diary, namely that this book doesn't talk back. It looks like an object, and Harry treats it as such. He is right to articulate the distinction between an annotated textbook and a bewitched diary mimicking human consciousness, but wrong to assume that because *Advanced Potion-Making* is a textbook rather than an enchanted diary, it is benign and trustworthy. The trio's attempts to solve the mystery of the marginalia's author reveals the limitations of a model of reading that objectifies, and therefore subordinates, books and their authors.

Prior to *HBP*, both approved and restricted textbooks share a similar use value and stability for the students who encounter them. The approved textbooks, as well as the canonical volumes that are not assigned for particular courses but are housed in the school library, are reliable sources of dependable information. For example, in *SS*, Ron assumes that the secret to outsmarting Fluffy the three-headed dog can be found in a book (*SS*, p. 180). Similarly, in *CoS* when the attacks begin, Hermione, along with a number of the other students, go straight to *Hogwarts, A History* because, as Hermione explains, everyone wants to acquire information about the Chamber (*CoS*, p. 148). The students understand books to be containers of information, needing only to be opened and read for their contents to be revealed and used.

Much like these readily available and approved volumes, the books found in the restricted section of the Hogwarts library might be dangerous, but they are nonetheless reliable in content. These books are quarantined in a strictly policed area of the library because reading them carelessly is risky for a wizard or witch's personal health and well-being, but not because they contain inaccurate information. Ron describes some of the menacing possibilities of reading books from the restricted section while the trio are considering stealing a book from its number in order to brew the highly volatile Polyjuice Potion in *CoS*, noting that the books therein might "burn your eyes out," make you speak in poetry, or literalize the cliché of a book you can't put down by compelling its reader to hold it open for the rest of his or her life (*CoS*, pp. 230–231). Though these books have demonstrable (and deleterious) effects on the humans who read them, there is nothing to suggest that their content is untrustworthy. In fact, *Moste Potente Potions*, the book Harry, Ron, and Hermione do decide to pilfer from the restricted section (*CoS*, p. 160), proves itself a good resource: the Polyjuice Potion Hermione brews by following the recipe contained therein is a success.

The Half-Blood Prince's *Advanced Potion-Making* textbook resists categorization as either an approved or restricted textbook, and challenges the foundational assumption that textbooks are neutral containers of information to be used by the reader. Though the book itself is part of the approved curriculum, the Half-Blood Prince transforms the text into something else entirely through his marginalia. This extra-textual space contains extra-curricular shortcuts and spells that subvert the "official" method of potion-making (*HBP*, p. 194). The Prince's notes augment, edit, and defiantly overwrite the recipes for the spells the text contains. As Harry realizes while engaging in the unprecedented activity of reading a schoolbook for fun, with the notes, his copy "hardly qualified as a textbook" (*HBP*, p. 237) at all. Harry, Ron, and Hermione wrestle with the ontology of the Prince's copy of *Advanced Potion-Making* throughout *HBP*, and in so doing learn that information itself is a space to explore, not a tool to master.

Hermione, the most academically inclined of the trio, shows the strongest inclination to apply a previous lesson to a new but similar situation. She learned in *CoS* that nonfiction books can be misleading, and authors might write for nefarious ends. Showing no willingness to be fooled again, she tries to "read" the character of the Prince through his notes. Her conclusions are damning. She proclaims him "a bit dodgy" (*HBP*, p. 240), and "not a very nice person" (*HBP*, p. 241). In another interpretive move that suggests Hermione considers *Advanced Potion-Making* to be on par with Riddle's diary, she begins to conflate the text with the body of the Prince, at one point giving the book "a nasty look as though it had been rude to her" (*HBP*, p. 305). Though Hermione is right to look at the spells the Prince creates in order to understand his personality and perhaps reveal his identity, she has no interest in exploring the book once she deems it unsuitable. Her unwillingness to enter the world of the Prince not only limits her capacity to understand the subtleties of his character, but also denies the very real advantages of his perspective on spell-making.

Ron and Harry, on the other hand, enjoy the benefits of the Prince's potion-making shortcuts and original curses far too much to discard or report the book, as Ginny and Hermione would prefer. Rather than viewing it as malevolent or dangerous, the boys consider the marginalia not only harmless but also fully available for appropriation: the book almost becomes an extension of Harry himself. Ron goes so far as to refer to Harry as the "Potions Prince" (*HBP*, p. 373), and Harry in turn begins to rely on the book to solve problems that have nothing to do with Potions class—for example, he instinctively turns to it as a resource for convincing Professor Slughorn to share a memory of Voldemort with him (*HBP*, p. 448).[8] This attitude is the logical extension of a reading philosophy that considers informational texts to be containers or all-purpose tools meant to enhance a witch or wizard, and blunt ones at that. The book's material is freely taken out of context with the assumption that it *must* exist only to aid the wizard reading it, in this case Harry. However, a book of magic is not a magic wand. Instrumentalizing a text in this way denies it its history, context, and purpose. In appropriating the Half-Blood Prince's writing for his own ends, Harry denies the book its autonomy, and consequently misunderstands and misapplies its contents.

Harry's appropriation of the Prince's marginalia not only gives him a reputation for mastery in Advanced Potions that he does not deserve, but also causes him to grievously injure and nearly kill Draco. In his extracurricular reading of *Advanced Potion-Making*, Harry comes across *Sectumsempra* in the marginalia, a spell designed and designated "For Enemies." He commits the curse to memory, intending to use it against a student who has been lately annoying him (*HBP*, p. 518). For Harry, the connotation of the word "enemy" remains largely limited to adolescent conflicts, and his imagination for "punishment" is similarly narrow and benign.[9] Harry ends up performing the spell in an impromptu duel with Draco, assuming it to be on par with the standard hexes and jinxes students use to torment each other in the halls of Hogwarts. However, when Malfoy begins bleeding uncontrollably and has to be saved by Snape, Harry realizes his mistake: his idea of what "enemies" deserve is dreadfully and dangerously different from the Prince's.

Harry has failed to consider that the Prince's text has a purpose and context separate from his own, and does not exist solely to improve his magical prowess. This negligence nearly makes him a murderer. In the aftermath of his attack on Draco, he is shocked, "as though a beloved pet had turned suddenly savage" (*HBP*, p. 525). The problem is, books are not companions, trained to serve the will and pleasure of their human masters.[10] Harry treats the notes not as a location for exploration and understanding, but like an animal subservient to his will. He berates himself for being "taken in" by the way the marginalia, and the author behind it, had "been so clever, had helped him so much" (*HBP*, p. 638). If he had more carefully considered the spells, notes, and addendums as a cohesive and coherent ecosystem, he would have seen that there was nothing "sudden" about their savagery.

The spells created by the Prince have three things in common: they are innovative, they are unauthorized, and they aim to establish dominance over another person. Even excluding the particularly wicked and injurious curse *Sectumsempra*, the Prince's spells are meant to impede another wizard's agency. The Prince's original hexes include causing toenails to grow too fast, preventing an enemy from walking; gluing the tongue to the roof of the mouth, which prevents someone from talking; and the spell most employed by Harry to Hermione's chagrin, the *Muffliato* spell that creates white noise to all surrounding the spell casters (*HBP*, p. 238), preventing others, including teachers, from hearing privileged conversations. "Levi-corpus," a spell that Harry sees his father employing through Snape's memory (*OotP*, p. 647), lifts a witch or wizard bodily and hangs them from the air by the ankle, helplessly displaying them to danger and ridicule. None of these spells is fatal, but they are designed to reduce a walking, speaking, perceiving person to a more easily managed and sensually deprived object. Similarly, the Prince's marginalia itself has the tendency to talk over and stifle the official spells, marking out ingredients, contradicting instructions (*HBP*, p. 189), and overwriting a list of antidotes with the aggressive scrawl "just shove a bezoar down their throats" (*HBP*, p. 377). Even the Prince's advice for healing is tinged with aggression and detachment. If any of the three friends had noted the subtleties of the spells rather than just their naughtiness and effectiveness, they might have realized that they are the magically manifested revenge fantasies of a victim of bullying capable of far more than idle mischief.

The Half-Blood Prince's moniker reveals the conflicted personality of the marginalia's author, as well as the complicated and paradoxical function of *Advanced Potion-Making* in the novel. Severus Snape reveals himself to be the author of the annotations in a furious stand-off with Harry after Snape has killed Dumbledore and is fleeing the Hogwarts grounds with a group of Death Eaters (*HBP*, p. 604).[11] Snape is a half-blood wizard, with a Muggle father and witch mother, Eileen Prince, with whom he primarily identifies. The "Half-Blood Prince" contains both the adolescent Snape's self-loathing and aspirations to grandeur—he is a marginalized person, and he uses the margins of his Potions book to promote and track his advancement in the wizarding world. He lacks the full-blood pedigree prized by other Slytherins, but he knows himself to be talented enough to join the wizarding meritocracy nonetheless. Snape himself is a confoundingly contradictory character, and a difficult and damaged man. He is one of the few wizards in the text who is forced to recognize, and atone for, the impulses within himself that made him embrace Dark Magic.[12] He is defined in equal parts by love for Lily Potter and melancholic mourning for both her loss and *his* loss of her love to James.[13] This pain leads him to acts of great heroism, though always tinged with an unwarranted disgust for Harry and other members of the Order of the Phoenix. Similarly, though the annotations reveal a wizard who delights in the pain of enemies, the book is not pure treachery, further distinguishing it from Riddle's diary. Its annotations save Ron's life from poisoning, and lead Harry to win a vial of Felix Felicis, which later proves invaluable in capturing Slughorn's crucial memory. The Half-Blood Prince's copy of *Advanced Potion-Making* is a psychobiographical document as well as an informative text, and reading it carefully, and radically, would reveal much about the older wizard and Dumbledore's trust in him that would have greatly helped Harry, Ron, and Hermione understand the events at Hogwarts in the series' final volume.

However, this deep and radical reading does not occur. After Snape's presumed execution of Dumbledore, the subsequent rise of Voldemort, and the fall of Hogwarts (along with the other primary civic institutions in the wizarding world) at the end of *HBP* and the beginning of *DH*, Harry, Ron, and Hermione have, to quote Dumbledore "enough responsibility to be going on with" (*OotP*, p. 844) with their charge to destroy the remaining Horcruxes and fulfill Harry's prophecy that he must duel to the death with the Dark Wizard. Snape's copy of *Advanced Potion-Making* drops out of the series, perhaps due to Harry's disgust at being so close to a book partially authored by a man he feels sure is an enemy. Nevertheless, the ability to situate a book in its appropriate context, and to read with a radical understanding of how texts operate as worlds of their own responsive to and within the world of the reader, will literally and figuratively unlock the answer to Voldemort's defeat in *DH*.

Part 3: A Reader Is a Seeker

The seventh and final novel of the series is largely concerned with the decisive battle with and defeat of Lord Voldemort through the destruction of his remaining material Horcruxes, and Harry's sacrifice of his body (the seventh Horcrux). Even this entirely extra-curricular plot is and has been connected to the concept of radical reading. Tom Riddle's above-quoted description of his possession of Ginny is a synecdochal enactment of Lord Voldemort's modus operandi (*CoS*, p. 310). For him, power results from consumption and incorporation. If the other has been ingested and integrated into Voldemort's mind and body, resistance is not only futile, but unthinkable. The connection between ethical reading and resistance becomes even more urgent in the fifth book of the series, *OotP* (2003). Tom's creation of a self-serving reality is intensified and refined by Voldemort's capacity for predatory "Legilimency": the ability to gain access to another's mind and not only uncover the victim's thoughts and emotions, but also to implant visions. Essentially, Voldemort is able to "manipulate and misdirect" Harry's perception of events without the aid of the diary (*OotP*, p. 827). Harry's susceptibility to this assault leads to an ill-fated attack on the Ministry, and Sirius Black's death (*OotP*, pp. 781–806). The word's etymology, as with most of Rowling's spells, comes from an evocative root: legere, to read. Voldemort is, of course, reading Harry's mind, but Harry is also "reading" the visions, and in the case of the vision of Sirius being tortured that spurs him to invade the Ministry, reading them badly. The necessity of radical reading only intensifies as Voldemort's power grows.

In *DH*, Harry, Ron, and Hermione are faced with three subversive texts, each resisting the stable definition of what a text should be and do, and each requiring exploration and interpretation to provide meaning. The Last Will and Testament of Albus Percival Wulfric Brian Dumbledore, *The Life and Lies of Albus Dumbledore*, and *The Tales of Beedle the Bard* are neither windows nor magic wands, though they in different ways appear to be. Harry, Ron, and Hermione must apply what they've learned in previous books in order to engage with these texts as radical readers. The stakes are not only to achieve understanding of themselves and others, but quite literally to save the wizarding world.

An early chapter of *DH* contains a dramatic and confrontational reading of Albus Dumbledore's will by Minister of Magic Rufus Scrimgeour to Harry, Ron, and Hermione (*DH*, pp. 123–129). The Minister had hoped the document would provide useful information in the fight against Voldemort, and had kept the text, and the bequeathed items, confiscated in order to discover the significance and possible application of the items Dumbledore left to the three friends. Unsurprisingly, Scrimgeour is unable to decipher the purpose and import of the document because he is an aggressive and suspicious reader. His approach objectifies the text by assuming it's a puzzle to be unlocked or a tool to be instrumentalized when in reality it is Dumbledore's last lesson to the three students. Because the headmaster's pedagogy is based in respectful and empathic give and take, the will is neither a set of instructions nor an enchanted weapon, but rather a map that provides emotional and introspective guideposts for the three as they attempt to locate Voldemort's remaining Horcruxes.

The will is a particularly subversive text as it cannot be understood, either epistemologically or ontologically, as solely consisting of words on parchment. The document points towards, and therefore hermeneutically includes, material objects, which in turn refer back to the will. For example, Dumbledore leaves Ron his personal Deluminator, "*in the hope that he will remember me when he uses it*" (*DH*, p. 125, italics Rowling's). The relationship between the object and the proviso only becomes clear through Ron's own experience during the trio's harrowing search for Horcruxes. The device's capacity to extinguish and contain light sources has an undeniable use value in the fight against Death Eaters, providing the three with an edge against Dolohov and Rowle when they are ambushed in a café soon after escaping the Burrow (*DH*, p. 166), and assisting in Harry and Ron's escape from the dungeons of Malfoy Manor (*DH*, p. 467). More important, though, is its capacity to return Ron to Harry and Hermione after frustration and jealousy prompts him to abandon the two while on the run from Voldemort's thugs. The Deluminator allows Ron to hear Harry and Hermione when they speak his name, and it proves able to reverse its function by providing a trail of light for him to follow back to his friends. This faculty produces a radical and collaborative reading from Harry and Ron of Dumbledore's proviso. Ron glumly offers the interpretation that Dumbledore predicted he would desert his friends, and Harry counters and completes his analysis by adding that he also knew he would always come back. To understand how this interpretation works, how Ron's arc fulfills Dumbledore's wish to "remember" him, it's necessary to employ a radical reading of another text: Rita Skeeter's unauthorized biography, *The Life and Lies of Albus Dumbledore*.

Harry's first impression of the book upon spotting it in Dolores Umbridge's office reveals both its irresistible appeal and its subversive potential. Harry is stopped in his tracks when in his periphery he sees "Dumbledore was staring at him from a small rectangular mirror" on Umbridge's bookcase (p. 252). What Harry actually sees is Dumbledore's face on the cover of a copy of *The Life and Lies of Albus Dumbledore*.[14] This momentary misapprehension is a neat encapsulation of how the text promises to provide (but actually distorts) an authentic portrait of Dumbledore, and how Harry initially, but completely, falls for it. He is seduced by the book's promise to hold Dumbledore steady within its covers, to objectify and expose him for Harry's perusal. After Dumbledore's death, Harry bemoans and regrets the many lost opportunities he had to learn more about his mentor's own boy- and young-adulthood and harbors anger and disappointment towards his mentor for not sharing more of his inner life with Harry. Skeeter's unauthorized biography, with its exclusive interviews and archival photographs, proves irresistible, despite Harry's firsthand knowledge of her tendency for salacious and melodramatic embellishments of fact, enabled by the Qwik Quotes Quill and her own appetite for the wizarding equivalent of clickbait content.[15] Hermione is able to secure Bathilda's copy from her home (*DH*, p. 352), and, demonstrating an insatiable and ruthless appetite for information, Harry devours it while in hiding. Though he has learned from Lockhart's performative faux-memoirs and Riddle's carnivorous diary that personal narratives can creatively frame, edit, and overwrite the truth, Skeeter's use of historical documents provides a story about Dumbledore's youth that initially captivates, confuses, and crushes Harry.

As earlier experiences with subversive texts have revealed, such a predatory and careless approach to reading is counterproductive at best, and dangerous at worst. The "savage pleasure" Harry experiences at possessing the volume stems from his belief that owning the book will be like owning the man: providing a window into Dumbledore's inner self and revealing information Dumbledore thought was unimportant to share with Harry, "whether Dumbledore wanted him to or not" (*DH*, p. 352). This desire not just to *know* Dumbledore but to master him is the same model of reading demonstrated by Scrimgeour, and produces the same results. He learns facts about the headmaster's early life while reading the biography in this way, but misses the depth of Dumbledore's motivations and the value of his experience.

Life and Lies subverts the principles of biographical writing by beginning with a preconceived purpose—to dismantle and diminish Dumbledore's reputation as an exemplary wizard and human being—and shaping facts into a narrative to support that story. Skeeter reveals Dumbledore's friendship with Gellert Grindelwald in their boyhood, and his flirtation with the proto-fascistic philosophy endorsing the superiority of wizards over Muggles that Grindelwald would later embrace and Voldemort would institutionalize (*DH*, p. 353). Harry, reading voraciously, suspiciously, and "savagely," feels infuriated and betrayed. He dismisses Ron and Hermione's appeal to Dumbledore's youth, pointing out that the three of them are also young, and have consistently rejected and defied Dark magic. However, a radical reading of this subversive text not only provides Harry with crucial information to continue his quest for Horcruxes, but also tells a very different story about Albus Dumbledore than its author intended.

However, *Life and Lies* is a subversive text not only because it purports to objectively relate the story of a life and instead manufactures scandal, but also because the autobiography itself refuses to reliably communicate its author's purpose. Rita Skeeter wanted to create a book that would devalue and denigrate Dumbledore, and used the textual trappings of truth—photographs and first-person accounts—to substantiate her story. What Rita could never have foreseen is that these documents ironically lead Harry, Ron, and Hermione to a deeper truth about their headmaster and friend through the very documentation meant to destroy him. Much like his will, Dumbledore's biography is valuable both as a material object and a multivalenced narrative, and requires radical reading. In terms of plot, Harry is able to recognize the young blonde thief appearing in his shared visions with Voldemort through a caption in the book (*DH*, p. 353). Identifying Grindelwald provides an invaluable clue in demystifying Voldemort's plan and the importance of the Elder Wand, which ultimately redeems Dumbledore. However, the narrative Rita provides of Dumbledore's intense friendship and disastrous falling out with Grindelwald is what makes the autobiography truly subversive.

The eighteenth chapter of *DH* is entitled *The Life and Lies of Albus Dumbledore*, and within it, Rowling inserts Skeeter's complete chapter from her book recounting the initial exuberance and ultimate violent end of Dumbledore and Grindelwald's friendship (*DH*, pp. 353–359). For all intents and purposes, the reader of *DH* is now also the reader of *Life and Lies*, holding the same book in his or her hands as Harry and Hermione, and able to draw his or her own conclusions about the events described. Skeeter's account relates a few indisputable facts: In Dumbledore's youthful arrogance, he made an error of interpretation breathtaking in its depth and breadth by embracing a philosophy that hierarchizes Muggles below wizards. By welcoming Grindelwald and his ideas into his life, he precipitated the death of his sister and estrangement from his brother. These incidents happened, and Skeeter uses them as evidence for her character assassination. An engaged and empathic reader might not stop at Dumbledore's mistake, though, as Harry initially does. The regret and heartbreak Dumbledore must have carried with him is unspeakable and unwriteable, at least in Skeeter's salacious and mean-spirited account of the episode. However, as Hermione realizes, by and through including this story, Skeeter unintentionally implies its redemptive end—Dumbledore "changed" (*DH*, p. 361) by dedicating his life to eradicating not only Dark Magic but injustice and ignorance in any form, perfectly encapsulated in choosing a career not as Minister of Magic, but Hogwarts teacher and later headmaster. This radical reading of the biography reveals not just the error, but also the atonement.

Life and Lies provides the context to show that when Ron used his Deluminator to rectify his mistake and return to his friends, he was truly an embodied remembrance of Dumbledore, just as the will requested. The biography similarly subverts the intent of its author in relation to Hermione's bequest. Putting a text in historical and emotional context is also what is required to understand Dumbledore's gift to Hermione: his copy of *Tales of Beedle the Bard*, with the hopes that she will find it "*entertaining and instructive*" (*DH*, p. 126, italics Rowling's). As the *Tales* are a collection of well-known wizarding fables and children's stories, Scrimgeour, as well as the rest of the trio, are unable at first to imagine how it could be either. However, Hermione, and eventually a community of readers, offer a radical reading of one of the stories that helps to ensure the defeat of Voldemort.

Dumbledore's copy of *Tales* is a subversive text not only because it requires its readers to take seriously a genre that is traditionally undervalued and marginalized,[16] but also because its meaning depends on its particularity—its unique position as a text that has been read by a specific person. Much like Snape's copy of *Advanced Potions-Making*, Dumbledore's book becomes a place to explore his intentions through marginalia. Hermione discovers a hand-drawn symbol above one of the story's titles (*DH*, p. 316) that she cannot translate. Harry recognizes the image as one their friend's father Xenophilus Lovegood wore, and which Viktor Krum identified as a symbol of dark magic. Hermione, again applying a previous experience with reading to a new situation, takes care to contextualize the annotation. Though Krum reads the symbol as an unambiguous and static symbol of Dark Magic, Hermione explores the communication between the note and the text, commenting, "if it's a symbol of Dark Magic, what's it doing in a book of children's stories?" (*DH*, p. 317). This question will lead Harry and Hermione first to Godric's Hollow, and then, joined by Ron, to the home of Lovegood, where *DH* enacts a truly radical model of collaborative meaning-making through reading.

Once the three arrive at the Lovegood home, Xenophilus encourages Hermione to read the annotated story aloud, as it is "much the best way to make sure we all understand" (*DH*, p. 406). Though Mr. Lovegood has his own definite interpretation of the story, his suggestion nevertheless opens up the text to the type of reading that is neither reductive nor compliant, but rather responsive to the text's capacity to entertain and inform its readers. The whole of the fable is reproduced in the twenty-first chapter of *DH* which, similar to *Life and Lies* in chapter eighteen, gets its title from the text it includes: "The Tale of the Three Brothers." As Hermione reads aloud, the italicized text of the tale is consistently and persistently "annotated" by the listeners. From Ron's correction of "twilight" to "midnight" (*DH*, p. 406), to Harry's recognition of Death's Invisibility Cloak (*DH*, p. 408), to Hermione's identification of the fantastical genre of the tale (*DH*, p. 409), the three inhabit the world of the story on its own terms while also bringing their individual perspectives to its narrative and meaning. Whereas Snape's annotations aggressively confront and overwrite the text that inspires them, reflecting his personal desire to trump and replace any voice that casts him as inferior, the commentary offered by Harry, Ron, and Hermione enrich the fable and make it personally and collectively relevant.

In contrast, Xenophilus demonstrates a mode of reading that diminishes and objectifies the text. After Hermione finishes the tale, he explains that the three objects Death bestows upon the brothers are known as the "Deathly Hallows" which gives the owner the power to overcome Death. When Hermione questions why the term doesn't appear in the text itself, Xenophilus's "maddeningly smug" response reveals his marginalization and misconception of the tale. He scoffs, "That is a children's tale, told to amuse rather than to instruct," and "those of us who understand these matters" have arrived at the correct interpretation (*DH*, pp. 409–410). Mr. Lovegood's belittlement of the story forecloses his ability to fully appreciate its emotional and social resonance. Dumbledore's will identifies a dual purpose for his text—entertainment *and* instruction. By dismissing the former, Xenophilus cannot fully apprehend the latter. The point of the story is not to "master" death, as he believes, but rather to accept it "as an old friend" (*DH*, p. 409) or, as Dumbledore believes, "the next great adventure" (*SS*, p. 297).

For Harry, Ron, and Hermione, this collaborative radical reading does not result in the reduction and objectification of the text to a simplistic riddle, or even as a tool in their fight against Voldemort. "The Tale of the Three Brothers" becomes a lens through which they organize and articulate their priorities in their quest to defeat the dark wizard, and how they view themselves. Hermione reveals the text's capacity for multiple meanings when she asserts that the superior gift from Death is "obvious" (*DH*, p. 414) and immediately (and humorously) all three friends simultaneously select a different object. Hermione chooses the Cloak, a practical tool that provides time for the contemplation and study that she regularly uses to benefit the group. Ron's choice, the unbeatable wand, reflects his propensity for action, and his drive to distinguish himself in relation to his brothers and famous best friend. Harry selects the stone, explaining that with the power to bring people back from the dead, the three could benefit from the great wizards, and beloved friends and family, lost to the battle against Voldemort (*DH*, p. 416). Harry's inclination to read the story as offering a way to establish and secure community is indicative of his impulses throughout the series, and points towards a metaphor for reading that is liberating for both text and reader.

Much as Quidditch players use their minds and bodies to find the Golden Snitch, radical readers must demonstrate a willingness to move throughout the playing field of a text in order to capture meaning. Harry Potter, the youngest Seeker in a century (*SS*, p. 152), finally demonstrates his ability to do just that with his reading of Dumbledore's bequest to him. Throughout *DH*, Harry has been obsessed with making his reading of *Life and Lies* and "Tales of the Three Brothers" "fit" perfectly into the situation in which he finds himself (*DH*, p. 429). However, this denies each text its own autonomy—neither the libelous biography nor the fairy tale can or should seamlessly slide into Harry's own narrative. Instead, he must search for and snatch the pieces from each that allow him to understand his relationships and responsibilities. Dumbledore leaves Harry the Snitch he secured in his first Quidditch match at school, "*as a reminder of the rewards of perseverance and skill*" (*DH*, p. 126, italics Rowling's). Frequently throughout the novel, Harry attempts to open the Snitch, knowing it contains sense memory, and can only be controlled by the player who caught it. He is unsuccessful until he understands the actual "rewards" of practice and accomplishment through a radical reading of its inscription: "*I open at the close*" (*DH*, p. 698). It is his imminent close, his willingness to die, that wins Harry the true prize of all his achievements: the presence and support of his dearest family and friends who have been lost. The stone, secured inside Harry's Snitch, falls away, ironically suggesting that the rewards of the Seeker are not nearly as precious as the relationships forged in the process of looking.

This willingness and capacity to surrender the prize and privilege emotional connection allows Harry to defeat Voldemort through sacrificing himself. It is a distinction that Dumbledore explicitly ties to reading when he speaks with Harry in an unplottable space between life and death. In this place, which Harry shapes as Platform 9¾, Dumbledore fervently explains what the dark wizard is incapable of "comprehending": "Of house-elves and children's tales, of love, loyalty, and innocence, Voldemort knows and understands nothing. *Nothing*" (*DH*, p. 709). Perhaps the vocabulary of magic is, ultimately, not adequate for understanding radical reading. Perhaps the best way to talk about how to read is to talk about how to love. In Dumbledore's diagnosis of Voldemort's weakness, he equates the ability to understand and love a being ontologically different from oneself, the willingness to open oneself to affection towards another creature, and *reading*. According to Dumbledore, radical reading is on some level the same skill as loving, with the same power to both challenge and shore up the self, to both recognize and embrace the other, and to overwhelm and disarm evil, "a power beyond the reach of any magic" (*DH*, p. 710).

Notes

1. The first novel in the series, *SS* (1997), previews the importance extra-curricular texts have for the rest of the series in its opening chapters. One of the novel's central mysteries is the identity of Nicolas Flamel, a wizard accidentally mentioned by Hagrid as connected with the titular stone (*SS*, p. 193). Despite Hermione's best efforts, she is unable to find his name in any of the library's encyclopedias and histories. He *does*, however, appear in a decidedly non-academic text: Albus Dumbledore's Chocolate Frog card, which Harry first encountered in chapter six (*SS*, pp. 102–103).

2. Because Lord Voldemort had yet to assume his anagrammatical and ominous moniker at the time he was producing his diary, I will refer to him as Tom Riddle throughout this section.

3. This impulse recalls the "Mirror of Erised" from the first book in the series. In the Room of Requirement, Harry encounters a mirror that magically reflects whatever the subject standing in front of it most wants to attain in life (*SS*, pp. 207–209). Both Lockhart and Riddle treat their manuscripts this way—as reflections of their lives as they *want* others to see them. However, just as the mirror is framed—cut off from reality—the borders of the books exclude much that would complicate and even contradict the textual world each writer creates.

4. Hermione, especially in the early volumes of the series, is often this type of reader—one who assumes books will contain reliable information for her later use to impress teachers and succeed at school, so consumes them wholesale. For example, she answers a question from Professor Sprout about mandrakes "sounding as usual as though she had swallowed the textbook" (*CoS*, p. 92).

5. Experientially, reading the diary is similar to what Harry will experience entering Dumbledore's Pensieve, the first of which occurs in book 4 (2000) when he witnesses the trials of several Death Eaters (pp. 582–596). The crucial difference is the Penseive replicates an individual's sensory perceptions, whereas the diary is written, and can therefore be manipulated.

6. For example, see the intense following generated by the personal revelations of Sylvia Plath's poetry, Francesca Woodman's photographs, or Marina Abramović's performance art.

7. This relationship, symbiotic at best and parasitic at worst, is a perverse literalization of the theory of authorship that understands a book to be a manifestation of the author's mind. In opposition to postmodern theories of textuality that insist on a book's life outside the author, here, the author has no life outside the book.

8. As I will later discuss, the book *does* prove invaluable in completing this task, but not through providing simple instructions for Harry to follow.

9. Interestingly, Harry does not immediately think of Lord Voldemort when encountering a spell for "enemies." At this point in the series, Hogwarts is still the somewhat sheltered sphere that organizes his relationships. However, even when Harry drops out of school and enters into the battle with Voldemort and his followers in the wider wizarding world, he still demonstrates an aversion to spells that maim or kill. His tendency to first disarm his opponents through the *"Expelliarmus"* spell rather than aim to injure them becomes a trademark that both identifies him to Death Eaters (*DH*, p. 70) and is the spell that defeats Voldemort in their final battle (*DH*, p. 743).

10. As many scholars in the field of animal studies and posthumanism would argue, we shouldn't conceive of pets this way either: see Yi-Fu Tuan's *Dominance and Affection* and Donna Haraway's *When Species Meet*. The series itself also actively undermines this retrograde assumption of the subservience of companion animals through its attention to and respect of the autonomy and agency of Fawkes, Hedwig, Crookshanks, Fang, Norbert, and Aragog, to say nothing of the subversive potential of Animagii, particularly Scabbers and Snuffles/Padfoot.

11. In fact, the book is so intimately connected with both Snape's painful personal history and his remarkable development as a supremely gifted wizard it's surprising he allowed it to be stored in the Potions classroom cabinet at all. Unlike Riddle's diary, the schoolbook and its annotations are not meant to be publicly distributed. One theory holds that he must have left the book behind in the shuffle of changing classrooms after he was appointed Defense Against the Dark Arts professor ("Severus Snape's copy," n.d.), though this seems unlikely from such a precise and careful man. Perhaps the best explanation is that the annotated copy of *Advanced Potion-Making* has agency separate from its author.

12. This is an existential moment Harry flirts with, though never has to fully face. His nearly uncontrollable anger and hatred are persistently referenced in both *OotP* and *HBP*, however these unsavory emotions are linked to his magically forged connection to Voldemort, not to his own capacity for wickedness.

13. Snape's insistence on wearing black robes and his Patronus, "always" (*DH*, p. 687) Lily's doe, reveals that he has refused to emotionally work through and move forward from her death.

14. As evidenced by the scandalous title, Rita Skeeter has not abandoned the preference for high readership over accuracy in reporting that she demonstrated in *GoF*. However, with the promise of extensive interviews with longtime friend of the Dumbledore family (and highly respected historian) Bathilda Bagshot, Skeeter's book is reliable enough to garner mainstream wizarding media coverage, and the understandable interest of Harry.

15. During Skeeter's "interview" with Harry in *GoF*, he watches in horror as his answers to her leading questions are transformed from bewildered non-responses to deeply emotional and revelatory textual confessions by the Quill (*GoF*, pp. 304–306).

16. For examples of literary critics undervaluing and marginalizing the Harry Potter series itself because it is marketed for young adults, see Harold Bloom (2003) and Anthony Holden (2000) among, unfortunately, many others.

References

Anatol, G.L. (2003). Introduction. In G.L. Anatol, ed., *Reading Harry Potter* (pp. ix–xxv). Westport, CT: Praeger Publishers.

Bloom, H. (2003, September 24). "Dumbing down American readers." *Boston Globe.* Retrieved from http://www.boston.com/news/globe.

Gaiman, N., & Holdengräber, P. (2014, October 31). *Live from the NYPL.* Podcast retrieved from http://www.nypl.org.

Holden, Anthony. (2000). "Why Harry Potter doesn't cast a spell over me." *The Guardian.* Retrieved from http://www.theguardian.com/books.

Hopkins, L. (2003). "Harry Potter and the acquisition of knowledge." In G.L. Anatol, ed., *Reading Harry Potter* (pp. 25–34). Westport, CT: Praeger.

Nabokov, V. (1980). "Good readers and good writers." In *Lectures on Literature* (pp. 1–8). San Diego: Harcourt, Inc.

Parks, T. (2014). "A weapon for readers." *NYR Blog.* Retrieved from http://www.nybooks.com/blogs/nyrblog/2014/dec/03/weapon-for-readers/.

Rowling, J.K. (1997). *Harry Potter and the sorcerer's stone.* New York: Arthur A. Levine.

Rowling, J.K. (1998). *Harry Potter and the chamber of secrets.* New York: Arthur A. Levine.

Rowling, J.K. (2000). *Harry Potter and the goblet of fire.* New York: Arthur A. Levine.

Rowling, J.K. (2003). *Harry Potter and the order of the phoenix.* New York: Arthur A. Levine.

Rowling, J.K. (2005). *Harry Potter and the half-blood prince.* New York: Arthur A. Levine.

Rowling, J.K. (2007). *Harry Potter and the deathly hallows.* New York: Arthur A. Levine.

Schanoes, V.L. (2003). "Cruel heroes and treacherous texts: Educating the reader in moral complexity and critical reading in J.K. Rowling's Harry Potter books." In G.L. Anatol, ed., *Reading Harry Potter* (pp. 131–45). Westport, CT: Praeger.

Severus Snape's copy of *Advanced Potion-Making.* (n.d.). Retrieved December 3, 2014, from the Harry Potter Wiki: http://harrypotter.wikia.com/wiki/Severus_Snape%27s_copy_of_Advanced_Potion-Making.

Political Economy of Media
in the Magical World
of *Harry Potter*

Jennifer M. Proffitt *and*
Juliann Cortese

You can't accomplish everything alone; avoid blind allegiance; people in power aren't necessarily in the right; injustices operate within systems. These are a few of the lessons learned according to "13 Lessons about Social Justice from 'Harry Potter,'" which, as a whole, suggests that social change ultimately comes from the motivations, determination, and actions of the collective (Yandoli, 2013). That is, in order to enact change, while one person can be considered the leader or catalyst or face of the movement, such as in the case of Harry Potter, it takes a collective of people working together for the betterment of society. To reach larger numbers of people, mediated communication is necessary. On the other hand, those with wealth and power certainly want to maintain the status quo that benefits them and their bottom-line. One way to do this is to gain the consent of the dominated to accept the current system of rewards (and punishment). This is often done through ownership or control of the means of communication. Mainstream media, as both part of the economic system and ideological supporters of it, often provide content that induces fear of others so that we are less likely to work together for change, celebrates the individual, particularly the wealthy (and if one is not wealthy or not striving to be wealthy, then he/she is the problem rather than the structural issues inherent in capitalist societies), and attracts and distracts people from their struggles through news and entertainment that focuses on celebrity culture, sex and violence, and sensationalism. As fiction often reflects reality, these same issues can be found in J.K. Rowling's wildly popular *Harry Potter* series. As such, we ask, what does the Wizarding world of Harry Potter have to say about the role of the media in maintaining and challenging oppressive systems of power?

In this chapter, we use a political economic approach to analyze how the political elite attempt to control knowledge and maintain power through pressure on the mainstream media as well as how the profit-driven and monopoly newspaper, *The Daily Prophet*, provides content that benefits the ministry and sells more newspapers. We also examine how alternative media (e.g., *The Quibbler*, the radio program *Potterwatch*) are used to challenge the political agenda set forth by the government and perpetuated by the mainstream media and to mobilize collective action against the state and ultimately affect change.

Political Economy of Media

As Robert McChesney (2004) explains, the political economy of media approach explores "how media and communication systems and content reinforce, challenge, or influence existing class and social relations" and "how ownership, support mechanisms (e.g., advertising), and government policies establish media systems and communication technologies and (directly and indirectly) influence media behavior and content" (p. 43). It examines how the pursuit of profit affects the types of cultural products audiences can choose from and how ideologies such as the free market, consumption, and privatization are propagated in those cultural products.

The media industry in the United States, and indeed globally, is highly concentrated. The first edition of Ben Bagdikian's (1983) seminal book, *The Media Monopoly*, raises concerns about concentration of the media as 50 companies dominated the industry. By the seventh edition, *The New Media Monopoly*, published in 2004, that number dwindled to just five (Bagdikian, 2004). This is the result of a flurry of mergers and acquisitions since the 1980s as the Federal Communications Commission relaxed or eliminated regulations that were meant to encourage diversity, competition, and localism. Through vertical and horizontal integration and conglomeration, media corporations such as Comcast, Disney, News Corporation, Time Warner, Viacom and CBS eliminate risk by diversifying and by creating barriers to entry for potential competitors, centralize production, and homogenize and routinize information and entertainment content (Croteau & Hoynes, 2006; Meehan, 2005). The near monopoly power of these transindustrial, transnational corporations and their pursuit of profits shape the nature, form, and content of media products that then influence audiences. This can be seen very clearly in the news industry, particularly newspapers, as one newspaper towns and large newspaper chains like Gannett result in less diversity, innovation, substance, and independence due to a lack of competition (Croteau & Hoynes, 2006).

To minimize costs and maximize profits, many news organizations have cut the number of journalists they employ, closed international bureaus, and tend to rely on syndicated and wire news and news that is cheaper to cover: crime, celebrities, disasters and fluff. Investigative reporting is expensive and time-consuming, and in today's 24-hour news cycle and social media that allow anyone to post "news," the time crunch becomes even more harrowing. As such, journalists tend to cultivate a "golden Rolodex" of official sources, mostly experts and politicians, who can provide them with a steady stream of news and quotes (Bettig & Hall, 2012, p. 19). The reliance on official sources narrows the range of viewpoints disseminated and demonstrates the symbiotic relationship between news and government, for journalists need politicians for information and politicians need journalists to help them spin their agendas and frame the debates. This close relationship can lead to avoidance of the tough questions, as one doesn't want to lose access to such a source (McChesney, 2008). Further, the parent companies of news outlets and trade organizations lobby governmental officials and agencies and make campaign donations to politicians in order to influence legislation. Being critical of those in power can affect one's ability to manipulate the process. Thus, commercial and government pressures often combine to influence the type of news audiences receive. And this is especially problematic as audiences rely on media outlets for information that they do not have the time or resources to gather themselves.

Some of these same issues are reflected throughout the *Harry Potter* series, within which the portrayal of media is quite discouraging (Barton, 2006; Curthoys, 2011; Douglas, 2008). In a framing analysis of media references in the book series, Sturgill, Winney, and Libhart (2008) conclude that the portrayal of journalism is largely negative with news stories that are "manipulated, inaccurate and unethical" (p. 11). The news profession is sullied in the books, and the most focused upon journalist, Rita Skeeter, is portrayed as having questionable morals and a tendency to retaliate in print against anyone who speaks out against her (Stewart, 2010). With regard to media portrayals in the Potter series in general, Snir and Levy (2005) note, "the worse [*sic*] kind of monopoly in the Potterian economics is the monopoly on information" (p. 14). With this in mind, we are interested in how the problems and pressures that face news media in the

Muggle world are evident in the Wizarding world, particularly in the monopoly newspaper, the *Daily Prophet*.

Ministry Manipulation: Creating the News, Squashing the News

As the main newspaper in the Wizarding side of London, the *Daily Prophet* benefits from its monopoly status because, no matter how much people complain about the accuracy or sensationalism of the *Prophet*, they still have to depend on it for news and information because it is the only widely-available newspaper in town. Its closest competition, it appears, is the *Weekly Witch*, a magazine for women that appears to be similar to *People* magazine, and *The Quibbler*, a magazine that appears to be similar to the now defunct *Weekly World News*, which included some strange-but-true stories but mainly focused on hoaxes and supernatural news that were presented as true, such as alien encounters, Elvis sightings, and Bigfoot and Loch Ness Monster photographs (Carlson, 2007). As the only mainstream newspaper available, the *Daily Prophet* bears a resemblance to U.S. news media, including its focus on selling the news and official sources. With its reliance on official sources, the paper often succumbs to pressure from the Ministry to create story lines that benefit the government's interests or to suppress stories that will embarrass or contradict the Ministry line.

For example, at the end of *GoF*, despite evidence to the contrary, such as the body of Cedric Diggory, the confession of Barty Crouch, Jr., and the word of Harry and Dumbledore, the Minister of Magic, Cornelius Fudge, refuses to believe Lord Voldemort has returned. He dismisses Harry's account as the words of a troubled boy who talks to snakes, has hallucinations, and makes up "crackpot" stories. As the students return home from Hogwarts on the Hogwarts Express, Harry, not sure whether he wants to know what might be reported in the *Prophet*, looks to Hermione's copy of the paper. Hermione tells him that she had been checking the paper regularly and there were no reports regarding the events that took place during the third task of the Triwizard Tournament, including the death of Cedric, except for a brief story noting that Harry won the tournament. She states, "If you ask me, Fudge is forcing them to keep quiet" (*GoF*, p. 726).

In the next book, *OotP*, Fudge continues to pressure the *Prophet* to suppress stories, such as the snake attack on Mr. Weasley in the Ministry building, or to blame the escape of the Death Eaters from Azkaban on Sirius Black rather than admit that Voldemort is behind these events. The

Prophet also turned on Harry and Dumbledore during the summer months after the Triwizard Tournament, making Harry seem like a "nutcase" and Dumbledore "senile" (*OotP*, p. 251). Hermione tells Harry that the *Prophet* characterized him as "this deluded, attention-seeking person who thinks he's a great tragic hero or something." She continues, "If some far-fetched story appears they say something like 'a tale worthy of Harry Potter' and if anyone has a funny accident or anything it's 'let's hope he hasn't got a scar on his forehead or we'll be asked to worship him next'" (p. 73). And the stories worked: focusing on discrediting Harry and Dumbledore kept people from believing that Voldemort was back. That is, people trusted the newspaper and the government to tell them the truth rather than a much loved and distinguished professor and the Boy Who Lived who was witness to Voldemort's return, in part because people are supposed to be able to trust that their newspaper is reporting reality. The framing of Harry and Dumbledore as crazy and irrational as reported in the *Prophet* left the Wizarding world largely unprepared for the return of the Dark Lord, his Death Eaters, and his allies such as giants and dementors. People who protest are discredited, such as in the case of Wizengamot elder Griselda Marchbanks, who was quoted in an article in the *Prophet* about the Ministry's Dolores Umbridge being named High Inquisitor of Hogwarts as saying, "Hogwarts is a school, not an outpost of Cornelius Fudge's office.... This is a further disgusting attempt to discredit Albus Dumbledore"; in parentheses, the author of the article notes Marchbanks' "alleged links to subversive goblin groups" (*OotP*, p. 308).

These tactics appeared to work and prevent people from mobilizing collective action. As Lupin explains, "While the Ministry insists there is nothing to fear from Voldemort, it's hard to convince people he's back, especially as they really don't want to believe it in the first place." He continues to explain that the Ministry is "leaning heavily on the *Daily Prophet* not to report any of what they're calling Dumbledore's rumor-mongering," leaving people unaware and therefore susceptible to the Death Eater's Imperious Curse[1] (p. 94). The continuous drumbeat of the *Prophet* discrediting Harry and Dumbledore causes conflict at Hogwarts; even some of Harry's friends are unsure of their credibility. His friend and roommate Seamus calls those who believed Harry (rather than the *Prophet*) "mad" (p. 219). By making Harry and Dumbledore out to be "nutters" and refusing to report on Voldemort's return, the *Prophet* violates the first rule of newspapers: tell the truth. Rather, the paper, perhaps inadvertently, works to prevent any type of action that would result in preparations against Voldemort's new army. The suppression of news about Voldemort and the advancement of inaccurate or incomplete information by the Ministry continue in *HBP* and *DH*, despite the battle in the Hall of Prophesy in the Ministry building and the Minister's admission, finally, that Voldemort is indeed back in the *OotP*, and despite the Death Eaters' attack on Hogwarts and the death of Dumbledore in *HBP*. Further, such distractions allow Voldemort's regime to surreptitiously and systematically take over institutions of power, including the government, the media, the bank, and the prison, without resistance from the general Wizarding public who remained largely unaware due to the arrogance, pride, and power-hungry nature of Minister Fudge, the attempt to create a false sense of security by Fudge's successor Rufus Scrimgeour, and the lack of critical reporting by the media. The mainstream media serve as a lapdog rather than a watchdog, which in this case has dire, deadly consequences.

The fear and anger toward Harry continues in the *DH*. As the Death Eaters quickly and quietly take over the *Prophet*, they attempt to turn people against Harry by blaming him for Dumbledore's death. The Ministry, also taken over by Death Eaters through a combination of faulty Ministry decisions and the Imperious Curse, dubs Harry Undesirable No 1, which gives them the "pretext" for torturing people for information about Harry's whereabouts, and the *Prophet* reports this as truth on the front page of the paper (*DH*, p. 207). News is also suppressed when the Death Eaters take over the Ministry, including a story regarding escaped prisoners and a story about students at Hogwarts trying to steal the sword of Gryffindor from Headmaster Severus Snape's office.

However, even those who know that stories in the *Prophet* are false, exaggerated, or suppressed still must rely on it for information. As Dumbledore states in the *HBP* when Harry tells him he saw a story in the *Prophet* about a fight between the new Minister Scrimgeour and Dumbledore: "The *Prophet* is bound to report the truth occasionally ... if only accidentally" (*HBP*, p. 357). Horace Slughorn, the new Potions professor in *HBP*, notes that "the *Prophet* has been known to print inaccuracies, make mistakes" and admits that "it is true the *Prophet* often exaggerates" (pp. 146–147). Despite this, Hermione takes out a subscription to the *Prophet* in *GoF* because she is "sick of finding everything out from the Slytherins" (*GoF*, p. 540); Harry had to depend on the *Prophet* for news when he was at home on Privet Drive in *OotP*; Hermione continues her subscription of the *Prophet* in *OotP* despite its reporting on Harry because "it's best to know what the enemy are saying" (*OotP*, p. 225); in *HBP*, Hermione searches the *Prophet* for obituaries and arrests; and in *DH*, Harry, Ron, and Hermione steal copies of *Prophet* out of people's briefcases in order to know what is going on when they are in hiding in Number 12 Grimmauld Place. For those readers not immediately or directly affected by the events in question, it becomes difficult to separate the truth from falsehoods.

The role of the newspaper should be first and foremost to tell the truth. But the news can be manipulated by the people journalists choose to interview, the quotes that they choose to print, and the stories they choose to cover, particularly when the news media depend on official sources with political agendas for news and information or when those who control the outlet have a strong ideological agenda.

Celebrating Celebrity, Seeking Sensationalism

In *OotP*, journalist Rita Skeeter admits to Hermione that the Ministry is leaning on the *Prophet* not to cover the news that Voldemort is back, noting that people won't believe Harry's "cock-and-bull" story because readers think he is "delusional" (*OotP*, p. 567). Skeeter also notes that the *Prophet* "won't print a story that shows Harry in a good light" because "nobody wants to read it." Further, she notes that "people just don't want to believe that You-Know-Who's back." Hermione challenges her by saying, "So *the Daily Prophet* exists to tell people what they want to hear, does it?" Skeeter replies, "The *Prophet* exists to sell itself, you silly girl" (p. 567). Actually, Rowling points outs that the use of "prophet" as a homonym for "profit" is a clue to the motivation for the media source (Rowling, n.d.). As noted previously, the media are part of the economic system, and in order to increase profit margins and reduce risk, sensational stories, celebrity watching, and conflict become more prominent, as they are cheaper to cover and easier to report.

Nothing seems to sell newspapers like a good story. And Skeeter knows how to write a good story, even if she has to exaggerate, obtain information illegally, or use questionable and unethical practices. We first meet Skeeter in the *GoF* when the Twiwizard champions first have their wands weighed and meet the press. Lugo Bagman, Head of the Ministry's Department of Magical Games and Sports, introduces her to Harry, stating, "She's doing a small piece on the tournament for the *Daily Prophet*." She responds, "Maybe not *that* small, Ludo" (*GoF*, p. 303). Skeeter asks to speak with Harry and without further ado—or an answer—she steers him into a closet and begins to interview him using her Quick-Quotes Quill, a handy writing utensil that doesn't exactly write verbatim what the interviewee says. Rather, it interprets what the interviewee says in sensationalistic, flowery wording and often embellishes or provides inaccurate information. She tells him to "Ignore the quill," reveals that the *Prophet*'s readers "love a rebel," and begins asking leading and personal questions, such as "Can you remember your parents at all?" (pp. 305–306). Harry becomes irritated, and even more so when he sees that the quill wrote, "Tears fill those startling green eyes…," even though there were no tears (p. 306). Her final article is several pages long and all about Harry, misspelling the other champions' names at the end and leaving out Cedric, the other Hogwarts champion, all together. Her article is largely erroneous, putting words in Harry's mouth and in the mouths of the other students she interviewed about him. Overall, the picture painted of Harry is sympathetic, unlike later articles she writes about him after she writes a terrible story titled, "DUMBLEDORE'S GIANT MISTAKE," which discusses Dumbledore's "controversial staff appointments," interviews disgruntled Slytherin students including Harry's nemesis Draco Malfoy, and calls Hagrid "an alarmingly large and ferocious-looking man" who "terrif[ies] the students," revealing that he is part giant. Later, Harry sees her in the Three Broomsticks; she asks him to join her and he doesn't hesitate to tell her what he thinks of her since reading that story. Hermione calls her a "horrible woman," which doesn't sit well with Skeeter. Ron warns Hermione about upsetting Skeeter, for Skeeter will "dig something up on [her]" (p. 451).

Ron is right. Skeeter writes a story for the *Weekly Witch* that claims Harry's love, Hermione, "a plain but ambitious girl," is two-timing him with Viktor Krum, the Seeker for the Bulgarian Quidditch team and fellow Triwizard champion, who asked Hermione to visit him in Bulgaria (*GoF*, p. 512). The trio cannot understand how Skeeter found out that Hagrid was half-giant or how she knew that Krum invited Hermione to Bulgaria. As a result of the story, Hermione receives hate mail that includes poisons, howlers, and letters that look like ransom notes cut from the newspaper. The largely invented stories in which some truth is embedded have real consequences, and as Hagrid reveals, he received hate mail as well after Skeeter's article about him. But we must remember that a story filled with gossip, sensationalism, provocative quotes, and conflict presumably attracts audiences, as the volume of hate mail demonstrates. And that, as Skeeter notes, is what sells papers.

Skeeter later writes a scathing article about Harry describing his collapse in class and "complains of pain in the scar on his forehead," deducing that Harry is "unstable and possibly dangerous" (*GoF*, p. 611). She says she saw him "storm" out of his Divination lesson due to his claims of pain that wouldn't allow him to continue sitting in class (p. 611); however, she was nowhere to be seen when the incident occurred. The trio questioned whether she had an invisibility cloak or planted bugs (which, according to Hermione's reading of *Hogwarts: A History*, will not work on Hogwarts grounds). It is finally revealed at the end of the book that Skeeter didn't plant bugs—she actually is a bug. Hermione finds out that Skeeter is an unregistered Animagus,[2] which is illegal, and Hermione catches her in her beetle state, keeping her in a jar to blackmail her into no longer writing stories about Harry or his friends. The unethical and even illegal means by which Skeeter obtains her stories and quotes are symptomatic of the goals of commercial media, for the pressure to be first with the scoop and attract audiences (and advertisers) can lead journalists to cross ethical boundaries, such as in the case of News Corporation's *News of the World* phone-hacking scandal in the United Kingdom (see Poynter, n.d.).

The focus on celebrity is most obvious in the *CoS* when we first meet Hogwarts' new Defense Against the Dark Arts professor, Gilderoy Lockhart. Lockhart, winner of *Witch Weekly's* Most-Charming-Smile Award five times, had authored several books, such as *Year with the Yeti*, *Traveling with Trolls*, and *Wanderings with Werewolves*, that regaled his readers with stories about his experiences with and defeat of dark creatures. A handsome wizard, he attracts women and the press. When Harry, Ron, Hermione, and the Weasley family go to the bookstore Flourish and Blotts to buy their schoolbooks, they see Lockhart signing copies of his autobiography titled, *Magical Me*. As a *Daily Prophet* photographer takes pictures, Lockhart sees Harry and exclaims, "It *can't* be Harry Potter?" (*CoS*, p. 60). Lockhart proceeds to grab Harry, pulling him to the front of the line of people waiting for Lockhart's autograph, and shakes Harry's hand for the photographer. Lockhart tells him, "Nice big smile, Harry…. Together, you and I are worth the front page" (p. 60).

After Lockhart gives Harry a pile of his autographed books, the trio and the Weasleys come face-to-face with Draco Malfoy and his father, Lucius. Lucius insults the Weasleys for befriending the Muggle Grangers, and Mr. Weasley, outraged, slams Mr. Malfoy into a bookshelf. Mrs. Weasley expresses concern regarding what Lockhart would think about the men fighting, but son Fred tells her that Lockhart asked the *Prophet* journalist to "work the fight into his report" because he said "it was all publicity" (*CoS*, p. 63). As one of the key news values, conflict ostensibly attracts audience attention, particularly when the conflict involves violence, and when one combines celebrity and conflict, the attraction factor presumably intensifies.

While Harry is famous for being the Boy Who Lived, Lockhart is a celebrity, or "a person known for his well-knownness" (Boorstin, 1962/1992,

p. 217). Lockhart's celebrity is self-constructed as he writes books about himself, promotes them and his image incessantly, and signs copies of photographs of himself winking and smiling. Following the adventures of celebrities makes for easy news, for stars like Lockhart encourage, sometimes create, and indeed thrive upon the publicity, and news outlets know that fans will watch or read about their exploits. Investigative news takes more time and resources; celebrity news does not.

Just as the *Prophet* uses a focus on celebrity to sell papers, it also uses sensationalized headlines to grab reader attention. In an attempt to shock and possibly frighten readers, the *Prophet* published the headline, "SCENES OF TERROR AT THE QUIDDITCH WORLD CUP," complete with photo of the Dark Mark looming in the sky (*GoF*, p. 146). Sensationalistic headlines are used to discredit both Dumbledore and Harry with such phrasings as, "DUMBLEDORE'S GIANT MISTAKE" (p. 437), a story about Dumbledore's decision to hire Alastor "Mad-Eye" Moody as Defense Against the Dark Arts teacher, and "HARRY POTTER 'DISTURBED AND DANGEROUS'" (p. 611), a story reporting on the odd behavior Harry engages in while at school. Even in death the *Prophet* continues to discredit Dumbledore with the sensationalized headline, "DUMBLE-DORE—THE TRUTH AT LAST" (*DH*, p. 22), a story that dredges up unflattering stories from Dumbledore's youth. Such headlines use emotionally charged words and judgmental overtones to interest readers and increase sales.

The focus on sensationalism and celebrity news distracts people from the other pressing issues of the day such as poverty, increased inequality, war, racism, misogyny, and so on. Sensational and celebrity stories are much simpler to report, for such stories are prevalent and do not require much time or research. They also tend not to upset advertisers, for advertisers want readers to be in the "right" frame of mind when they view the advertisements. Critiques of structural and political factors that affect our daily lives do not attract advertisers, who, as Meehan (2005) suggests, are really the primary focus for news media, for such criticisms do not sell products.

Non-Mainstream Media and the Collective Voice

As noted, the commercial news media have a symbiotic relationship with the government, which makes it more difficult to ask hard questions that may challenge the official line, and rather than providing hard-hitting investigative news, news media tend to provide easy and cheap sensationalistic and celebrity news. The focus also tends to be on the individual, rather than the collective. In the search for truth and social, economic, and political change, U.S. alternative media sources such as the magazine, *The Nation*, or the radio and television program, *Democracy Now!*, take on the investigative stories the mainstream media gloss over or ignore. In the *Harry Potter* series, the magazine, *The Quibbler*, and the radio program, *Potterwatch*, play this role. And both lead to collective action to enact change.

We first hear about *The Quibbler* in *OotP*. Harry meets Luna Lovegood, the daughter of *The Quibbler's* publisher, on the Hogwarts Express. She is described as a girl who has "an aura of distinct dottiness" (*OotP*, p. 185). *The Quibbler*, as noted previously, is much like the *Weekly World News* with its strange headlines and focus on the bizarre and the imaginary. Harry's first encounter with the magazine is an article titled, "SIRIUS-Black as He's Painted? Notorious Mass Murder OR Innocent Singing Sensation?" (p. 191). Hermione calls the magazine "rubbish," but Luna defends her father's magazine and apparently believes all that is reported in its pages, even the sightings of Crumple-Horned Snorkacks.

In *OotP*, Hermione calls upon journalist Skeeter, who, as stated previously, does not want it to be known that she's an unregistered Animagus, to write a story—for free—about Harry's encounter with Voldemort and the Death Eaters who joined him at the end of the Triwizard Tournament. The story would be published not in the *Prophet* but in *The Quibbler*. Despite Skeeter's protests that no one will take the story seriously in *The Quibbler*, she writes the story. As Hermione predicted, people do read it—in fact, no other copy of the magazine sold out quicker—and many finally believe Harry's versions of events. When Umbridge finds out that Harry spoke to the press, telling his "lies" as she proclaims, she forbids students to read *The Quibbler* story, creating another decree that states, "Any student found in possession of the magazine *The Quibbler* will be expelled" (*OotP*, p. 581). Nothing makes people want to read something more than being told they can't, as Hermione explains, and of course, everyone does. And many, including his friend Seamus who did not believe him before, ultimately accept the truth and eventually rally around Harry in his fight against evil.

In *DH*, *The Quibbler* supports Harry and provides the truth while the *Prophet* suppresses or distorts the news. When Harry, Ron, and Hermione are in hiding, they hear people talking around a campfire. These people are also on the run from the Death Eaters, including Tonks' father Ted, a muggle-born wizard named Dirk who worked for the Ministry, the trio's classmate Dean Thomas, and two goblins. As they talk, the conversation turns to whether Harry is the Chosen One. Dirk believes the *Prophet*'s version of events, and Ted says, "*The Prophet?* You deserve to be lied to if you're still reading that muck…. You want the facts, try the *Quibbler*" (*DH*, p. 299). Upon hearing this, Dirk chokes on his food then states, "*The Quibbler?* That lunatic rag of Xeno Lovegood's?" (p. 299). Ted explains that *The Quibbler* is printing the news that the *Prophet* is not and is inspiring people to help Harry. Unfortunately, the Death Eaters kidnap Luna to stop her father's news reporting, and, resultantly, he tries to turn Harry in to save his own daughter.

Though *The Quibbler* is known for its unbelievable stories, it ended up being the voice of truth in the struggle to defeat Voldemort's regime. When it became too noisy, the regime struck back, threatening Lovegood by taking Luna in order to silence the magazine that was supporting Harry and encouraging collective action against the despotic government. As with mainstream news in the United States, threats by the government or by advertisers can silence or attempt to silence news, such as the case of Monsanto threatening Fox over a story about the negative effects of rbGH ("Fox," 2000) or the U.S. government threatening the *New York Times* regarding the printing of the leaked Pentagon Papers in 1971. And more recently in the United Kingdom, the British government threatened *The Guardian* regarding the publishing of National Security Agency (NSA) documents provided by Edward Snowden (Taibi, 2014). These threats have serious consequences for democracy and free speech, creating a chilling effect and making the media much more cautious or timid, for being sued or losing major advertisers is costly. But so is self-censorship.

Another alternative media source in the *DH* is *Potterwatch*. Ron informs Harry that there's a radio program that "tells the news like it really is," but in order to avoid a raid by the Death Eaters, the show's hosts need to continuously change locations, and the audience needs a password to listen to the program. When the trio is finally able to tune in, they hear their friends and family talking about those who were killed, missing, or escaped and providing commentary about what is really going on in the Wizarding and Muggle worlds. The "popular feature" titled "Pals of Potter" reports that Lupin, aka Romulus, believes Harry is still alive and "remains a symbol of everything for which we are fighting," including "the need to keep resisting" (*DH*, p. 441). The segment ends with "Keep each other safe: Keep Faith" (p. 444).

It is clear that Harry's supporters are indeed listening to *Potterwatch*; encouraged by the reports, they are engaging in resistance of their own. When Harry, Ron, and Hermione return to Hogwarts to find another Horcrux, they find many of their friends and classmates in the Room of Requirement in their resistance to the rules and punishment allocated under the new administration. One of them tells Harry that the students had "been trying to keep up with [him] on *Potterwatch*" (*DH*, p. 578). They tell Harry unequivocally that they are all ready to help him defeat Voldemort, and they do bravely fight the evil forces that penetrate the school.

Unlike in the case of *The Quibbler*, those hosting the *Potterwatch* program learn that the key to staying on the air is not to get caught. Despite the threats to their lives, reporting the truth regarding the struggle is paramount. But like *The Quibbler*, the radio program supports the cause and encourages collective action to defeat a tyrannical government. Though Harry is the symbol of the resistance, the revolution cannot occur without the courage of others to stand and fight for what is right. And in order to provide accurate information to others, alternative media that are not bound by profits maximization or political ties are essential.

Conclusion: Muggles and Wizards Unite

J.K. Rowling has created a magical world of wizards, spells, villains and heroes, yet this fantastical world is still grounded in elements of reality—pieces of the Muggle world that we see represented in the Wizarding world. The focus of this chapter is the depictions of media in these novels. A political economic analysis of these portrayals brings to the fore the elements of government influence, celebrity portrayals, sensationalism in stories, and the importance of alternative media.

Most of the references to media in the *Harry Potter* series focus on the *Daily Prophet*, which holds a monopoly over information in the Wizarding world. This newspaper is portrayed negatively throughout the series as it provides mostly inaccurate and misleading information to the public, especially evident in the writings of Rita Skeeter, a journalist of questionable morals who will make up story details in order to write a compelling story for the reader to ensure sales for the newspapers. Other tactics used to drive sales include the presentation (and sometimes attempted creation) of celebrities such as Gilderoy Lockhart and Harry (who transforms from celebrity to deviant then back to celebrity in the course of the series). In addition to questionable journalistic practices, the *Prophet* suffers from control by the Ministry of Magic as information is often misleading or stifled so as not to have wizards lose faith in their Ministry. This trend becomes dangerous in the end of the series as Voldemort and his followers take over the Ministry and the *Prophet*. With the continued suppression and manipulation of news, readers aren't motivated to align themselves against Voldemort and don't prepare for the coming battle.

With this type of control over the primary media outlet, Harry and his friends are forced to seek out alternative press to get out the truth to the public, which they do through *The Quibbler* and *Potterwatch*. And these two outlets continued to thrive even when facing attempts to silence their messages (from Dolores Umbridge's decree to punish students who were found in possession of a *Quibbler*, to the kidnapping of Luna Lovegood to silence the views of the publication producers, to the need for *Potterwatch* to stay hidden to avoid punishment by the Death Eaters).

The *Harry Potter* series also shows why news media monopolies are problematic, for diversity of viewpoints suffers when only one voice—which is profit-driven and susceptible to the influence of political ideology—is disseminated. As in the Wizarding world, the Muggle world needs more print and broadcast news sources unencumbered by commercial pressures. While the Internet and new media technologies have allowed for alternative voices and an increase in the number of citizen journalists, many people still tend to rely on traditional media sources as their primary source of information (Pew, 2012). It is difficult to enact social, political, and economic change when traditional news media distract audiences with celebrity news, sex and violence, crime, and fluff rather than inform them with investigative news that points to the structural factors that lead to the problems we need to address as a society. While this is in part by design so that the status quo is maintained, it is also due to the logic of capitalism and the pursuit of profit by any means. Let's take a page from Harry Potter and work together to enact change, starting with the commercialized media system that would marginalize the hero as a deranged little boy and would hide the real dangers we need to face.

Notes

1. The Imperious Curse is one of the Unforgivable Curses; it allows the castor of the spell to control the actions of another person.

2. An Animagus is a wizard or witch who can change him- or herself into a particular animal when he/she wishes.

References

Bagdikian, B.H. (1983). *The media monopoly*. Boston: Beacon Press.

Bagdikian, B.H. (2004). *The new media monopoly*. Boston: Beacon Press.

Barton, B.H. (2006). "Harry Potter and the half-crazed bureaucracy." *Michigan Law Review 104*(6), 1523–1538.

Bettig, R.V., & Hall, J.L. (2012). *Big media, big money: cultural texts and political economics*, 2d ed. Lanham, MD: Rowman & Littlefield Publishers, Inc.

Boorstin, D.J. (1962/1992). *The image: a guide to pseudo-events in America*. New York: Vintage.

Carlson, P. (2007, August 7). "All the news that seemed unfit to print." *The Washington Post*. Retrieved from http://www.washingtonpost.com/wp-dyn/content/article/2007/08/06/AR2007080601293_pf.html.

Croteau, D., & Hoynes, W. (2006). *The business of the media: corporate media and the public interest*. Thousand Oaks: Pine Forge Press.

Curthoys, A. (2011). "Harry Potter and historical consciousness: Reflections on history and fiction." *History Australia 8*(1), 7–22.

Douglas, T. (2008). "All the minister's men: Analyzing power and the press in Harry Potter." *Terminus: Collected papers on Harry Potter 15*(3), 120–135.

"Fox network on trial." (2000, July 28). *Democracy Now!* Retrieved from http://www.democracynow.org/2000/7/28/fox_network_on_trial#.

McChesney, R.W. (2004). "Making a molehill out of a mountain: the sad state of political economy in U.S. media studies." In A. Calabrese & C. Sparks, eds., *Toward a political economy of culture: capitalism and communication in the twenty-first century* (pp. 41–64). Lanham, MD: Rowman & Littlefield.

McChesney, R.W. (2008). *The political economy of media: enduring issues, emerging dilemmas*. New York: Monthly Review Press.

Meehan, E.R. (2005). *Why TV is not our fault: television programming, viewers, and who's really in control*. Lanham, MD: Rowman & Littlefield.

Pew Research Center. (2012). *Trends in news consumption: 1991–2012*. Retrieved from http://www.people-press.org/files/legacy-pdf/2012%20News%20Consumption%20Report.pdf.

Poynter. (n.d.). "News of the World phone hacking." Retrieved from http://www.poynter.org/tag/news-of-the-world-phone-hacking/.

Rowling, J.K. (n.d.). "Daily Prophet." Pottermore.com. Retrieved from http://www.pottermore.com/en-us/book4/chapter18/moment2/the-daily-prophet.

Snir, A., & Levy, D. (2005). "Popular perceptions and political economy in the contrived world of Harry Potter." Retrieved from http://dx.doi.org/10.2139/ssrn.817346.

Stewart, D. (2010). "Harry Potter and the exploitative jackals: How do JK Rowling's books about the Boy wizard impact the salience of media credibility attributes in young audiences?" *Image of the Journalist in Popular Culture 2*, 1–33.

Sturgill, A., Winney, J., & Libhart, T. (2008). "Harry Potter and children's perceptions of the news media." *American Communication Journal 10*(1). Retrieved from http://ac-journal.org/journal/2008/Spring/1HarryPotter.pdf.

Taibi, C. (2014, March 27). "UK government reportedly threatened to close down Guardian coverage over Snowden stories (Updated)." *Huffington Post*. Retrieved from http://www.huffingtonpost.com/2014/03/27/guardian-shut-down-edward-snowden-leaks-close_n_5041853.html.

Yandoli, K.L. (2013). "13 lessons about social justice from 'Harry Potter.'" *BuzzFeed*. Retrieved from http://www.buzzfeed.com/krystieyandoli/essons-about-social-justice-from-harry-potter#.vnmBzx4k13.

Political Activism and *Harry Potter*

Kalen M.A. Churcher *and*
Meghan S. Sanders

From child labor, to desegregation, anti-war counter-culture crusades and immigration reform, the youth of the world have a well-documented history of advocating social change. Similarly, young people throughout the world have often served as *the* or at least *a* change agent for a particular cause or issue. And, as we shall see in this chapter, such activism through the power of the printed word and big screen has manifested itself beyond the world in which most of us live, in a world where wizardry and magic cannot alone change a societal structure.

Where would Hogsmeade, Diagon Alley and Hogwarts School of Witchcraft and Wizardry be today were it not for the determined, and antiestablishment-minded young wizards who rejected the status quo and challenged authority at almost every turn? Harry Potter, Ron Weasley and Hermione Granger may have not have planned initially to launch a counter revolution when they first boarded Platform 9¾ at King's Cross Station. However, their ultimate charge in gathering support—physical and other-wise—against the politics attacking Hogwarts and its governance is indicative of historic youth activism in the Muggle world.

Like many of the notable U.S. social movements of the 1960s and 1970s (e.g., gay rights, free speech, civil rights, feminist, etc.), the activism presented in the *Harry Potter* series draws leadership from committed youth, politically conscious and civic-minded individuals who organize to safe-guard the quality of life and safety of an entire culture. Furthermore, similar to techniques used by youth activists in the 21st century, the young wizards in *Harry Potter* use their own forms of media to study the political climate and advance their cause. Following a close reading of the *Harry Potter* series, the authors detail some of the similarities between the politically motivated and socially focused actions of the Hogwarts students and recent international uprisings. In addition, identity is explored as the Hogwarts' students mature throughout the series and work toward the self-actualization process (Bennett, 2008; Dalton, 2008)—individuals opting for civic participation through community work, unconventional political activities, and various mediated forms of political expression (Dalton, 2008). Case in point—in perhaps the most obvious example of this self-actualization, we witness Harry Potter and friends rebelling against institutional hierarchies in order to (ironically) save one of the very institutions they rebel against—their world of wizardry. Finally, this chapter explores the changing role media have played in recent uprisings and a parallel with the Potter texts. Particularly, we explore ways in which the characters attempt to bypass government-controlled media to reach the masses and coordinate a successful movement (Marwell & Oliver, 1993).

Youth Participation in Politics

Before one can become a part of a movement, one must first feel a citizenship in the society in which he or she lives, and this citizenship can take multiple forms. Dalton (2009) defines citizenship as a "shared set of expectations about a citizen's role in politics" (p. 21). This includes public participation in political decision-making, but also an emphasis on the authority of the state wherein state sovereignty and the role of loyal subject are emphasized. Citizenship also involves social concern for others or solidarity in the form of ethical and moral responsibility to others. At times, personal values and norms will be at odds with one another, which is arguably where activism may quite often live. We see this occurring within the wizarding world, where there is an avoidance and reluctance by the Ministry of Magic and others within the government to acknowledge the dark occurrences and a restriction of basic rights, conflicts with the personal values of freedom of expression and need for securitization of the wizarding world held by the students of Hogwarts and members of the Order of the Phoenix.

Referencing McAdam, Tarrow & Tilly (2001, pp. 342–343), Morrill, Zald & Rao (2003) define political conflict as "a form of 'contentious politics' in which challengers contest authorities over the 'shape' and governance of 'institutionalized systems of power,'" (Morrill, Zald & Rao, 2003, p. 393). Such conflicts may occur within or alongside "social, economic, ethnic, historical or cultural" institutional entities (Barber, 2009, p. 23). There is an expectation of power inequities among groups and a focus on identity of group members, as they establish their citizenship (or loyalties) and distinguish themselves from other (perhaps opposing) groups (Morrill, Zald & Rao, 2003). Ultimately, we see a clash between those without power exercising their agency to reacquire power from those who have taken it. If those without succeed, they topple the hegemonic regime that had once oppressed them.

This political unrest may begin small, with one or a few individuals haphazardly taking on a particular cause. However, as we move along a continuum, the cause becomes more attractive to a whole and eventually becomes a collective political movement with (hopefully) a more structured mission (see Morrill, Zald & Rao, 2003, p. 400). It is worth noting that the unorganized beginnings of these conflicts are common and expected. In the case of youth activism, such unpreparedness could be seen as being indicative of reckless youth. Barber (2009), however, notes that many scholars have disputed this characterization and urges a closer examination of such work.

Despite Barber's (2009) assertion that an actual focus on youth activism is a relatively recent phenomenon, young people have been paramount in historic political movements, including, but not limited to, the French Revolution, China's Tiananmen Square, Northern Ireland's conflicts and the Arab Spring uprisings throughout the Middle East and North Africa. The more current focus on youth participation may be attributed to the increased coverage of such conflicts on television and other media outlets (Barber, 2009), particularly social media. The (perceived) increase of youth activism should not be seen as a shift or detachment from older generations; rather Youniss, et al. (2002) posit that the various demographic groups must work together and acknowledge the present and the past. This means understanding the political precedent of the past, harnessing it, and using it to succeed in future political goals.

Youth see a role for themselves and their government in improving their society. But, in the case of youth, they do so in ways that are different from their predecessors (Dalton, 2009). According to Dalton (2009) there are multiple norms of citizenship. Duty-based citizenship reflects those activities of citizenship that are more obligatory in nature (voting, etc.) and stress limited participatory roles, those rights that have traditionally been defined and practiced by older generations that were arguably split into more hierarchical, definitive social demarcations. Norms ranging from volunteerism to public protest reflect engaged citizenship, a form of citizenship that promotes other forms of political action. These norms reflect the empathetic and moral elements of citizenship as they pertain to helping those within and outside of the polity.

Early in the series, Hogwarts' students are not necessarily concerned with the political environment in which they live; however, it is within the earlier novels that readers witness the characters beginning to understand and connect with their identity. The Sorting Ceremony in *SS* illustrates this as the young wizards wait—some uneasily—to hear into which house they will be placed. From a sociological/psychological standpoint one could argue whether the young wizards' identities are shaped through their placements or if their politics were predetermined. Nonetheless, the Sorting Hat explains that Gryffindor's are "brave at heart," Hufflepuffs are "just and loyal," Ravenclaws have "a ready mind" and those in Slytherin represent "(t)hose cunning folk (who) use any means to achieve their ends" (*SS*, p. 118). Charp et al. (2006) argue that education and understanding about the self is "key to social transformation because it helps individuals identify and articulate what it is that needs to be changed" (p. 23), but it also serves as a mechanism to engage youth in issues that are most relevant to them. Hence the negative reaction by Harry when he is first placed into Slytherin before ultimately securing a spot in Gryffindor.

SS begins by presenting a counternarrative, presenting the wizard identity as a marginalized one—using phrases such as "their kind" and "unwelcome" and Harry's unwitting use of magic explained as strange occurrences. Soon, readers begin to see a change from the wizard identity being an outgroup identity, to an ingroup one. The Dursleys and Muggles become "them" and "less like us" (*SS* p. 13) and the world of wizards is owned though the use of words like "our," "your" and "my." And having lived in the world of humans, Harry and students with "non-magical parents," have to learn the norms of the society in which they now find themselves. The identity formation is strengthened during the Sorting Ceremony. By *CoS*, what was once a source of shame to Harry, becomes a source of pride as he feels at home and excited to return to school and his friends the next year.

We are introduced to the term, "mudblood" in *CoS* and later learn it is the most derogatory name you can call a person with non-magical parents. We further learn the importance of this term in a form of perceived hierarchy within the wizard world—one that separates "pure bloods" from "half-bloods," "mudbloods" and "squibs" (wizards with magical parents, who do not possess powers themselves). One of the most popular legends within the school involves these perceptions—that wizarding education and power should be reserved for only those from fully magical families. This legend, which we later learn to be true in *HBP* and *DH*, ends up being the foundation for activism—protection of the magical world from those who seek to control it and keep it for "pure bloods" at any cost—including various forms of disenfranchisement and abuse. The politics spurring this movement is akin at minimum to segregation and at worst, to ethnic cleansing. Though J.K. Rowling has stopped short of saying her series pulls from specific political events, she has acknowledged a definite political metaphor in Voldemort's killing of Muggles (Vieira, 2007).

It is in the fifth book, Harry Potter's fifth year at Hogwarts, that readers are privy to the start of some of the most involved examples of activism—particularly youth activism—in the collection. Rowling's books succeeded in growing as her readers did. In *OotP*, readers experience a darker, more grown up Harry Potter and friends, as well as the looming threat of He-Who-Must-Not-Be-Named. Because the Ministry of Magic fears that Dumbledore is set to launch his own upheaval and overthrow the Minister, Cornelius Fudge, the group sends one of its own to infiltrate Hogwarts under the guise of a new Defense Against the Dark Arts teacher: Professor Dolores Umbridge. Umbridge's ultimate role is to thwart any possible movement against the ministry by not educating her students with current/relevant material. "[P]rogress for progress's sake must be discouraged, for our tried and tested traditions often require no tinkering" (*OotP*, p. 213). Umbridge's presence at Hogwarts serves as a pivotal point for Harry Potter and could be seen as an impetus for the counter-hegemonic attacks on the governing ministry. It is here where Harry and his peers begin to formulate their covert plans to save Hogwarts and the world of wizardry.

Waging a Wizarding War

Drawing on social movement theory, Morrill, Zald & Rao (2003) define covert political conflicts as including four components: a "contestation of institutionalized power and authority, perceptions of collective injury, social occlusion, and officially forbidden forms of dissent" (p. 391). These four characteristics are seen throughout the entire *Harry Potter* series and peak in *OotP*, where we see many of the characters go through an identity transformation and readers witness a newfound maturity and seriousness develop among the characters. Though young Harry, Hermione, Ron, George and Fred rebel against authority figures and friends in earlier books, such actions are much more easily attributed to youthful pranks or curiosity. Even when the characters lose points for their houses because of their mischief—unsanctioned magic, etc.—their actions are eventually rewarded or indirectly praised. Similarly, Harry's use of the Marauder's Map and Invisibility Cloak, Hermione's Time Turner and Polyjuice Potion, and Ron's theft of the family car seem to leave little—if any—permanent harm to young wizards, save a possible Howler sent from an angry mother. Such youthful playfulness morphs into deliberate disobedience and outright rebellion as the series progresses (i.e., breaking school rules to investigate the Chamber of Secrets, breaking into the restricted section of the library, saving Buckbeak and Sirius in *PoA*, etc.). The momentum begun in *OotP* continues through *HBP* and *DH*, illustrating directly Morrill, Zald & Rao's first and fourth points.

The actual Order of the Phoenix can be seen as a civic activism group that facilitates collective action and nurtures collective forms of identity, allowing the students to make systematic, tangible changes on issues that are meaningful and relevant to them. In this case it is an active form of rebellion in response to education reform they feel is not within their best interests. Knowing that Dumbledore has become a target for the Ministry and that Umbridge is not providing an apropos education to defend against Voldemort, Hermione urges Harry to create Dumbledore's Army. All houses, with the notable exception of Slytherin, form the underground group of young dissidents who meet regularly in the Room of Requirement to prepare for battle. Though Dumbledore's Army appears to have disappeared or disbanded in *HBP*, readers learn in *DH* that the group is still very much active and led by a new group of witches and wizards—Ginny Weasley, Neville Longbottom and Luna Lovegood. Thus, the youth movement was not a knee-jerk reaction to a particular instance, but rather an organized caucus of resistance. Were it not for the longevity and consistency of Dumbledore's Army, one could assume the series might have ended very differently. Leadership from within is valued, and similar to grassroots efforts (Alinsky, 1971), the students are involved with the decision-making. This strengthens the movement's growing efforts because the decisions are based on their own experiences and enable them to mobilize their peers in ways the adults cannot (Charp et al., 2006). This involvement continues in later novels, when adults such as Mr. and Mrs. Weasley, Professor McGonagall and Remus Lupin join forces with the students leading into the final battle. It is through their involvement with the Order and other activist efforts, that the students are "pushed to extend their thinking, to confront their own biases, and to ask hard questions of the leaders within and outside of their community … creat[ing] a sense of purpose in young people to take a civic activist stances and to work with others in their communities to end various forms of oppression" (Charp et al., 2006, p. 27).

Although political unrest and uprisings may be viewed as unorganized and individualistic (Barber, 2009) at first, it is not until there exists a perceived consensus that an entire group will be impacted that such conflicts will proceed with strength. This is similar to Morrill, Zald & Rao's (2003) requirement of knowledge of collective injury as part of covert political conflicts; however, as previously mentioned, the end battle manifests itself in *DH* as an overt, publicized act. In *OotP*, it is the Order that first agrees that Voldemort has returned to destroy Hogwarts and assume control. Later, the young wizards of Gryffindor, Hufflepuff and Ravenclaw must be convinced to eschew the new establishment's rules and work against Umbridge, their new headmistress, as they recognize their own safety has been compromised and that Dumbledore must return to Hogwarts to regain stability and order. In *DH*, readers again see this behavior as most of the young wizards fight to save Hogwarts. Those who may impede the fight, specifically those within Slytherin House, are gathered and locked away. As the final battle at Hogwarts continues and Slytherin members are released, readers are largely left to decide for themselves where the members' loyalty rested or will rest. Even Draco Malfoy appears to have some trepidation as he eventually leaves Hogwarts to join his parents who show their allegiance to Voldemort. Draco's final stand of uncertainty as to whether to join the resistance or support the Dark Lord is foreshadowed throughout the latter half of the series when he does not disclose Harry's identity in *DH* and when he accepts Harry's help as the Room of Requirement burns.

(Magical) Media and Political Conflict

Call them what you will: political conflicts, protests, uprisings, revolutions. The commonality among the terms relates to their potential to effectuate change. That change is impossible if leaders cannot relay information to their audiences and likewise gather support for their cause. The marketplace of ideas is not much of a marketplace without the product or consumers. Because of this, leaders must not only possess the knowledge to formulate ideas, but they must also have the means to transmit that knowledge over distances. In essence, such political leaders must be part journalist and part public relations practitioner; they must set the political agenda and then market said agenda as a call to action (Bennett, 2007).

Media were—and still are—crucial components to political activism. We learn from legal history that the First Amendment, particularly the ideals of free speech and press are necessary for an informed citizenry and successful government (Bennett, 2007; Graber, 2012). Even detrimental forms of media (i.e., Nazi propaganda) have been studied and taught for their persuasive techniques. As media technologies have advanced throughout the decades, so too, have the forms of media used to convey information and solicit support for political causes. The popularity of pamphlets and traditional newspapers has fallen to posts, tweets and videos. Just as television placed the Vietnam War into America's living rooms, events like the Arab Spring have placed liberation and strife in our social media accounts.

In discussing media, we are not just referring to "traditional" forms that involve communicating from one entity to the masses, but also to those mechanisms that enable one-to-one, one-to-many and many-to-many interactions and transmission of information. All provide the opportunity to serve as a center for political activism. For youth, it is those media and technologies they use most and are most fond of that allow for initial and reconnections with civic life (Skoric & Poor, 2013). Throughout the *Harry Potter* series, Harry and others of similar viewpoints use the communication tools at their disposal to find one another, act together, organize, and take action (Jenkins, 2006). Giving the setting of the books, these media technologies are specific to the wizarding world.

Because mainstream politics—and therefore mainstream media—tend not to be reflective of youth political ideologies (Diemer, 2012), younger generations search out less traditional vehicles for transmitting information—sometime commandeering mainstream media and repurposing it to meet their ends. Although it is far from the only conflict to utilize social media and networking, the Arab Spring uprisings played a crucial role in understanding how new media may shape political events. Millennials were able to utilize modern technology to spawn interest and awareness online prior to initiating more traditional protests, riots and other counter-hegemonic activities. The sharing of Khaled Said's brutal death via the Internet, specifically Facebook, rallied crowds of young people to protest the Egyptian government. Within days, President Hosni Mubarek resigned, but the resignation came too late for the hundreds of non-violent protesters who died during protests (Barber & Youniss, 2013). Yet the mobilization of youth is not always a guaranteed success. While Tunisian youth mobilized quickly and in number despite a lack of formal structure, others acknowledge that the Egyptian youth movement was not always successful in mobilizing forces, though it still represents some of the strengths of the youth movements (Ottaway & Hamzawy, 2011). Ottaway & Hamzawy (2011) note that one of the major groups, while boasting 100,000 members online, saw only several hundred participating in on-the-ground protests.

Similarly, Lim (2012) states it is an "oversimplification" to describe the Egyptian uprising as either a Facebook or "people's revolution" (p. 232).

Indeed, the mobilization of youth and others to fight the Ministry and Voldemort was no easy task, and one could easily argue that personal relationships and interpersonal communication played more of a role than media in mobilizing forces against the Dark Lord. Were it not for the core group of revolutionaries—Harry, Ron, Hermione, Ginny, Neville, Luna, Lupin, Sirius, the Weasleys—and their personal connection to the cause, the outcome of the final battle could have been entirely different. Though the students of Hogwarts came together to save the castle and that for which it stood, there was little formal planning or training to prepare them for what is about to occur. And, similar to the Egyptian youth movement, though there are a number of young wizards who supported Harry and the politics surrounding him, when it comes to the actual fighting, we see a much smaller group engaging in combat. One could argue that the traditional media's role may have inhibited larger-scale participation, especially early on.

Political communication scholars have identified journalism as an integral part of the political process as it helps to provide and legitimate the standard against which we compare various forms of discourse (Edy & Snidow, 2011). As Edy and Snidow (2011) state, "the institution of journalism is a set of social practices that produce and define knowledge and that legitimate ways of knowing about political and public life" (p. 818). The larger scale, national media have a large capacity to influence the saliency and frame in which issues are thought of (Skoric & Poor, 2013). This in turn, aids in controlling the population, both in thought and action. Media are not simply about information transmission but also about the shared belief systems and experiences that become ritualized through their consumption (Carey, 1992). These roles are not mutually exclusive, and both should be viewed as important. With this in mind, we see how wizards and witches herald the *Daily Prophet* as an accurate source of information, and Harry and colleagues' concern and disappointment when the paper seems to turn against them and the objective journalistic values they hoped the paper to possess. This creation of a shared experience provides the group members with common cause for which to fight.

The Daily Prophet may be the primary media vehicle featured throughout the series. It is the most widely-read vehicle and even respected in earlier novels—although some of the headlines and stories are questioned. It is not until *GoF* that we really see Harry and the other students begin to question the integrity of the paper, when they become the focus of the stories as part of the coverage of the Triwizard Tournament in year four.

They get a glimpse of the behind-the-scenes machinations that lead to publication of half-truths and fabrications. Before heading back to Hogwarts in year five, Harry has already given up on the predictable mainstream news of *The Daily Prophet*, recognizing it would not be until "(T)he idiots who ran the paper finally realized that Voldemort was back (that) it would be headline news..." (*OotP*, p. 8). Harry's attitude is not surprising, as young people tend to equate traditional, more mainstream politics and media as not identifying with their particular needs. However, when those needs are met, we witness a spike in interest within that demographic (Youniss et al., 2002). With *The Daily Prophet* no longer meeting his needs, Harry turns to more magical means of obtaining information. As usual, the Dursleys oppose Harry's skills and magic in general, and when the wizarding owls plague the Dursleys' neighborhood early in *OotP*, they are kept at bay by Uncle Vernon, who knows the birds could be bringing news from a dissident source, or at the very least, a wizarding one.

We also begin to see a reliance on a dominant bias against youth in that wizards such as Lucius Malfoy and particularly Dolores Umbridge use "youth" in a more pejorative way, painting the picture of youth through the government-run media (*The Daily Prophet*) as wild, incorrigible and even dangerous individuals with no knowledge of what their educational needs are and therefore in need of the strictest guidance and regulation. This strategy taps into anxieties held for and about youth, and eventually about Harry and his friends as they are presented in the general market media and government/ministry reports as volatile, ticking time bombs whose activities are detrimental to the safety of wizarding society. This mirrors media's portrayal of Latina/o youth during the 2006 anti-immigration fights where the youth were described as "uninformed" and "acting out" so as to cause trouble or skip school (Vélez et al., 2008, p. 8). Not surprising, those who support the state and its hegemonic belief system (like Bellatrix Lestrange or Lucius Malfoy) are not admonished by *The Daily Prophet* despite their destructive behaviors. Interestingly, even those with Harry's best interests in mind display their disapproval of youth being made aware of adult business. Harry, Ron and Hermione are made aware of this when they must convince Mrs. Weasley to allow them to hear about the Order of the Phoenix, Dumbledore's secret society comprised of those who fought Voldemort in the past. This is Harry's first real entre into an established political group beyond Hogwarts.

Harry is also equally disappointed when he learns that opposing viewpoints are not always welcome in *The Daily Prophet*, and in fact, the newspaper has become propaganda for the Ministry of Magic, providing legitimization for those who wish to deny or avoid information suggesting the Dark Lord's return and the danger this represents. The government-controlled media paint a picture in which all is safe, and those who state and behave otherwise are dissidents who seek to use scare tactics to further the fame of Harry Potter. Anyone who claims that Voldemort has returned is subject to mudslinging—or worse. The headlines are more critical (Boyle et al., 2004) and names such as "undesirable #1" are used to further marginalize Harry and his supporters from the rest of the wizarding world (Shoemaker, 1984). Thus, state media has gone beyond its gatekeeping role and has disappointed—if not failed—Harry again. *The Daily Prophet* is acting in support of a nation-building cause rather than the watchdog role. As with many activist groups, the students find it impossible to control how the news frames them and their cause (Ryan, Carragee, & Meinhofer, 2001). So, the students and their allies turn to alternative, grassroots or participatory media.

Haas (2004) argues that alternative media provide "representations of issues and events which oppose those offered in the mainstream media" (p. 115). Activists create spaces and forums in which they can define the issue in their own terms. In her paper on the use of youth media in Palestine, Norman argues that media, particularly media created by youth, provide a space for empowerment, advocacy and activism. It is within this space that alternative narratives that challenge the dominant discourse emerge. As a result, a wider range of experiences and voices are represented, and more holistic and detailed understanding of the conflict is presented (see Debrix 2003; Gregory 2006). However, such media still have to negotiate for that space in such a way that doesn't destabilize or weaken the autonomy they are trying to establish in the first place.

Alternative media can take many forms including newspapers, magazines, radio, films, and documentaries (Downing, 2001). "Numerous alternative periodicals have given voice to cultures and viewpoints not expressed in the mainstream press. This alternative press tradition includes many vigorous social movement advocacy publications which have challenged the dominant culture to consider new ideas and issues and to foment change" (Roberts, 1996, p. 16). However, songs/music, people's radio, comics and posters are all also forms of grassroots media (Jenkins, 2006).

We see many of these forms throughout the series. *The Quibbler*, the castle and other paintings, the pirate radio station, the Pensieve, the diary of Tom Riddle, a simple fire, and even owls serve as a form of social networking tools through which the dissidents stay connected. And some of them, such as owls, later become a source of concern because of the possibility of messages being intercepted. *The Quibbler*, surprisingly, becomes a form of alternative media. Edited by Xenophilius Lovegood, the magazine's main focus is on conspiracy theories and mythical, magical creatures. Despite these stories, it is still considered an outlet that becomes of value to the movement as it also does not shy away from publishing truth. In *HBP*, Harry admits to "a certain fondness for the magazine, having given it an exclusive interview the previous year" (p. 137). Recognizing the importance of this channel of information and its influence on mobilization, the Death Eaters force Xenophilius to publish anti–Harry stories by kidnapping Luna in *DH*.

One could argue that paintings inside and outside of the Hogwarts castle create a form of social networking system through which Harry and his supporters may communicate. They are used to communicate with the Muggle Prime Minister and even reconnect Harry, Ron and Hermione with the Order in *DH*. Social networks are based on trust between friends, so mobilization calls through this network are given more credence and trustworthiness (Skoric & Poor, 2013). It is not the availability of this communication mode that leads to greater participation by the students, rather the impact of it is more noticeable because of the seriousness the upheaval in Hogwarts has presented. As a result, we see more message amplification, mobilization and organization on the part of the students and select others. Similarly, communication with those beyond Hogwarts is possible through more clandestine and nontraditional means. Tom Riddle (Voldemort) communicates with Harry via a seemingly blank diary in *CoS*, and Sirius Black uses a glowing fireplace as a technological mode to speak with Harry in *GoF*. The students have a resource for communicating and networking, even with engaged supporters outside of the castle walls that does not need to conform to state regulations or requirements.

In many ways, we can see that the use of alternative and networked communications tools is successful in garnering support for their activism efforts. However, we could argue that you do not see more widespread support because mass-oriented media is still necessary for far-reaching distribution and legitimization (Jenkins, 2006; Skoric & Poor, 2013). Rather than the complimentary relationship we saw in Singapore, the Arab Spring, and many others, we see the antagonistic relationship between the communications systems.

Self-Actualization

Imagination, quality of writing, and universal themes are just some of the reasons the *Harry Potter* book series has remained so popular. J.K.

Rowling's ability to grow the story, characters and plotline as her audience aged is surely another. In *SS* and *CoS*, the stories are much lighter and the students' actions much more fanciful than in later books. The wizards and witches are young and in a number of cases, still coming to terms with who they actually are: For Harry, it is that he is not only a wizard, but also a wizard who (as just a baby) was able to defeat Voldemort; Ron, who coming from a large family has his own hurdles to overcome, appears as if he will be in Harry's shadow throughout his time at Hogwarts, never quite living up to his friend's history; and Hermione, who presents as an overachiever, struggles with being Muggle-born at a time when the Ministry of Magic is questioning if only pure-bloods should be privy to a Hogwarts' education. Even secondary characters like Neville Longbottom and Ginny Weasley first present as very uncomfortable or uncertain as to whom they are. Fast forward to *HBP* and *DH*, and all experience a sharp change in personality and emotional development in part because of the natural maturation process but also out of the necessity as they fight to save Hogwarts and the ideological foundation established by Dumbledore.

Situated atop Abraham Maslow's hierarchy of needs, though first introduced by Kurt Goldstein, self-actualization refers to one achieving his or her self-fulfillment or maximum potential. Presumably, the process of reaching this potential is ongoing; therefore, the desire to continually *do better* is constant (Boeree, 1998; Maslow, 1965). "Self-actualizing people are … involved in a cause outside their own skin, in something outside of themselves. They are devoted, working at something, something which is very precious to them—some calling or vocation in the old sense, the priestly sense" (Maslow, 1965, p. 110). It is not likely this process will happen exclusively in youth or only once in one's life. For example, one would not become self-actualized in his or her 20s and remain self-actualized through doing nothing else for the rest of his or her life. Thus, a more appropriate term might be self-actualizing, referring to a continuum instead of a fixed point.

For first years at Hogwarts, achieving one's maximum potential may seem unlikely, what with failed spells and youthful foolishness. Yet the young wizards know what (they think) will prevent them from succeeding. Harry fears of being placed into Slytherin House in *SS* and later, in *CoS*, is ashamed and somewhat frightened that he is able to speak Parseltongue. Hermione resorts to using a Time Turner to allow her to accomplish all she must do to prove herself a worthy Muggle-born student at Hogwarts, and Ron struggles to have his own identity in the large Weasley family and as a friend to Harry Potter. Yet as the series progresses, Harry's Parseltongue abilities become an asset; Hermione proves to be a promising young witch and Hogwarts' prefect; and Ron establishes himself not only as a capable Quidditch player and prefect, but as a wizard independent of Harry Potter. Each success—no matter how small—plays a role in the self-actualization process. We see this in *SS* when Dumbledore awards the introverted Neville Longbottom 10 house points for standing up to his friends, allowing Gryffindor House to beat Slytherin for the House Cup. Later in *DH*, Neville reveals his mature, more confident self when he risks his life in the fight against Voldemort.

Maslow (1965) also states that young people "suffer from too little selflessness, too much self-consciousness, self-awareness" (p. 111) to fully commit themselves to the self-actualization process. Several young wizards in *Harry Potter*, however, may be an exception. This may be most evident in *DH* when Harry not only realizes he is the final Horcrux that holds Voldemort's soul—and thus, must die in order to destroy him—but when he physically takes himself into the Forbidden Forest to face Voldemort and his (presumed) death. We also see the self-actualizing process taking place within Ron and Hermione, as well as members of the Order, including Lupin and his wife, Nymphadora Tonks. For the young wizards, the courage needed to participate in the self-actualization process did not simply happen. J.K. Rowling carefully crafted their turbulent transformations throughout the series. Whereas Barber (2013) views political conflict as posing a "risk to development" (p. 337), Harry, Ron and Hermione appear to have overcome any obstacles despite having left Hogwarts and been subject to isolation, in addition to lacking basic resources and complete knowledge as to what they were to face.

Not all young wizards had similar experiences, however. From Day One, Draco Malfoy is portrayed as destined for dark magic. From his placement in Slytherin House to his aggression in the Quidditch arena, Malfoy's goals are much more self-focused than the other wizards. Although we witness glimpses of a possible character transformation in Malfoy, the changes never fully develop. Always one to hold out hope for his young witches and wizards, Dumbledore explains to Snape that Voldemort has planned for Draco Malfoy to kill him—soon. Dumbledore asks Snape do it in his place because "the boy's soul is not yet so damaged ... I would not have it ripped apart on my account" (*DH*, p. 683). Yet in the end, as Voldemort stands before Hogwarts and calls for support from the young wizards, we see a reluctant Draco Malfoy walk meekly toward Voldemort and his parents who eventually turn their backs on Hogwarts and retreat slowly. They no longer fight on any side, and Draco's identity becomes more of a traitor than rebel or dissident.

With the critical mass of their social network still at Hogwarts and a lack of confidence in *The Daily Prophet* to provide or disseminate credible news, the trio of young wizards, as addressed earlier, takes to using magical means of message making and distribution to keep in touch and abreast of crucial information. This is not unlike youth political activists from other causes who lean more toward social media and other less traditional technologies to crowdsource material (Bennett, Well & Freelon, 2011). Bennett et al. (2011) also address the concept of dutiful citizenship where "individuals participate in civic life through organized groups, from civic to political parties, while becoming informed via the news and generally engaging in public life out of a sense of personal duty" (p. 838). Again, we see this as Harry assumes it is his duty to rid the world of Voldemort because of his past. Of course, Harry's past also encompasses revenge for the death of his parents, as well as revenge for the death of Dumbledore and Sirius Black, both of whom served as father figures to Harry at some point in the series.

Death and coming to terms with death is a recurring theme throughout the series and the death of Severus Snape in *DH* is another moment of poignancy in Harry's quest for self-actualization. The contentious relationship between Snape and Harry that begins in *SS* continues throughout the series, escalating when Harry witnesses Snape kill Dumbledore in *HBP*. After collecting the tears of weak and dying Snape, Harry uses the Pensieve to view a sort of video timeline that explains (through Snape's memories) years of questions Harry my have had. Harry must come to terms that neither Snape, nor Dumbledore, may have been the men the once young and impressionable wizard though they were. Both had their faults and their strengths, something Harry is able to digest and process in *DH*. The extent to which Harry accepted those memories is plain when, in the *DH* epilogue, Harry addresses the concerns of his son, Albus Severus, who is fearful of being placed into Slytherin House once he arrives at Hogwarts: "...you were named for two headmasters of Hogwarts. One of them was a Slytherin and he was probably the bravest man I ever knew" (*DH*, p. 758).

In the final pages of the *DH*, following the defeat of Voldemort, Harry displays the ultimate act of selflessness when he snaps the Elder Wand— the most powerful wand in the wizard world—and throws the pieces off of a bridge. This ensures that no one can use the wand's magic to rise to the power that Voldemort had acquired prior to his death. This is, indeed, a selfless act and example of an established moral and civic identity (Youniss & Yates, 1999) because since it was Harry who disarmed Draco Malfoy, the true master of the Elder Wand, the power would have lain with him. After Voldemort's defeat, Harry did not view himself as heroic but instead portrayed a sense of moral duty (Bennett et al., 2011; Youniss & Yates, 1999). One can speculate that Harry may have questioned if so much power was worthwhile; we can assume that he thought not.

Final Thoughts

"Youth around the world share the burden of forging a civic order that must be attuned as much to the evolving future as to the past. Young people need to collaborate with the older generation in bridging tradition with these new forces" (Youneiss et al., 2002, p. 123). In the *Harry Potter* series, Harry and the youth of Hogwarts realize they must learn—and work with—the past if they are to save their future. Were it not for magical technologies used and institutional histories learned, it is unlikely Voldemort would have been defeated and Hogwarts School of Witchcraft and Wizardry saved from destruction. Though hidden under a guise of wands, mythical beasts and magical spells, the youth activism in the *Harry Potter* series not only shares comparable attributes to current youth movements (see the events noted in Valenzauela, Arriagada, & Scherman, 2012; Skalli, 2013; Skoric & Poor, 2013; Zhang, 2013), but also illustrates possible motivating opportunities to engage youth in socio-political activities. Similar to the Arab Spring uprisings, the youth activists in *Harry Potter* cast aside traditional media like *The Daily Prophet* and used instead more independent forms of media technologies that are not so tightly controlled by the state.

In addition, the transformation of multiple key characters from *SS* to *DH* illustrates a pathway to self-actualization and identity, despite the young age of the wizards. We witness acts of selflessness, as well as sincere dedication to moral and civic responsibilities. The creation of the rogue, yet well intended, Dumbledore's Army provides a space, no matter how temporary, for youth to identify, organize, learn and strategize (Rogers, Mediratta & Shah, 2012). In the case of the *Harry Potter* series, it allows for a counter-hegemonic movement to be born. True, the army was burdened by a lack of official support (as in many social movements), leaving its members to gather at unpredictable times. It also suffered setbacks when Harry, Ron and Hermione left Hogwarts to wage the war against Voldemort. Yet, in the final pages of *DH*, we see loyalty to the army and Harry return when the war hits home.

From a youth activist perspective then, where does the end of the *Harry Potter* series leave us? It should leave readers with a great deal to consider with regard to youth as engaged citizens and their potential roles in policy-making and society. Politics should not be an "us-them" situation, but rather an organized, communal movement toward a greater good, where strengths are celebrated and shortcomings supported by others. The lessons of *Harry Potter* need not be relegated to governmental political spheres, however. Sociopolitical causes are equally important and addressed within the narrative. Diversity and inclusiveness should be embraced and valued, whether a Pureblood or Muggle-born; languages, however 'strange' should be respected; and backstories should be explored, as the can often explain first impressions. Informed participation by all groups is necessary for quality societal governance (Flanagan & Sherrod, 1998). Youth should not be underestimated in their aspirations, and their quest toward self-actualization should not be minimized. In short, listen and learn; keep close to family and friends; and do not let the possibility of power consume you. If those mantras are kept, to paraphrase the narrator, all will be well.

References

Alinsky, S. (1971). *Rules for radicals*. New York: Random House.

Barber, B.K., ed. (2009). *Adolescents and war: How youth deal with political violence*. New York: Oxford University Press.

Barber, B.K. (2013). "Political conflict and youth." *The Psychologist 26*(5), 336–339. Retrieved from http://www.thepsychologist.org.uk/archive/archive_home.cfm/volumeID_26-editionID_225-ArticleID_2266-getfile_getPDF/thepsychologist/0513barb.pdf.

Barber, B.K. (2013). "Egyptian youth make history." *Harvard International Review*. 68–72.

Bennett, W.L. (2007). *News: The politics of illusion*, 7th ed. New York: Pearson Education.

Bennett, W.L. (2008). "Changing citizenship in the digital age." In W.L. Bennett, ed., *Civic life online: Learning how digital media can engage youth* (pp. 1–24). Cambridge: MIT Press.

Bennett, W.L., Wells, C., & Feelon, D. (2011). "Communicating civic engagement: Contrasting models of citizenship in the youth web sphere." *Journal of Communication 61*, 835–856. DOI: 10.1111/j.1460–2466.2011.01588.x.

Boeree, C.G. (1998). "Abraham Maslow: Personality Theories." Retrieved from http://www.lake.k12.fl.us/cms/lib05/FL01000799/Centricity/Domain/3306/Abraham_Maslow.pdf. Last viewed on January 28, 2015.

Boyle, M.P., McCluskey, M.R., McLeod, D.M., & Stein, S.E. (2005). "Newspapers and social protest: An examination of newspaper coverage of social protest from 1960 to 1999." *Journalism & Mass Communication Quarterly 82*, 638–653.

Dalton, R. (2008). *The good citizen: How a younger generation is reshaping American politics*. Washington, D.C.: CQ Press.

Diemer, M.A. (March 2012). "Fostering marginalized youth's political participation: Longitudinal roles of parental socialization and Youth sociopolitical development."

American Journal of Community Psychology 50, 246–256. DOI: 10:1007/s10464–012–9495–9.

Downing, J. (2001). *Radical media: Rebellious communication and social movements.* Thousand Oaks: Sage.

Edy, J.A., & Snidow, S.M. (2011). "Making news necessary: How journalism resists alternative media's challenge." *Journal of Communication 61*(5), 816–834. DOI: 10.1111/j.1460–2466.2011.01584.x.

Graber, D. (2012). *Media: Making sense of politics.* Boulder: Paradigm.

Haas, T. (2004). "Alternative media, public journalism and the pursuit of democratization." *Journalism Studies 5*, 115–121.

Jenkins, H. (2006). *Convergence culture: Where old and new media collide.* New York: New York University Press.

Lewis-Charp, H., Yu, H.C., Soukamneuth, S. (2006). "Civic activist approaches for engaging youth in social justice." In. S. Ginwright, P. Noguera & J. Cammarota, eds., *Beyond resistance: Youth activism and community change, new democratic possibilities for practice and policy for America's youth* (pp. 21–35). New York: Routledge.

Lim, M. (2012). "Clicks, cabs, and coffee houses: Social media and oppositional movements in Egypt, 2004–2011." *Journal of Communication 62*, 231–248.

Marwell, G., & Oliver. P.E. (1993). *The critical mass in collective action: A micro-social theory.* New York: Cambridge University Press.

Maslow, A. (1965). "Self-Actualization and beyond." Proceedings of the Conference on the training of counselors of adults. May 22–28, 1965, Chatham, MA.

McAdam, D., Tarrow, S., & Tilly, C. (2001). *Dynamics of contention.* Cambridge: Cambridge University Press.

Morrill, C., Zald, M.N. & Rao, Hayagreeva R. (2003). "Covert political conflict in organizations: Challenges from below." *Annual Review of Sociology 29*, 391–415. DOI: 10.1146/annurev.soc.29.010202.095927.

Norman, J.M. (2009). "Creative activism: Youth media in Palestine." *Middle East Journal of Culture and Communication 2*, 251–274.

Ottaway, M., & Hamzawy, A. (2011). "Protest movements and political change in the Arab world." *Carnegie Endowment for International Peace: Political Outlook*, 1–14.

Roberts, Nancy. "'Ten Thousand Tongues' Speaking for Peace: Purposes and Strategies of the Nineteenth-Century Peace Advocacy Press." *Journalism History 21*, no. 1 (Spring 1995): 16–28.

Rogers, J., Mediratta, K., & Shah, S. (2012). "Chapter 3: Building power, learning democracy: Youth organizing as a site of civic development." *Review of Research in Education 36*, 43–66. DOI: 10.3102/0091732X11422328.

Ryan, C., Carragee, K.M., & Meinhofer, W. (2001). "Theory into practice: Framing, the news media, and collective action." *Journal of Broadcasting & Electric Media 45*, 175–182.

Shoemaker, P.J. (1984). "Media treatment of deviant political groups." *Journalism Quarterly 61*, 66–75, 82.

Skalli, L.H. (2013). "Youth, Media and the Politics of Change in North Africa: Negotiating Identities, Spaces and Power." *Middle East Journal Of Culture & Communication 6*(1), 5–14. DOI: 10.1163/18739865–00503001.

Skoric, M.M., & Poor, N. (2013). "Youth engagement in Singapore: The interplay of social and traditional media." *Journal of Broadcasting & Electronic Media 57*(2), 187–204. DOI: 10.1080/08838151.2013.787076.

Valenzuela, S., Arriagada, A., & Scherman, A. (2012). "The Social Media Basis of Youth Protest Behavior: The Case of Chile." *Journal of Communication 62*(2), 299–314. DOI: 10.1111/j.1460–2466.2012.01635.x.

Vélez, V., Huber, L.P., Lopez, C.B., de la Luz, A., & Solórzano, D.G. (2008). "Battling for human right and social justice: A Latina/o critical race media analysis of Latna/o student youth activism in the wake of 2006 anti-immigrant sentiment." *Social Justice 35*(1), 7–27.

Vieira, M. (2007). "Harry Potter: The final chapter." *NBC News.* Retrieved from http://www.nbcnews.com/id/20001720/ns/dateline_nbc-harry_potter/t/harry-potter-final-chapter/#.VM6OzGRg67o. Last accessed on January 30, 2015.

Youniss, J., & Yates, M. (1999). "Youth service and moral-civic identity: A case for everyday morality." *Educational Psychology Review 11*(4), 361–376.

Youniss, J., Bales, S., Christmas-Best, V., Diversi, M., McLaughlin, M., & Silbereisen, R. (2002). "Youth civic engagement in the 21st century." *Journal of Research on Adolescence 12*(1), 121–148.

Zhang, W. (2013). "Redefining youth activism through digital technology in Singapore." *International Communication Gazette 75*(3), 253–270. DOI: 10.1177/1748048512472858.

About the Contributors

Dr. Tracy L. **Bealer** teaches literature and composition at Borough of Manhattan Community College. She specializes in the twentieth- and twenty-first-century American novel with a particular interest in pop culture and genre fiction. She has published on William Faulkner, Alice Walker, Quentin Tarantino and the *Harry Potter* and *Twilight* series, and she co-edited *Neil Gaiman and Philosophy* for Open Court's Pop Culture and Philosophy series.

Dr. Bronwyn E. **Beatty** teaches and researches at the New Zealand Broadcasting School, CPIT, Christchurch, Aotearoa/New Zealand. She has published on the political economy of the *Lord of the Rings* film trilogy, the televised YouTube political debates of 2008, and the value of media events for broadcast television. Other research interests include cultural policy, transmedia storytelling and audience studies.

Dr. Christopher E. **Bell** is an assistant professor of communication at the University of Colorado–Colorado Springs, teaching both theory and methodology courses in critical analysis of popular culture, rhetorical theory, representation theory and mass media. He specializes in popular culture, focusing on the ways in which race, class and gender intersect. He is the chair of the Southwest Popular/American Culture Association's *Harry Potter* Studies division.

Dr. Kalen M.A. **Churcher** is an assistant professor in the Communication Studies Department at Wilkes University, Wilkes-Barre, Pennsylvania, and adviser to the award-winning student newspaper *The Beacon*. Her research lies at the intersection of cultural studies and journalism. Her work has been published in various journals, including *Communication* and *Culture & Critique*, and has been presented at national and international conferences.

Dr. Elizabeth Morrow **Clark** is an associate professor of history at West Texas A&M University. She is an inaugural member of the *Harry Potter* Studies division of the Southwest Texas Popular/American Culture Association. She publishes on such topics as east European history, Polish diplomacy and the history of Gdańsk/Danzig as well as *Harry Potter*.

Kelly E. **Collinsworth** is an associate professor of legal studies at Morehead State University. She received a juris doctor degree from The Ohio State University in 1997. Her legal work focused primarily on foreclosure defense, family law and juvenile court matters. She is an avid *Harry Potter* fan and enjoys teaching a class on Harry Potter and Law in which students prepare and perform *Harry Potter*–based mock trials.

Dr. Juliann **Cortese** is an associate professor in the School of Communication, College of Communication and Information at Florida State University. She studies mass media uses and effects with a particular focus on Internet use and eHealth. She has published in several journals including *Journal of Health Communication, Cyberpsychology, Behavior, and Social Networking, Human Communication Research* and *Patient Education and Counseling.*

Megan **Farnel** is a second year PhD candidate at the University of Alberta. She works in the fields of new media, affect and materialist scholarship, with a particular focus on fans and crowds as subcultural affective labor formations. Her dissertation is also a public writing project and is being blogged on HASTAC (the Humanities, Arts, Science and Technology Alliance and Collaboratory).

Tolonda **Henderson** is an instruction and reference librarian at George Washington University. Her conference presentations include "Student Driven Library Instruction" (Lilly Conference on College and University Teaching, 2011), "Restricted Access: The Gendered Role of the Library at Hogwarts" (Southwest Popular/American Culture Association, 2014), and "Glad of Your Absence, or, Why Nobody Writes about Ron" (Harry Potter Conference, 2014).

Christine **Klingbiel** is a senior lecturer at the University of Wisconsin–Milwaukee, where she teaches English composition for the Academic Opportunity Center. She writes both fiction and non-fiction. She has had short stories published in *Doorways, Twisted Ink* and *Lady Churchill's Rosebud Wristlet.* Her interests include women's images in art and media, myth, folklore and fairytales, and contemporary rhetoric and spin.

Chin-Ting **Lee** received a master of global media communication degree from the University of Melbourne. Her research interests are *Harry Potter*, literature and anime/manga fandoms, social media and memory studies.

Dr. Jennifer M. **Proffitt** is an associate professor in the School of Communication, College of Communication and Information at Florida State University. Her research interests include political economy of media, broadcast history and regulation, popular culture and labor coverage. Her work has been published in several journals.

Dr. Meghan S. **Sanders** is an associate professor in the Manship School of Mass Communication at Louisiana State University. Her research focuses on the psychological effects of media content as they pertain to cognition, emotion, and psychological and subjective well-being. Her work has been published in top-tier journals such as *Communication Theory* and presented at national and international conferences.

Dr. Amy M. **Von Lintel** is an assistant professor of art history at West Texas A&M University. Her research explores the popular origins of art history in the 19th century and the modern art of the Texas Panhandle. She has published an article in *Modernism/modernity* on wood engravings as well as several essays on women art historians in Britain and America, on art history exhibitions in 1850s England, on Robert Smithson's *Amarillo Ramp,* and on Georgia O'Keeffe.

Index